David Goodman Croly

Seymour and Blair

Vol. 2

David Goodman Croly

Seymour and Blair
Vol. 2

ISBN/EAN: 9783337216092

Printed in Europe, USA, Canada, Australia, Japan

Cover: Foto ©Thomas Meinert / pixelio.de

More available books at **www.hansebooks.com**

Truly yours,
Horatio Seymour

SEYMOUR and BLAIR

THEIR

LIVES AND SERVICES

WITH AN APPENDIX CONTAINING A HISTORY OF

RECONSTRUCTION

By DAVID G. CROLY
OF "THE NEW YORK WORLD"

NEW YORK
RICHARDSON AND COMPANY
4 BOND STREET
1868

PREFACE.

In the compilation of this work, I have had the following aims in view :—

1. To give a truthful and accurate *résumé* of the personal and political careers of Hon. Horatio Seymour and General Francis P. Blair, Jr., the Democratic candidates for President and Vice-President in the contest of 1868.

2. To state fairly and succinctly the issues now before the country, upon which the people are asked to give their verdict next November.

3. To deal honestly by my readers, making no unfair appeals to passion or prejudice, giving currency to no doubtful statements merely because they might damage the Republican party or its candidates, at the same time claiming no more for the Democratic party, its platform and ticket, than I think is honestly their due. Wherever it has been possible, I have made use of Governor Seymour's public utterances to explain his views.

In short, my design has been to compile a book, which, while it will be a storehouse of facts invaluable to Democrats during the campaign, will yet be so candid in its spirit, and careful in its statements, that no fair-minded citizen, of any party, will be repelled from reading it. Such a work, I humbly conceive, will be far more effective as a means of proselyting inquiring or wavering Republicans, than one filled with strong party appeals, and abounding in the reckless charges so common in the prints usually put forth by political parties upon the eve of important elections.

The contest has opened very bitterly. Nor is this surprising. There are vast material interests at stake. A question of race-superiority is involved, while the passions and prejudices generated during the war have been stimulated into a new life, so as to affect the result. It is the duty, however, of the great body of the American people, who are neither office-holders nor office-seekers, whose only concern is to see our financial system reformed, the revenues collected, and the Union restored in its integrity, to discountenance these exhibitions of party folly and fury, and address themselves to the task of discussing the candidates and the issues of the campaign temperately and candidly, in order that a wise and honest verdict may be given at the polls next November. To this class the following work is respectfully addressed and dedicated.

Many of the facts, and all the speeches, orders, messages, and documents, are taken directly from Governor Seymour's private papers, to which he has been kind enough to allow me access, and from which, for lack of space, I have been able to make only such extracts as are absolutely essential to a fair exhibit of his career as a public man. His official secretaries have also given me valuable assistance. So far, this work may be considered authorized. But for the language used, opinions expressed, statements made, as well as the arrangement of the matter, I am wholly responsible.

Whatever shortcomings may be noticed in the composition of this work, can easily be accounted for when it is known that it was written within a week, and that week the warmest known in the history of the country.

For valuable assistance in the preparation of the work, I am indebted to Messrs. Salem Dutcher, Henry E. Sweetser, A. C. Wheeler, St. Clair McKelway, and Hiram Calkins—all members of the *World* Editorial Staff.

DAVID G. CROLY.

JULY 17, 1868.

CONTENTS.

LIFE OF HON. HORATIO SEYMOUR.

CHAPTER	PAGE
I.—ANCESTRY AND EARLY LIFE	7
II.—SOCIAL, LITERARY, AND FARM LIFE	15
III.—HIS LEGISLATIVE CAREER	25
IV.—MR. SEYMOUR'S ELECTION AS GOVERNOR	30
V.—THE TERM OF 1853–'54—VETO OF THE LIQUOR LAW AND ROVING COMMISSION ACT—ANECDOTES	33
VI.—ELECTION OF 1854	43
VII.—GOV. SEYMOUR'S SPRINGFIELD SPEECH—THE DEMOCRATIC THEORY OF GOVERNMENT	47
VIII.—FROM 1854 TO 1861—CINCINNATI CONVENTION	66
IX.—THE BREAKING OUT OF THE WAR	71
X.—ELECTION OF 1862	77
XI.—MESSAGE OF 1863, AND INVASION OF PENNSYLVANIA	91
XII.—THE CONSPIRACY AGAINST NEW YORK	101
XIII.—MEASURES FOR THE RELIEF OF SOLDIERS—NEGRO RECRUITING	118
XIV.—GOV. SEYMOUR'S EFFORTS TO PROCURE THE SOLDIERS THE RIGHT OF VOTING, AND TO PROTECT THEM AGAINST FRAUD	124

CHAPTER	PAGE
XV.—The Outrage on the New York State Agents—Their Arrest, and Long Incarceration and Subsequent Acquittal and Vindication	131
XVI.—Proclamations during the War	138
XVII.—Prison Discipline	141
XVIII.—Public Faith	145
XIX.—Governor Seymour and the Western States	149
XX.—Gov. Seymour and the Interests of Labor	154
XXI.—The Election of 1864	156
XXII.—Gov. Seymour's Cooper Institute Speech of 1866	160
XXIII.—Speech of the Convention of 1867	168
XXIV.—The National Democratic Convention	180
XXV.—The Democratic Party and Horatio Seymour	193
XXVI.—Horatio Seymour as a Man, an Orator, and a Statesman	205
XXVII.—Looking ahead—Result of the Election	208

LIFE OF GEN. FRANCIS P. BLAIR, JR.

CHAPTER	PAGE
I.—His Birth, Boyhood, and Early History	219
II.—His Professional and Early Political Career—He Leads the Free Soil Movement	227
III.—His War Record	234
IV.—His Recent Political History	247
Appendix	255

LIFE OF
HON. HORATIO SEYMOUR.

CHAPTER I.

ANCESTRY AND EARLY LIFE.

The Seymour family were among the earliest settlers of Hartford, Connecticut. Richard Seymour, as we find in the preserved history of that place, figured extensively in its primitive struggles. The history of the family, however, assumed a broader character with Major Moses Seymour, the fourth lineal descendant of Richard, and grandfather of the subject of our memoir, who was born in 1742.

Early in the war of the Revolution, he was commissioned as captain of the troop of horse attached to the Seventeenth Regiment, Connecticut militia, and took an active part in the principal events of the war. He distinguished himself in the decisive battle which culminated in the surrender of Burgoyne, and in the establishment of American Independence.

Major Seymour had five sons and a daughter. In the "History of Litchfield" we read:—"Of these five sons, one became distinguished as a financier and bank president; two became high sheriffs of this county; one was a representative, senator, and canal commissioner in the State of New York ; and one was for twelve years a United States Senator from Vermont—the most remarkable family of sons ever raised in Litchfield. The daughter, Clarissa Seymour, married the Rev. Freeman Marsh, for many years rector of St. Michael's Church, in this town."

Among the relatives of Governor Seymour, well known in public life, may be mentioned his uncle, Horatio Seymour, LL. D, of Middlebury, Vt., who was a member of the State council from 1809 to 1816, and of the United States Senate from 1821 to 1833, and Origin S. Seymour, at present a judge of the Superior Court of Connecticut, and for many years Speaker of the House of Representatives of that State, and Member of Congress. He was the democratic candidate for governor a few years since. Col. Thomas H. Seymour, late governor of Connecticut, and formerly United States Minister to Russia, is a cousin, and was the classmate of Horatio. General Seymour, of the United States Army, is also a relative, as was the late Hon. David L. Seymour, of Troy, N. Y.

No less distinguished and patriotic were his maternal ancestry. His grandfather on that side was Lieut.-Col. Forman, of the First New Jersey Regiment in the Revolutionary Army. His grandmother was a niece of Col. William Ledyard, who commanded at Groton when that place was sacked and burned by British and tories under command of the notorious Arnold, on the 6th of September, 1781, and where the Ledyard family was nearly extirpated. It is said that Arnold stood in the belfry of a church, while the town was burning, and looked upon the scene with the satisfaction of a Nero. After the place surrendered, Major Bromfield, a New Jersey tory, at the head of a band of bloodthirsty savages, entered the fort, and demanded, "Who commands this garrison?" Col. Ledyard, who was standing by, mildly replied, "I did, sir, but you do now," at the same time handing his sword to the victor. The tory miscreant, says the historian, immediately murdered Ledyard running him through the body with the weapon he had just surrendered.

Governor Seymour as the lineal descendant of Col. Forman, is now a member of the ancient and honorable Society of the Cincinnati. Col. Forman spent all his property in support of the Revolutionary cause. At the close of the war he moved to Cazenovia, N. Y., and received a commission as a general of this State, signed by the governor.

Henry, the father of Horatio, was born in 1780, and soon after reaching his majority removed to Onondaga County, in the State of New York, then little better than a wilderness.

On May 31, 1810, was born their son, the subject of our biography; and about nine years after, the family removed to Utica. Mr. Henry Seymour, then in the heyday of life, was already conspicuous in those greater interests of the commonwealth which need practical wisdom and personal character in their development and trust. He was one of the earliest and most efficient canal commissioners, a colleague of Dewitt Clinton, was member of the council of appointment, mayor of Utica, representative and senator, and was president of the Farmers' Loan and Trust Company, in all of which positions he exhibited fidelity and talent.

The Seymour family have always been distinguished for their ability, and renowned for their patriotism. Democratic by education, by tradition, and by instinct, there is no variableness nor shadows of turning in their political history and relationships. In Connecticut, they were ever among the most advanced of the liberal party, bravely resisting the blue-laws and church rites, imposed upon the State by the early Puritans. It was in this contest that the democratic party of that State had its origin; and with it in Connecticut grew up the Methodist, Episcopal, and other anti-Puritan churches. In that State, as elsewhere, democracy and liberal Christianity, have ever gone hand in hand,—and Horatio Seymour was educated in, and has grown up a firm believer in the faith of each. The State has no more consistent Christian. Associations and physical surroundings have much to do with forming the intellectual and moral character. The curious in such matters, in contemplating the pure character, commanding intellect, and lofty patriotism of Horatio Seymour, will not fail to connect him with the many strong men that have sprung from Litchfield, the home of his ancestry; with the Wolcotts, the Talmadges, the Masons, the Sedgwicks, the Pierponts, the Kirbys, and others that will occur to the intelligent reader.

Onondaga County, New York, the birthplace

of Governor Seymour, was settled by men of a very high order. One of the first things done by the pioneer settlers was to mortgage their lands in order to raise funds for the erection and endowment of an academy. In this academy Horatio Seymour received the rudiments of his education. Few academies can boast a nobler body of students. The Jeromes, the Marshes, the Litchfields, the Sedgwicks, Fargoes, Charles Mason (late Commissioner of Patents, who graduated at West Point, first of a class in which Robert E. Lee stood second), Senator Williams, of Oregon, Elliot, the painter, and Palmer, the sculptor, were students here. Pompey Hill was also the home of the distinguished lawyers, Daniel Gote, and Victory Birdseye, and among many successful business men who came from there were John R. Yelverton, and Erastus Partridge, of Seneca Falls, two of the most eminent and successful bankers in the State. Mr. Partridge frequently speaks of his early days at this place, and of his favorable recollection of Governor Seymour and his distinguished father and estimable and accomplished mother.

At the age of ten, he was sent to the Oxford Academy, then one of the foremost educational institutions of the State, where he remained for two or more years in the family and under the instruction of the late David H. Prentice, a most successful educator, who, as principal of the Oxford Academy, and subsequently as a leading professor in Geneva (now Hobart) College, gave the impression of his virtues and ability to many of the leading minds of the country. Governor Seymour preceded his distinguished tutor from Oxford to Geneva, and spent two years of his school-life in that beautiful village, amid the wild, romantic, and almost classical scenery of the lovely Seneca,—the finest of all the lakes which adorn and beautify the landscape of Western New York.

From Geneva, the subject of this sketch went to the Military Academy at Middletown, Connecticut, then under the able management of Captain Partridge. It was probably the discipline of this school, that matured Governor Seymour's mind, while it gave to his person that elegance of style, which has always rendered him a marked man in any popular assemblage. Here too he acquired his taste for philosophical and out-door pursuits, which have ever been among his leading characteristics. Here were laid broad and deep the foundations of that strong, intellectual and moral development which has made Governor Seymour the polished gentleman, the graceful orator, as well as the foremost statesman of his day and country.

After graduating at this Military Academy, where his cousin, the Hon. Thomas H. Seymour, of Connecticut, was his classmate, Governor Seymour, returned to Utica, New York, and entered upon the study of the law, under the guidance of those celebrated jurists, Greene C. Bronson and Samuel Beardsley, then in their prime. These men ranked among the legal giants of those days. They each subsequently filled the highest judicial posts in their State, besides leaving their mark on the legislation and jurisprudence of the nation.

After a thorough preparation, Governor Seymour was admitted an attorney and counselor of the Supreme Court of the State of New York, as a member of the Oneida bar. About this time his marriage occurred with Mary, the daughter of John R. Bleeker, of Albany.

The cares of business soon after thrown upon him, tended, rather than political pursuits, to withdraw him from the practice of a profession, to which he was so well adapted, and in which he was so certain of success. It is said of him, by those who know him well, both as a lawyer and subsequently as a business man, that his adaptation to business, and his dispatch were remarkable, showing, as has been remarked, his versatility of talent—eminent at the bar, in the forum, the senate, the counting-room, and the executive chamber.

When the late William L. Marcy became governor of New York, and Martin Van Buren was at the head of affairs, state and national, the keen eye of Mr. Van Buren espied in young Seymour the elements of a great popular leader, and at his special instance, Governor Marcy placed Horatio Seymour —then just arrived at man's estate—upon his staff, and made him his Military Secretary, in which position he naturally became his confidential friend. The intimate personal relations thus established between Mr. Seymour and Governor Marcy, and the other great leaders of the then triumphant democracy, continued unbroken until the death of Governor Marcy. During this time, Horatio Seymour acquired an intimate knowledge of public men and public affairs, and also cultivated and matured his literary tastes. Few men possessed the genial scholarship and masterly ability of Governor Marcy, and at this perennial spring of logic and of knowledge, Horatio Seymour freely drank. He retained Marcy's confidence to the end, and the latter never failed to urge his favorite pupil to devote himself more entirely to public affairs. Secretary Marcy and President Buchanan each expressed a wish to send Governor Seymour abroad in an honorable diplomatic position, but their offers, though highly appreciated, were declined.

It has been remarked by many that Governor Seymour in his mode of treating public questions, is very like Governor Marcy. An intimate and active correspondence was ever kept up between them. Governor Seymour was Marcy's spokesman in the National Convention of 1852; and shortly before the death of the latter he sent for Seymour, to visit him at Ballston Spa, where they had a long interview, in the course of which the political history and condition of the country was thoroughly canvassed; and the dying statesman urged Seymour to continue and complete that great work of conciliation and national development which Marcy had so well begun. The words of wisdom which were uttered upon that occasion the world can never know, but they sank deep into the mind and heart of the appreciative auditor, and now form a part of that store-house of statesmanship upon which the present champion of Democracy so copiously draws.

CHAPTER II.

SOCIAL, LITERARY, AND FARM LIFE.

NOTWITHSTANDING Governor Seymour's opportunities and acquirements as a politician, he has never been a mere party man. His statesmanship has been on a more elevated plane, and he has only appeared in public when the public voice called him—when the public good required his services—and when duty left him no alternative but to yield. In the pursuit of polite and classic literature—in the cultivation of the higher arts—in the quiet discharge of social duties—in devising ways for the promotion of agriculture, of popular education, and of sound morality—he has always taken the greatest delight.

His zeal as a sportsman, in the true sense of that term, has always been keen and appreciative. The great North Woods of Northern New York have been to him a familiar and pleasant retreat; its lakes, its rivers, and its almost impenetrable forest-recesses, are to him as familiar as the school-room—they have been the school-room of his maturer years; but they have not been the limit of his wanderings. He has roamed yearly over the prairies of the far West, penetrated the wilds of the upper and lower Mississippi, and is almost as familiarly known to the hardy inhabitants of Minnesota, Wisconsin, and Nebraska as to the citizens of his own New York.

Much of his time has been devoted to agriculture, and his large and beautiful home-farm on the northern bank of the Mohawk, opposite the city of Utica, has been the scene of many useful and practical experiments, which in his various addresses before different agricultural societies, State and county, have been given to the world. He is President of the American Dairymen's Association, and has done much to direct the attention of the farmers of the South and West to this branch of domestic industry. No less ardent has been his devotion to the educational interests of his State. He has long been an active trustee of Hamilton College, and his address upon the induction of President Fisher, and on various other occasions, and particularly his remarks at Albany before the Regents of the University, upon the educational system of the State, show a familiarity with the subject, and an enthusiasm in the cause, that commend their author to the consideration and confidence of the friends of popular education throughout the land. In this connection the attention of the reader is called to his eloquent address before the Mercantile Library Association of the city of New York, and his no less eloquent lecture before the New York Geological and Statistical Society, upon the history and topography of his native State. Both are remarkable productions, and should be studied by every one who would acquire an intimate knowledge of the history and characteristics of the Empire State, or would nourish and cherish a proper pride of country. On reading the latter, Governor

Marcy, then Secretary of State of the United States, addressed its author the following note:—

WASHINGTON, April 13.

MY DEAR GOVERNOR—I have received your lecture on the topography and history of New York, and read it with more pleasure than I can well express. You have given us a charming and beautiful sketch. I could not, on reading it, help reproaching myself for being so ignorant of the many interesting facts which you have brought out. We have I find, many claims upon the consideration of our sister States which were unknown to me. The manner and the matter are alike deserving of high commendation. I owe you thanks for the pleasure the perusal of the lecture has given me.

Yours truly,

W. L. MARCY.

As has been stated, Governor Seymour was educated a Democrat and an Episcopalian, and to his party and his church he has ever adhered with unwavering fidelity; though the most tolerant of men, quietly, yet firmly maintaining and defending his own views, he is never impatient of opposition, nor unjust to others. Recognizing the great good there is in varied organizations, he would co-operate with each wherever the interests of his country or of humanity demand such co-operation, trusting to the Master of the harvest in His own good time, to gather in the wheat and to destroy the tares. There is not a denomination which has not been aided by his liberality in the erection of houses for public worship. He has been for years a leading vestryman of Trinity Church, Utica, and generally a delegate to the annual diocesan convention, and a delegate from Western New York in the national or triennial convention of the Church of the United

States. The late Bishop De Lancy always recognized Governor Seymour and the late Governor Hunt as his right-hand and chief supporters. Shortly before his death, Bishop De Lancy visited Governor Seymour at Albany, and spent several days in his family.

Before leaving this interesting portion of his career, to enter upon the more tumultuous scenes of his political life, it may be well to draw a rapid sketch of his home as it appeared at the time of his nomination. About three years ago he built upon the range, known as the Deerfield Hills, which rise gently on the north of the Mohawk Valley, and about three miles from Utica, his present home. It is a modest frame house, standing on the highest point of the farm of three hundred acres, which stretches down to the river. Approaching it from the lane which leads off the main road, it is almost hidden from view by an enormous black cherry tree of native growth. Once fairly on the rise, it is found to be a plain story and a half cottage, one of those unpretentious but roomy affairs, that stretch away from a façade of porch that seems to spring from the grass and flowers into spacious rooms without any intermediate halls or vestibules.

Standing on this porch and looking down the long slope to the river, the whole of the farm, with the exception of a grove at the north of the house, lies mapped out in pleasant alternations of hillock and meadow, field and forest-trees, with the valley beyond, and the white houses of Utica showing through the elms in the background. A fine pear orchard, planted by the proprietor himself, is one of its features, and the clean cut hedge of English hawthorne running by the road-side, is an indication of careful and thrifty husbandry. He is said to take especial delight in the development of this estate, adding constantly the best stock, and supplying it with needed implements of improved design.

The indications of character which one will look for are uniformly simple. The spruce-tree at the side of the house, curiously bifurcated near its root and forming a rude chair, is unadorned by grotesque contortions of limbs, but is the governor's favorite seat. So with the house. There is nothing extrinsic or purely ornamental about it. This peculiarity, so conspicuous among the staid old settlers of Utica, seems to have been cherished particularly in this home. Immediately at the side of the front door, and projecting across the porch, is the well preserved and mounted head of an enormous moose—a trophy of the proprietor's skill some twelve years ago in the Adirondacks. Entering the parlor, odorous with the balmy breath of flowers that throughout the season are placed upon the little side-table, and the pleasant taint of the India matting upon the floors, one sees at a glance that all is of the old school. Although of very recent construction, the house is not conformed to recent follies. Its air is that of a manor-house, staid and venerable, but suggestive of comfort withal. There is a spacious fireplace of the olden time, begirt with a brass-headed dogs and glistening fender, and set in veritable Dutch tiles, sacred to the memory of some old inheritance in Albany, and a great carved mantel-piece restored and preserved out of respect to departed honesty, that reckoned carving better than stucco, and good oaken devices better than iron that pretends to be marble. Upon this quaint old mantel, quite as high as one's head, lie crossed the horse pistols of the Revolutionary grandfather. On the corner towers the old Dutch clock, tall and somber, and useless save as a reproach to the modern toys that seem to delight in frisking away the precious moments with impertinent levity. The furniture is black and grotesquely carved in a forgotten fashion. The pictures are portraits of relations, and have a wholesome sober look that is not to be trifled with. However, there are a solar microscope, a telescope, and other scientific apparatus in the same room, which effectually remove any idea that the owner pays servile homage to things of the past, or is amenable to the flippant epithet of "old fogy." In his moments of recreation he uses these instruments skillfully. It may be stated that Mr. Seymour always evinced a strong interest in the subject of the naturalist. For scientific investigation he has too much of the vigor which plans and executes to ever devote himself exclusively to these patient and atomic studies; but with that love of nature which invariably marks the man of evenly balanced faculties, he devotes his moments of leisure, when at home to the study of the phenomena upon his grounds, and it is said that there is not a tree nor an insect in the vicinity that he is not familiar with.

The remainder of the house is exactly in keeping. An air of solid comfort is apparent everywhere.

The library is small but valuable, and rich in old authors and religious works. There are few ornaments, and they are generally natural flowers or a stray trifle of art that must have been an heir-loom. The absence of conventional gewgaws and upholstery, the rustic freedom which is toned, combined with the evidences of culture, the exquisite simplicity, in a word, and the good taste wrought together in this house have an attraction for the visitor that is indescribable.

It is the genial grace of Mr. Seymour's manner, combined with his undoubted sincerity, and his clear, practical insight into the affairs of the hour, which constitutes the charm of his society, whether at home or in public life. One may not agree with him, but it is impossible not to respect his opinion, seeing that it is the result of careful observation and mature reflection, and is advanced in the interests of the many with the candor and sobriety of a thorough gentleman.

Mr. Seymour has shown in his political life, that decision of character and strength of will are compatible with gentleness of speech and moderation of manner. In his life, Mr. Seymour is thoroughly temperate. He was never known to indulge to excess in any thing. Inheriting a strong, vital temperament and sinewy frame, he has preserved his health amid the excitements and temptations of a long political career by prudence, and is to-day in the full exercise of every faculty of mind and body.

Mrs. Seymour presides over this home with true grace. She is a lady of most winning address and thorough culture. Familiar with the highest circles of our State from girlhood, with every opportunity that affluence afforded to strengthen and store a mind with knowledge, and possessing in a marked degree the virtues and accomplishments which were the pride of her ancestors, it may readily be seen that she is a lady fit to occupy the highest position in our country.

The visitors at the cottage have not been numerous. Outside of the circle of relatives residing in Utica, and the old friends of his father's family, the visitors have been mainly from abroad. The duties of the farm, when he is at home, occupy Mr. Seymour's time. He goes to the village seldom, and then only on business, or to Trinity Church of a Sunday. There have been fête days at the farm — festivals of children, one of which occurred early in the summer, when Mr. Seymour invited the orphans of St. John's Asylum in town to spend the day on the grounds. On this occasion, the master, no less than the mistress, devoted himself to their enjoyment with a personal zest that could only belong to a warm and kindly heart, and he was heard to declare that it was one of the really happy days of his life. How well the children appreciated his endeavors was shown afterward. They were out at Waterville on a picnic when the news of his nomination flashed through the valley, and a shout of shrill trebles went up from immature throats, that would have thrilled him, could he have heard it, with its honesty, as no lusty acclaim of men will ever do.

We have thus endeavored to sketch the early

career of the man, and his social position at his home. The story of his active life in the broader field of politics remains to be told. That he preferred the modest joys of this quiet home to the exciting arena of national politics and the distractions of a life at Washington, is not unreasonable. He had told his most intimate friends, before leaving Utica to attend the Convention, that he would not accept the nomination. Those who were in his confidence paid him a visit at the cottage the night before he left for New York; they used all their eloquence and pathos to induce him to alter his determination, but in vain. He was suffering with an attack of diphtheria, which became aggravated a few days later, and it was hardly possible for him to reply to the earnest words that they used. But late into the night, while he lay upon a lounge, they beset him, and fairly begged for the sake of the party and the country, that he would accept the nomination if it were offered.

He persistently refused, and did not hesitate to say that it was repugnant to him.

But let it not be supposed that he was actuated in this by any fear of his health. That consideration, at least, never entered into the question. Whatever may be the excitements of a campaign, Mr. Seymour is not the man to waste his strength in violence of words or action, or to suffer with alternate hopes and fears of a result. His whole life has shown most uniformly that his practice is to do his duty equably and honestly, and let the result take care of itself. It is a curious fact, worth stating here, that

Mr. Seymour's health has always been the best during a campaign in which he had plenty of work given him. In this use of vital energy he is happy.

CHAPTER III.

HIS LEGISLATIVE CAREER.

In 1841, Mr. Seymour accepted a nomination for the Assembly from the county of Oneida, and was elected by one of the largest majorities ever given a democratic candidate in that ancient stronghold of the party. At this period, just twenty-seven years ago, commenced his public career.

Mr. Seymour entered the Assembly the recognized friend of Governor Marcy, and an adherent of the established and national organization of the Democratic party. In the Legislature, he was a bold and efficient defender of the time-honored principles of the Democracy.

Judge Hammond, in his "Political History of New York," referring to Mr. Seymour at this time, says:—

"We have seldom known a man who possessed higher and better qualifications for usefulness and success in a popular government than Horatio Seymour. Kind and social by nature, affable in his deportment, possessing a shrewd, discerning mind, fluent, and at times eloquent in debate, enlarged in his views, liberal almost to a fault to his opponents, and fascinating in his address, no man seemed better calculated to acquire an influence in a legislative body than he, and few, indeed, at his time of life, have, in fact, acquired a better standing or more substantial moral power. He had early made himself well acquainted wth the great and varied interests of the State of New York, an acquisition which aided him much in debate, and gave him an advantage over older members, and which, at the same time, enabled him to render services in legislation highly useful and beneficial to the State."

Mr. Seymour had previously been a member of local and State Conventions, but this was the first position in which he attracted the attention of the public outside of his county. The Assembly of 1842 comprised many talented men such as John A. Dix; Lemuel Stetson, of Clinton; Geo. A. Simmons, of Essex; John A. Lott, of Kings; Levi S. Chatfield, of Otsego; Michael Hoffman and Arphaxad Loomis, of Herkimer; Solomon Townsend, William McMurray, Sandford E. Church; John Kramer, of Saratoga; Charles Humphrey, and others. Levi S. Chatfield was elected Speaker. Mr. Seymour at once took rank as a prominent and leading member. The great contest of the session took place on the passage of the celebrated bill of Michael Hoffman in relation to the finances. It was an act to provide for paying the debt and preserving the credit of the State. The bill passed the Assembly by a large majority, Mr. Seymour voting for it with Michael Hoffman. In 1842, Mr. Seymour was elected Mayor of Utica. He was, however, a member of the Legislature of 1843, and of each succeeding session until and including that of 1865. At the session of 1843, Gov. Bouck's Administration was met at the threshold by opposition, and a bitter sectional feeling sprang up. Mr. Seymour exerted his influence to prevent the schism which ultimately destroyed the democratic ascendancy in the State. In 1843, a large democratic majority was returned to both houses. One wing of the party urged for Speaker Michael Hoffman, while the other wing was anxious to present the name of Horatio Seymour. Mr. Seymour, however, withdrew in favor of Elisha Litchfield, of Onondaga County. It was at this session that the great contest took place between Michael Hoffman and Horatio Seymour on the canal and financial policy of the State. On the 23d of April Mr. Seymour made a report as Chairman of the Committee on Canals, on that portion of the Governor's message relating to that subject. This report covers seventy-one large octavo pages, and has been pronounced one of the ablest and best written documents ever presented to a legislative body.

Accompanying it was a bill making a practical application of the theory advanced and supported in the report. This passed both houses, Mr. Seymour's friends and nearly all the Whigs voting for it; Mr. Hoffman's friends voting against, but Mr. Hoffman himself refusing to vote. This was a great triumph for Mr. Seymour. A writer, speaking of this session, says:—

"In the excited and somewhat acrimonious contests that occurred in the Assembly, Mr. Seymour very soon became looked upon as the champion of the friends of the democratic administration. In this, as in the performance of the regular duties that devolved on him on the floor as well as a member of important committees, he acquitted himself with marked ability. Mr. Hoffman was a powerful antagonist, and had been universally regarded as the most formidable man in debate in the legislature. Such, however, was the charm of Mr. Seymour's manner, and such the manliness and frankness of his general course, that he secured from Mr. Hoffman the most respectful consideration, and it was regarded by many as a remarkable sight to behold the dictator of the house defer to the commanding courtesy of his competitor."

At the session of 1845, Mr. Seymour was elected Speaker, and filled the chair with great ability. He had declined the position at the previous session. At this session the bill providing for a convention to revise the Constitution was adopted. This was originally a Whig measure; and though the Democracy desired to effect certain changes in the Constitution they wished to accomplish it in the manner provided by the Constitution itself. This was Mr. Seymour's view, and the debate between him and John Young, the leader of the Whigs, was characterized by great eloquence. Time has confirmed all the objections made to the new Constitution as well in its political aspects as upon the interests of the people of the State. With this session ended Mr. Seymour's legislative career, and ended also the ascendancy of the party in the legislative and executive departments of the Government. Divisions had done their work, and in the State elections of 1846–'47 and '48, the Democratic party of New York sustained a series of defeats. Soon after the election of 1848, in which Mr. Seymour ardently supported Cass and Butler, he co-operated in movements to close the breach between the different sections of the party; and in the work of reconciliation became more prominent than any other of the National Democracy. He spared no honorable efforts to unite and consolidate the party upon a broad and consistent National platform. In this laudable work he for the time alienated the feelings of some of his old friends, and subjected himself to much unjust suspicion, but the end justified his course, and vindicated his sagacity and magnanimity. In 1849, the Democracy of the State partially regained their power, but soon lost it by a local and temporary issue in reference to the immediate enlargement of the Erie canal. We close our necessarily brief review of Mr. Seymour's early legislative career and his exertions in behalf of the union of the Democratic party of New York, by recalling the remarks made at the time by a leading opponent in reference to his social and personal qualities:—

"The courtesy and liberality of this leader of the Democracy in public life, were not more distinctly marked, than were his urbanity and generosity in private intercourse. His troops of friends, among all of those with whom he is brought in contact, constitute a cloud of witnesses to bear testimony to his general kindness of heart, and the many acts of delicate courtesy and considerate benevolence, which eminently characterize him as a citizen and as a man."

CHAPTER IV.

MR. SEYMOUR'S ELECTION AS GOVERNOR.

In recognition of Mr. Seymour's exertion in behalf of the union and integrity of the Democratic party of New York, he received in 1850 a unanimous nomination for governor; and associated with him on the ticket was the Hon. Sandford E. Church, then and ever since a popular leader in Western New York. At this time there existed in different localities in the State, but mainly in the neighborhood of Albany, a powerful organization, known as Anti-Renters. An Anti-Rent State ticket was selected from the candidates of both parties, and placed in nomination, with Washington Hunt, the Whig candidate for governor, at its head. The canvass was an animated one, and the anti-rent movement operated in favor of those adopted by them, as they were elected by large majorities. Hunt, notwithstanding this support, had only 262 majority in a total poll of nearly 429,000, Seymour running ahead of those of his associates who were not on the anti-rent ticket.

The gallant bearing of the Democratic champion in this contest, endeared him still more strongly to the masses; and in the great contest of 1852 he was again unanimously placed in nomination for governor, and after making a thorough canvass of the

State in person, he was triumphantly elected over his former competitor by 22,596 majority, carrying with him all his associates, and securing the electoral vote of the State to Pierce and King. In this, as in all great contests in the State, Governor Seymour appealed directly to the people, and he seldom appealed in vain. No man called out greater crowds of persons to listen, and no other man uniformly made a stronger or more favorable impression upon his hearers.

Although he and the late lamented Washington Hunt were opposing candidates in 1850 and in 1852, and the contest in each case was exciting and bitter, the personal relations of these two distinguished popular leaders were at all times intimate and friendly. Mr. Seymour always did full justice to the ability and integrity of his rival, with whom he had commenced political life, but who separated from the Democratic party on the United States Bank question. Before his death, Gov. Hunt become a warm political friend of Seymour, and during his last days he expressed a wish for his nomination and election to the Presidency. Had Washington Hunt been spared to the people of the country until this day, his voice would now be heard in behalf of the Democratic nominees. Horatio Seymour and Washington Hunt knew each other well; they had long communed at the same altar, their religious and political views entirely harmonizing. Together they had acted in the diocesan conventions of their church; together they were elected delegates to its triennial convention. In that convention they uniformly acted in harmony for peace, union, and the promotion of their Master's kingdom.

They were both members of the Chicago Convention, of which Gov. Seymour became the presiding officer; and while the latter advocated the nomination of Chief-Justice Nelson, Gov. Hunt as ardently desired Gov. Seymour to become the candidate. The writer well remembers the earnest and conciliatory speech he made to the assembled delegation from New York while it was deliberating upon the course it should take in carrying out the instructions of the State convention to vote as a unit.

The administration of Governor Seymour in 1853-4 was eminently successful, though in a time of great party peril and difficulty. The temperance agitators of the day had resolved themselves into a political party in favor of a system of coercive legislation, commonly known as the Maine law. The repeal of the Missouri Compromise had opened anew the schisms of the Democratic party of the North, and involved the administration of President Pierce in an angry and bitter contest for existence. The Whig party—that party of many virtues—was abandoned by its leaders, and upon its ruins had sprung up the National American and the Sectional Republican parties, each earnest and aggressive. All of these elements were bravely encountered by Governor Seymour's administration.

CHAPTER V.

THE TERM OF 1853-'54.—VETO OF THE LIQUOR LAW AND ROVING COMMISSION ACT.—ANECDOTES.

At the session of the Legislature of 1854, a prohibitory liquor law was proposed, framed similarly to one that had recently been passed in Maine, and after considerable discussion it received the sanction of the New York Legislature. The opposition party had then a majority in both houses, and as this subject was one engrossing public attention throughout the States, the Governor in his annual message at the opening of the session, had referred to it and substantially stated that while he was willing to co-operate in any effort to impose greater checks on the use of intoxicating liquors, yet that legislation in regard to it should be judicious or it would increase the evils it was intended to prevent, and that " any measures adopted should be framed so as not to conflict with well settled principles of legislation or with the rights of our citizens."

On March 31st, 1854, the governor transmitted a message to the senate, in which he stated the reasons why he could not approve the bill. He took up the sections consecutively, and showed in what respects they were unconstitutional, oppressive, or impolitic. The general views of Gov. Seymour upon the subject of the suppression of intemperance by peremptory and intermeddling legislation, are expressed very fully in the speech delivered at Springfield, Mass., in 1856, which is given in a subsequent chapter.

We may quote the following paragraphs from the veto:—

"The idea pervades the bill, that unusual, numerous, and severe penalties, will secure enforcement; but all experience shows that the undue severity of laws defeats their execution.

"After the excitement which enacted them has passed away, no one feels disposed to enforce them, for no law can be sustained which goes beyond public feeling and sentiment.

"I have omitted any notice of many defective provisions in the bill, as they might be corrected by future legislation. I have confined my objections to those which are radically wrong; which are inconsistent with the principles of justice, with the rights of persons and of property, and which so pervade the bill that they can not be stricken out without destroying its entire fabric. The bill is wrong, because it directs unreasonable searches of the premises and dwellings of our citizens under circumstances calculated to provoke resistance; it deprives persons of their property in a manner prohibited by the Constitution; it subjects them, on mere suspicion of knowledge of a suspected crime, to an inquisitorial examination.

"For one act of alleged violation of law, a citizen may be proceeded against as a criminal—be fined or imprisoned, and his property seized or forfeited; he may be proceeded against in civil suits by various parties with whom he has had no dealings, and subjected to the payment of damages where none have been averred or proved. To all these prosecutions he may be subjected without the benefit of trial, in the usual and judicial meaning of that term.

"The Constitution makes it my duty to point out the objectionable features of this bill, but I owe it to the subject, and the friends of the measure, to add the expression of my belief that intemperance can not be extirpated by prohibitory laws. They are not consistent with sound principles of legislation. Like decrees to regulate religious creeds or forms of worship, they provoke resistance where they are designed to enforce obedience.

"The effort to suppress intemperance by unusual and arbitrary measures, proves that the Legislature is attempting to do that which is not within its province to enact or its power to enforce. This is the error which lies at the foundation of this bill—which distorts its details, and makes it a cause of angry controversy.

"Should it become a law, it would render its advocates odious as the supporters of unjust and arbitrary enactments. Its evils would only cease upon its repeal, or when it became a dead letter upon the statute-book. Judicious legislation may correct abuses in the manufacture, sale, or use of intoxicating liquors; but it can do no more.

"All experience shows that temperance, like other virtues, is not produced by law-makers, but by the influences of education, morality, and religion.

"While a conscientious discharge of duty, and a belief that explicit language is due to the friends of this bill, require me to state my objections to the measure in decided terms, it must not be understood that I am indifferent to the evils of intemperance, or wanting in respect and sympathy for those who are engaged in their suppression. I regard intemperance as a fruitful source of degradation and misery. I look with no favor upon the habits or practices which have produced the crime and suffering which are constantly forced upon my attention in the painful discharge of official duties. After long and earnest reflection, I am satisfied reliance can not be placed upon prohibitory laws to eradicate these evils. Men may be persuaded—they can not be compelled to adopt habits of temperance.

"I concur with many of the earnest and devoted friends of temperance in the opinion that it will hereafter be a cause for regret, if the interest which is now excited in the public mind upon that subject, should be diverted from its proper channels and exhausted in attempts to procure legislation which must be fruitless."

The storm of denunciation which followed this message, was a sufficient evidence of the moral courage and decision of character which were required to veto the bill. The press, the pulpit, and other agencies of public opinion, opened upon him with all their batteries of epithet and invective, which was kept up, with but little cessation, until after the gubernatorial election in the fall of '54.

On the other hand, many Republican newspapers acknowledged the justice of his action. The New York *Times* said:—

"There are very few sober people who will not confess that the Governor's objections to the details of the bill are substantially sound, and entitled to weight."

A Republican organ of Oswego, shocked at the indecencies of the press of its own party, made this protest:—

"Against Gov. Seymour personally, we have not one syllable to say. We know him well, and will not yield to the Palladium in respect for his worth or in admiration for his talents. In all the relations of private life he is blameless and above reproach. His moral character has never been tainted by the breath of slander. At home he is proverbial for his urbanity, kindness of heart, and integrity. We never knew the man whom he had wronged in business or personal relations, and do not believe such can be found. To urbanity of manner and extreme courtesy toward all who have intercourse with him, he adds unflinching honor. Warm in his attachments, and manly even in his hostilities, he possesses the faculty in a wonderful degree of attaching political associates by personal ties.

"Thus much we know and believe of Horatio Seymour. Can the Palladium say more? We oppose him in politics not from prejudice, but from conviction. We oppose him openly, manfully, and because we differ from him. Did it ever occur to that sheet that it is within the bounds of honorable warfare, politically, to oppose one whom you may personally esteem and admire?"

As we shall have occasion to record, the same act, when passed after the election of Gov. Clark, was soon after declared unconstitutional, by the highest Court of the State, and in after years, when the law had proved a failure, the action of Gov. Seymour was acknowledged by many who had assailed him most bitterly, to have been dictated by sound judgment, and a profound sense of duty.

Another important veto which the Governor issued, is also proved, by the proceedings of every subsequent session of the Legislature, to have been well-timed and judicious. Had the suggestions therein contained been followed, the State would have been saved the thousands of dollars, which have been expended by roving commissions.

The act in question provided for the appointment of a commission to investigate the pecuniary affairs of the State Prison. We quote from the veto message:—

"By the Constitution of this State, three Inspectors of State Prisons are elected by the people, and are paid from the public treasury for performing the duties which this bill confers upon the commissioners to be appointed by this Comptroller. The powers of the Inspectors are clearly defined by our laws, and they embrace every object contemplated by this bill. The information which it is proposed to get by this expensive commission can be obtained from public officers who are liable to be impeached if they are guilty of any neglect of duty. The practice of appointing legislative or other commissions to be paid for the performance of duties which belong to public officers, has been attended with great expense and no practical benefits. They are frequently got up for the purpose of giving employment or bestowing patronage at the expense of the State.

"A committee was appointed in 1851 to examine the condition of our prisons, and their able and elaborate report, made in 1851, has never been acted upon nor referred by the Legislature. These commissioners are governed by no rules nor fixed objects of inquiry. They usually become mere partisan inquisitions, and their reports are regarded with but little respect by the public, while their assumptions of powers, which belong to public officers, release the latter from the appropriate responsibilities. Sound policy requires that public officers should be held to a strict performance of their duties. If the State Prison Inspectors have neglected theirs they should be impeached. Our laws provide, if they are guilty of misconduct or malversation in office, that the Executive shall remove them.

"The bill, which I return, is also objectionable because it conflicts with the distribution of powers and duties of the several branches of the State Government, made by the Constitution. The different departments derive their clearly defined powers from a common source, and they should be kept within their respective and proper limits. For this reason I have not responded to legislative resolutions of inquiry, which have been addressed to me, respecting the performance of the duties conferred upon the Governor of this State by the Constitution. For the same reason I object to this bill. In order to animate all branches of the State Government with a sense of their appropriate duties, it is important that the rights of each should be understood by themselves and the public.

"The constitutional distribution of power among the legislative, judicial, and executive departments should be observed and respected. It enables the people of the State to attach the proper responsibilities to the different public officers. It is essential to wise and intelligent legislation, to the faithful performance of duty, and the protection of private rights and public interests. All the objects of the bill are amply provided for by constitutional directions and statutory enactments. The bill will cause useless expense, and is not consistent with sound policy. I do not doubt that the State Prison Inspectors will perform their duties. If they do not, I shall 'take care that the laws are faithfully executed.'"

We can only give a passing reference to some of the many addresses delivered by Governor Seymour during this term. He delivered the oration at the celebration of the erection of the monument at Tarrytown, in commemoration of the capture of Major Andre.

He delivered an address at the opening of the New York House of Refuge.

He gave an oration before the State Normal School.

He was present at the anniversary dinner of the New England Society, where speeches were made by Rev. R. S. Storrs, Hon. John P. Hale, and Henry Ward Beecher, and where he responded to the toast to the State of New York.

He delivered historical lectures in various towns of the State.

At the National Horse Fair, at Springfield, Mass., 1853, he responded to the toast of the State of New York, in which reference was made to the "urbanity, energy, and ability of her chief magistrate."

Governor Seymour also attended the inauguration, at the Church of the Puritans, of the Mercantile Library, an institution that has done a more practical work in the dissemination of literature than any in the city. Governor Seymour made a most eloquent speech on the occasion, from which we make the following extracts:—

"I deemed it an official duty to accept an invitation to be present on this occasion to manifest my admiration of the liberality of the merchants of New York toward this institution, and my respect for its numerous members, who have associated themselves together for the purposes of self-improvement. I have had placed in my hands the constitution of this society, which states its objects to be "to facilitate mutual intercourse, extend information on subjects of mercantile and general utility, promote a spirit of useful inquiry, and qualify ourselves to discharge properly the duties of our profession and the social offices of life." I know of no object that can more commend itself to our sympathy and approval than the efforts of young men who are about to enter upon the grave duties of life, to store their minds with useful knowledge, not only for the purpose of rendering themselves successful in their honorable pursuits, but to make themselves educated and respected citizens. They do not intend to sink themselves into subordination to their business affairs, but to render these subservient to their advancement as men. If this institution is to be regarded only with reference to its individual members, it would deserve all the sympathy and support which it now receives in this intelligent and enterprising community. But I desire to consider it, on this occasion, in another light—not merely of individual or local, but of State and National interest. In order to estimate its importance to our whole country—to its commerce, to its prosperity, and to its affairs—it is necessary to regard the relationship which this great city bears to the rest of our common country. But, before I proceed on that topic, let me for a moment advert to one of its objects—to facilitate mutual intercourse among its members—by which I understand it is their design to promote that honorable pride of their profession which will induce them to elevate it to its best estate—to render it subservient, not only to their individual interests, but also to the honor and welfare of this great commercial metropolis. This community has heretofore evinced a want of pride in its numerous institutions, and of that local attachment which has characterized some of its commercial rivals. * * * I have glanced briefly at some of the commercial advantages which this city enjoys, to show that its harbor is not to be regarded merely as the mouth of the Hudson, but as the point where the productions of the vast regions of our country are to be exchanged for those of other climes. The inhabitants of our own State, and of the fertile valleys of the West, must in a few years intrust the products of their labor and their skill to the care of those who now constitute the members of this society. Their intelligence and fidelity will be considerations of national importance. The extent to which the productions of our soil will be sent into the different markets of the world, will depend in a great degree upon their skill and enterprise as merchants. The profession in which they are about to engage has been regarded as one of great dignity and interest in all periods of the world's history. Heathen mythology exalted the early navigators to the ranks of heroes and demigods. Commerce furnishes many of the most striking figures in the history of the Old Testament, and for the sublime verse of Milton. But at no period since the wisest and wealthiest monarch sent ships to the isles of the sea to bring back myrrh, and gems, and gold, has commerce exerted a greater influence than at present upon the condition of the world and the progress of events. At this time the mightiest nations of Europe are exerting all their energies to send out disciplined armies and naval forces to maintain what they deem to be their national rights and liberties. And yet these mighty efforts will fall far short of the influences which the merchants of this city are exerting in the ordinary course of their pursuits in bringing annually to this port three hundred thousand persons who are seeking the protection of our laws, the advantages of our institutions, and the benefits of our fertile and productive soil. Whatever may be the result of the present European war, it will fall far short of the influences which immigration to this country will exert upon the relative strength and power of nations. While the ranks of European armies will merely serve to whiten with their bleached bones some battle-field, those whom commerce brings to our shores will build up flourishing cities and States, and constitute an enduring source of national wealth and greatness. I have glanced briefly and imperfectly upon the great responsibilities to soon devolve upon the members of this association. If they shall possess the requisite intelligence, liberality, and enterprise, they may render this city not only the emporium of our own land, but it may be hereafter said of her as of commercial Venice:—

> "'Her daughters had their dowers
> From spoils of nations, and the exhausted East
> Pour'd in her lap all gems in sparkling showers;
> In purple was she robed, and of her feast
> Monarchs partook, and deemed their dignity increased.'"

We have spoken of the abuse to which Governor Seymour was subjected. This settled purpose on the part of political preachers and others, to look at every act of his in an unfavorable light, sometimes led to amusing results. On one occasion, when he was about to issue a thanksgiving proclamation, an eminent doctor of divinity came into his room. As it was to be an appeal to the religious sentiments of the people, the governor asked him to draw it up, which he did, in suitable terms. No sooner was it printed than it was assailed, particularly by the paper which was the organ of the church to which the doctor belonged, which declared that it had read the proclamation with pain and mortification: that it was evidently written by a man of infidel tendencies, and one who had never experienced vital piety. While the governor did not deem it his duty to let the public know who the author was, it was quietly suggested to his brother clergymen that they should look closely after the heretical views of their associate, and the worthy doctor has never heard the last of this criticism on his orthodoxy.

These constant attacks upon the character, habits,

and person of the governor are not without their advantages, as he constantly meets those who have formed their ideas of him from what has been said in the pulpit and the press; and who, shocked by the grossness of the falsehood, have ever after looked upon him more favorably than perhaps they would have done if they had not felt how indecently they had been cheated and misled.

But the prejudices of some men are so strong that they will not believe their own eyes. Upon one occasion, when Governor Seymour was traveling with a prominent Republican official, and a vehement advocate of the Maine Law, some one pointed him out to one of these men so full of vindictive piety and malignant philanthropy. The latter, mistaking his Republican friend for the governor himself, exclaimed, with great feeling, that he was just such a looking man as he expected to see; that it was clear he drank himself, and wanted everybody else to drink, and there was vice upon every lineament of his countenance. The governor's Republican friends were silent upon the subject of the Maine Law during the rest of their journey.

CHAPTER VI.

ELECTION OF 1854.

With the close of his term as governor, in 1854, Mr. Seymour earnestly desired to retire from official life; but he had acquired too strong a hold upon the affections and confidence of the people to be thus relieved. The State convention of his political friends, against his earnest remonstrance, unanimously placed him in renomination, putting Colonel William H. Ludlow, then late speaker of the assembly, and more recently chief-of-staff to General Dix, on the ticket with him, as the candidate for lieutenant-governor. So determined were the great leaders of the Union Democracy of the State of New York at that time, that Governor Seymour should not decline the candidacy, that they suppressed the messages passing between him at Albany, and his friends at Syracuse, where the convention was in session.

At this period the internal feuds of the party in the Empire State were at their height. The administration of Mr. Pierce, and the course of Mr. Douglass on the Kansas-Nebraska Bill, were bitterly assailed. Each section seemed to have implicit confidence in the sound patriotism and integrity of the governor; but great jealousy was manifested of his friends and surroundings; and a determined effort was made by rival leaders to get control of the national patronage, in many cases without regard to the local feelings and interests of the party. Finally, these dissensions culminated in putting into the field Judge Bronson, as an opposing candidate.

The temperance question had become a disturbing element in party politics. Many ministers of the gospel, and others, misled for the time by a single idea, and overlooking the great distinction between that which is simply plausible and that which is constitutional, and lawful, and right, took ground against Governor Seymour, on account of his veto of the coercive Temperance Law, and ignoring the purity of his morals and his strictly temperate habits (his example at all times affording the most effective argument for their cause), assailed him from their pulpits and through the public press, and in public meetings, as the great apostle of intemperance, pauperism, and crime. These things, unfounded, vile, and silly as they were, were not without their influence. Thousands formed false ideas of Seymour's true character and position, and became possessed of prejudices which controlled their political action and associations.

Myron H. Clark, a State Senator, was the Whig and Temperance candidate; and Daniel Ullman the candidate of the American or Know-Nothing party, then in the vigor of its youth and the zenith of its power. The quadrangular contest was exciting and animated, and notwithstanding these attacks, Governor Seymour exhibited a personal popularity unequaled by that of any other public man of the time, receiving some 30,000 votes more than his associates on the ticket. Clark was declared elected by an apparent plurality of 309 votes in a grand total of 469,431. It is due to the truth of history to state that it was then intimated that the State officers, though politically opposed to Governor Seymour, would have given him the certificate of election, and thus secured him the office, had he consented to file objections to certain returns which were manifestly irregular, and probably tampered with by some of the unscrupulous men aiming at the control of public affairs. This contest Governor Seymour refused to make, inasmuch as his associates on the ticket were defeated, and he cheerfully welcomed Clark as his successor, placing in his hands the insignia of power, and throughout his administration contributing in many pleasant ways to make his position respected and comfortable.

We should fail to do justice to the ability of Seymour at this time, if we omitted to state that "the Maine Law," vetoed by him, but re-enacted and approved by Governor Clark, was declared unconstitutional and void by the concurrence of all but one of the Judges of the Court of Appeals of the State, and that the leading opinions of the eminent judges who passed upon the question sustained each and every of the principal objections to the bill enumerated in the veto message, which has been heretofore given to the reader. Thus this measure of pains and penalties, which cost the people of the State so much litigation, became a dead letter upon the statute-book, and was ultimately given up by the very men that originally passed it. All were compelled to acknowledge the legal acumen and sound constitutional views of the governor; but how few of "the Scribes and Pharisees" that made the welkin ring with their denunciations of him have publicly admitted their own error or his vindication—more of them subsequently found the drunkard's level, and now fill dishonored graves—a warning to all who habitually assume morals superior to the rest of mankind, and when they pray, if they ever do, thank God they are not as other men.

During the first gubernatorial term, Governor Seymour felt many defects in the organization of the executive department of the State. After his retirement and surrender of office to a Republican successor, he urged upon the State Legislature a complete reorganization of the office—and an increase of office force to meet the growing wants of the State."

In accordance with his suggestion, the office was created, a Department of Record, and its efficiency greatly improved by the legislation thus suggested.

To bring about this change, although for the benefit of his political opponents, he spent much time and effort at Albany, as he felt it was due to the dignity of the State, and he was unwilling that his successors should be crippled, as he had been, by the want of a sufficient clerical force and of laws to to preserve records and papers of great value.

CHAPTER VII.

GOV. SEYMOUR'S SPRINGFIELD SPEECH.—THE DEMOCRATIC THEORY OF GOVERNMENT.

In 1856, soon after the nomination of Buchanan and Breckinridge by the Cincinnati Convention, leading members of the Democratic National Committee, solicited Governor Seymour, whose eloquence had made a deep impression upon that Convention, to make a speech which should give the key-note to the campaign, and be received, as Governor Seymour's speeches have ever since been received, as the platform, in fact, of the party. In response to this invitation, Gov. Seymour, at Springfield, Massachusetts, on the 4th day of July, 1856, before assembled thousands, uttered his views of "the Democratic Theory of Government," in a speech which was received with universal acclaim, and which was published and republished throughout the land, as a campaign document, contributing, in no small degree, to the brilliant victory of that year.

The reader will find that the extracts we give from this speech are as fresh and applicable to the present condition of things, as on the day of its first publication, showing the catholicity and immutability of the principles expounded.

The speech was as follows:—

"For the purpose of standing upon the soil of Massachusetts, to defend the principles of our party, and the honor and interests of our whole country, I declined the invitations to meet on this day the Democracy of Philadelphia, exulting in the nomination of Mr. Buchanan, or to unite with thousands who cluster around the time-honored halls of St. Tammany, in the city of New York. In a great battle, we love to stand where our ranks are thinnest, and our opponents muster in their might. We seek out the adversaries of religious and political freedom in their strongholds, and we raise the standard of our Union where sectional jealousy, bigotry, and hate are most rife. I honor those who stood up manfully in this State against the overwhelming numbers of the advocates of Alien and Sedition laws; against those who preached and practised treason in the last war with Great Britain; against those who prayed that our armies in Mexico might be met with bloody hands and hospitable graves; against those who have persecuted defenseless women for their religious faith; against those whose chief effort at this time is to teach one half of our common country to hate the other half. I have lately been upon the shores of the great lakes at the North, upon the banks of the Mississippi at the West, in the valley of the Potomac at the South, and upon the margin of the Hudson in New York, and it gives me pleasure to say to you who live along the course of the Connecticut, and amid the hills of New England, that but one sentiment animates the great national party to which we belong; and to tell you, the true men of Massachusetts, that however small your numbers may be here, that you belong to a brotherhood who, like yourselves, love our whole country, and who are strong enough to defend it against either foreign assault or domestic treason.

"We meet upon a day thick clustering with memories sacred to American patriots. These will animate us upon this occasion. No word will be uttered here which will jar with the recollections of the past. If those who, eighty years ago, came from the North, the West, and the South, to rescue Boston from hostile hands, and to drive destroying armies from the soil of Massachusetts, could have heard, in anticipation, our words, telling of the greatness of our country, and of our devotion to its preservation, their hearts would have thrilled with joy and pride. If, on the other hand, their hearing had been cursed by the appeals to passion and prejudice which are made, even now, in a neighboring assemblage, how would that patriotic array have been struck down by the base ingratitude! The strong heart of Washington would have given way as he listened to the revilings of his native State and of the descendants of those who had followed him from Virginia, to peril their lives for this State in the day of its trial and distress.

"At this time our country is convulsed with moral disorders, with religious dissensions, and political agitations. Denunciatory language and violent conduct disgrace our national capitol. Most of the great religious denominations are divided, and glare across a sectional line with fierce hatred, withholding from each other the charity and courtesies which they extend to their co-religionists from foreign lands. Another tie which has heretofore held our country together, has been disbanded, and from its ruins has sprung a political organization trusting for its success to sectional prejudices. It excludes from its councils the people of nearly one half the Union; it seeks a triumph over one half our country. The battle-fields of Yorktown, of Camden, of New Orleans, are unrepresented in their Conventions, and no delegates speak for the States where rest the remains of Washington, Jefferson, Marion, Sumter, or Morgan, or the later hero, Jackson. They cherish more bitter hatred of their own countrymen, than they have ever shown toward the enemies of our land. If the language they hold this day had been used eighty years since, we should not have thrown off the British yoke. Our national Constitution would not have been formed, and if their spirit of hatred continues, our Constitution and Government will cease to exist.

* * * * * * * * * *

"The democratic theory takes away control from central points and distributes it to the various localities that are most interested in its wise and honest exercise. It keeps at every man's home the greatest share of the political power that concerns him individually. It yields it to the remoter legislative bodies in diminishing proportions as they recede from the direct influence and action of the people. The principle of self-government is not the demagogical idea that the people, in their collective capacity, are endowed with a wisdom, patriotism, and virtue superior to their individual characters. The people, as a society, are as virtuous or as vicious, as intelligent or as ignorant, as brave or as cowardly, as the persons who compose it. The great theory of local self-government under which our country is expanding itself over a continent, without becoming weak by its extension, is founded on these propositions. That Government is most wise, which is in the hands of those best informed about the particular questions on which they legislate; most economical and honest, when controlled by those most interested in preserving frugality and virtue; most strong, when it only exercises authority which is beneficial in its action to the governed. These are obvious truths, but how are they to be made available for practical purposes? It is in this that the wisdom of our institutions consists. In their progress, they are developing truths in government which have not only disappointed the hopes of our enemies and dissipated the fears of our friends, but give promise in the future of such greatness and civilization as the world has never seen.

"The legislation which most affects us is local in its character. The good order of society, the protection of our lives and our property, the promotion of religion and learning, the enforcement of statutes, or the upholding the unwritten laws of just moral restraints, mainly depend upon the virtue and wisdom of the inhabitants of townships. Upon such questions, so far as they particularly concern themselves, the people of the towns are more intelligent and more interested than those outside of their limits can be for them. The wisest statesman living and acting at the city of Washington, can not understand these affairs, nor can they conduct them as well as the citizens upon the ground. What is true of one town is true of the other ten thousand towns in the United States. When we shall have fifty thousand towns, this system of government will in no degree become overloaded or complicated. There will be no more then for each citizen to do than now. Our town officers in the aggregate are more important than Congressmen or Senators. Hence the importance to our government of religion, morality, and education, which enlighten and purify the governed and the governor at the same time, and which must ever constitute the best securities for the advancement and happiness of our country. The next organization, in order and importance, are boards of county officers, who control questions of a local character, but affecting more than the inhabitants of single towns. The people of each county are more intelligent, and more interested in what concerns their own affairs than any amount of wisdom, or of patriotism, outside of it. The aggregate transactions of our supervisors are more important than those of our State Legislature. When we have secured good government in towns and counties, most of the objects of government are gained. In the ascending scale of rank, in the descending scale of importance is the Legislature, which is, or should be, limited to State affairs. Its greatest wisdom is shown by the smallest amount of legislation, and its strongest claims for gratitude grow out of what it does not do. Our General Government is remarkable for being the reverse of every other system. Instead of being the source of authority, it only receives the remnants of power, after all that concerns town, county, and State jurisdiction has been distributed. Its jurisdiction although, confined within narrow limits, is of great dignity, for it concerns our national honor, and provides for the national defense. We make this head of our system strong, when we confine its action to those objects which are of general interest and value, and prevent its interference with subjects upon which it can not act with a due degree of intelligence. If our General Government had the legislative power, which is now divided between town, county, and State jurisdiction, its attempts at their exercise would shiver it into atoms. If it was composed of the wisest and purest men the world ever saw, it could not understand all the varied interests of a land as wide as all Europe, and with as great a diversity of climate, soil, and social condition. The welfare of the several communities would be sacrificed to the ignorance or prejudices of those who have no direct concern in the laws they imposed upon others. Under our system of government, the right to interfere is less than the disposition many show to meddle with what they do not understand; and over every section of our great country, there are local jurisdictions, familiar with their wants, and interested in doing what is for the right. It required seven centuries to reform palpable wrongs in enlightened Britain, simply because the powers of its government, concentrated in Parliament, were far removed from the sufferings and injuries those wrongs occasioned. Under our institutions, evils are at once removed, when intelligence and virtue have shown them in their true light to the communities in which they exist. As intelligence, virtue, and religion are thus potential, let us rely upon them as the genial influences which will induce men to throw off the evils which encumber them, and not resort to impertinent meddling, howling denunciations, and bitter taunts, which prompt individuals and communities to draw the folds of wrong more closely about them.

"The theory of local self-government is not founded upon the idea that the people are necessarily virtuous and intelligent, but it attempts to distribute each particular power to those who have the greatest interest in its wise and faithful exercise. It gives to every township the right to direct its own local affairs, the people of a town being more intelligent about their own affairs than the public of any other locality. In the same way it leaves to every county the legislation that pertains to the county; and to every State the legislation that pertains to the State. Such distribution of political power is founded on the principle that persons most interested in any matter, manage it better than even wiser men who are not interested therein. Men act precisely thus in their private concerns. When we are sick we do not seek the wisest men in the community, but the physician who is best acquainted with our disorder and its remedies. If we wish to build, we seek not the most learned man, but the man most skillful in the kind of structure we desire to erect; and if we require the services of an agent, the one is best for us who is best acquainted personally with our wants, and most interested in satisfying them. The Bible intimates this course, when it says: 'That a man can judge better in relation to his own affairs than seven watchmen on a high tower.' Acting upon these simple principles, the tendency of democracy has constantly been to remove power from great central agencies, and to distribute it among the localities who have the best intelligence for its exercise, and the highest personal interest in exercising it judiciously.

"This system not only secures good government for each locality, but it also brings home to each individual a sense of his rights and responsibilities; it elevates his character as a man; he is taught self-reliance; he learns that the performance of his duty as a citizen, is the best corrective for the evils of society, and is not led to place a vague, unfounded dependence upon legislative wisdom or inspirations. The principle of local and distributed jurisdiction, not only makes good Government, but it also makes good manhood. Under European Governments, but few feel that they can exert any influence upon public morals or affairs, but here, every one knows that his character and conduct will at least affect the character of the town in which he lives.

"The conviction gains ground that the General Government is strengthened and made most enduring, by lifting it above invidious duties, and by making it the point which rallies the affections and pride of the American people, as the exponent to the world at large of our common power, dignity and nationality.

"Under this system our country has attained its power, its prosperity, and its magnificent proportions. Look at it upon the map of the world. It is as broad as all Europe. Mark its boundaries. The greatest chain of fresh water lakes upon the globe bathe its northern limits—the Atlantic and Pacific wash its eastern and western shores, and its southern borders rest upon the great Mediterranean Sea of Mexico. Our policy of government by localities meets every local want of this vast region; it gives energy, enterprise and freedom to each community, no matter how remote or small. And this is done so readily and so peaceably that the process resembles the great and beneficent operations of nature. See how it tells upon the individual citizen; how it develops manhood; how it makes our whole land instinct with energy and virtue. In the world's history no such exhibitions have ever been made of intellectual vigor, power and enterprise, as are now shown by the commercial men of these United States, or by its artisans and its agriculturists. These are owing to the principles of local self-government and freedom of individual action. Each man understands this in his own affairs, and he prays to be freed from legislative interferences. When all men concede to others what they thus ask for themselves, the democratic policy will have no opposers. As a party, we reject legislative legerdemain. We have but one petition to our lawmakers—it is, to be let alone. We have one reliance for good government, the intelligence of the people; one source of wealth, the honest, thinking labor of our country; one hope for our workshops, the skill of our mechanics; one impulse for our commerce, the untrammeled enterprise of our merchants; one remedy for moral evils, religious education; one object for our political exertions, the common good of our great and glorious country."

THE MEDDLING THEORY OF GOVERNMENT.

"In antagonism to the democratic creed of local and individual freedom, there has always existed a pragmatic organization, which under different names has sought to build up a system of political meddling. Its purposes may have been good; its claims have been high toned and exacting. Constantly defeated by the results of its erroneous principles, its instincts lead it to renew its attempts at power by new projects. It is as confident and as denunciatory today, as when it sought to uphold national banks and high tariffs. It now claims the exclusive championship of morals, religion and liberty, as it once did the guardianship of the finances and industry of the country. We deny that the meddling system of politics is favorable to morals, religion, or liberty. History proves the contrary. It has ever been the bane of each. It has always furnished the pretexts of tyrants. The fires of bigotry, the iron rule of despots, the leaden weight of ignorance and degradation, came from pragmatical doctrines.

"Political meddling has done nothing for religion here. It has hung Quakers—it persecuted Roger Williams—it has driven pious women into exile—it has tried to uphold a theocracy in New England—it has divided the church of our land—it has caused bitter sectional hate. It has done no good. We need not go back into the past to show this—it is proved by the questions of the day. *We have political meddling with morals in coercive temperance laws; politi-*

cal meddling with religion in Know-Nothingism and divided churches; political meddling with rights of local legislation by the Republican party. They each sprung from a common sentiment. The man of the South who supports Know-Nothingism, upholds the spirit of bigotry which calls Republicanism into existence. The man of foreign birth who aids in the attempt to disfranchise the emigrant to the West, will find that he is laboring to take away the right of citizenship from the emigrant from the eastern world. He who interferes with those a thousand miles away, must not object to the intermeddling of his neighbors with his domestic or personal affairs. Those who fan the fires of fanatism in any of its forms, will find their homes invaded by its flames.

"It is remarkable that the doctrine of local self-government is most bitterly assailed in some of the New England States, which owe their political power to this principle. Equal representation is given to each State in the Senate, the most important branch of the federal system, for it has not only the law making power in common with the House of Representatives, but also the power to confirm treaties (which are superior to laws), and to restrain the Executive by rejecting official appointments. The Senate holds in check every other department of Government.

"If New England was asked to give up its disproportionate power in the Senate, it would point to the constitutional compact. Then let New England see that the compact is respected where it gives as well as where it takes. If it was urged that, with a population less than that of New York, New England has ten Senators and ten electoral votes beyond its proportionate share, and that the Constitution should be amended to do away with this inequality, the answer would be, that it was the wise policy of our Constitution to uphold State sovereignties; that the organization of the Senate was designed to prevent interference with local affairs by the General Government; that representation by States was intended to keep alive the principles of local self-government. For these reasons the small States are allowed a disproportionate share of power in the Senate. Without these reasons, the disparity would be intolerable. But the power was given only for defensive, not for aggressive purposes. Nor will it be tolerated for other purposes. The disproportion of power becomes greater each year. Most of the new States have, each of them, land fit for cultivation equal to the aggregate of the six New England States. Many of them far exceed that amount. In a few years they will fill up with population, while your numbers will not increase. If a meddling policy is to prevail in our country, an undue share of power will not be allowed. Your remote and sequestered position, touching the rest of the Union only on the borders of New York, will lessen your influence. The principle of interference may be brought home to you, and in defense you will be compelled to urge the principles of local self-government and State rights, which has ever been the creed of the democratic party. Yet, blind to these considerations, the legislators of this State have been violent in their action against the principle of local sovereignty, which alone give it power, and most declamatory against the compromise of the Constitution, which alone give it influence, for the whole number of the citizens is only equal to the annual increase in the population of the United States."

COERCIVE TEMPERANCE LAW.

"I will present for your consideration the different phases of this spirit of political interference. We have forced upon us in many of the States a coercive temperance law, which is claimed by its advocates to be a new and certain remedy for most of the evils which affect society, but which is an oft-repeated and always futile effort to extend the jurisprudence of statutory laws beyond their proper bounds.

"The objections to this measure are twofold. It violates constitutional laws, and it will increase the evils it claims to abolish. At this time many speak lightly of constitutional law. They are impatient that their peculiar views are checked by its barriers, not bearing in mind that it is their only safeguard against unjust or hasty legislation, affecting their lives, their liberties, and their rights of conscience. We are made free by written constitutions restraining majorities and protecting minorities, and forbidding the legislators from touching a single right of a single citizen. In these days of legislative encroachment and legislative corruption, it is the duty of every citizen to uphold constitutional law. It is strange that those who demand respect for coercive temperance laws should show contempt for the more sacred obligations of constitutions—that those who call for submission to legislative enactments denounce and revile the higher decision of judicial tribunals. The objections to this legislation are of the gravest kind. It is not merely against drinking, but against thinking. It is a mere precedent full of evil. It is well described by an eminent clergyman as a 'lazy philanthropy which tries to get rid of the duties of life by declaring its evils are abolished by act of Legislature.'

"Its first and greatest mischief is the demoralization and disorganization of temperance efforts. No cause can receive a blow more deadly than that which degrades the passions and motives of its advocates. The efforts of those engaged in promoting temperance by reason and persuasion, were 'twice blessed.' They enlarge their own intellect, and improve their own characters, while they influenced and benefited others. But when the law gives them power over their fellow-men, poor human nature shows its wonted weakness. Pride and passion are aroused, and provoke resistance where persuasion has heretofore prevailed. I do not mean to urge against this measure that it has unworthy advocates or indiscreet friends, but that its tendency is to arouse bad passions in the breasts of men who have heretofore been humane and charitable—that the power which it gives them over the consciences and actions of others, creates a vindictive spirit on the one hand and calls forth resistance on the other.

"What are the effects on the minds of good men when excited by the idea of coercion? They become inflamed with passion, and indulge in reckless assertions against character—evil imputations against motive—and flippant denunciations of judicial decisions. These passions have been exhibited even in the pulpit, and teachers of a meek and charitable religion adopt the very language of the enemies of its author, when denouncing men as wine-bibbers and friends of publicans and sinners. It is hard to believe when listening to their invectives, that they are servants of Him who was thus reviled because He proposed to do away with the laws which restrained the actions of men, and to introduce in their place the principles which purify the hearts and motives. The statute giving them power over their fellow-men, like Ithuriel's spear, touches the love of power lurking in the heart of all, and evil spirits spring into full force and stature.

"The reasoning urged by the advocates of this statute is this: 'Intemperance is an evil. It is the duty of Government to suppress evil; therefore, a coercive law is right.' The evil is conceded, and those who feel its magnitude can not and will not consent to any measures which increase it. But we must not stop with depicting these evils in glowing and exciting terms. The great question is this: Is coercion a rightful and effectual remedy? This question is usually overleaped in order to reach the denunciatory exercises. The remedy is either a new one, or one which has heretofore failed. In either event, its advocates are hasty in vilifying those who doubt its efficacy. The arguments upon which it is founded have caused most of the political, social, and religious evils which oppress mankind. Those who hold or usurp power, are wont to say that they deem heresy, or infidelity, or dangerous habits of thinking freely, evils, and that it is the duty of a State to remove evils, and therefore they may punish freedom of thinking, as well as freedom of drinking. In all these cases the real question is overlooked. What are the right remedies?

"The bad effects of this law upon its advocates have been seen. Another objection is, that it creates a spirit of resistance which increases the evil it claims to root out. This fact is shown by the experience of different periods in the world's history. The use of particular narcotics amongst most nations, has been confirmed by efforts to suppress their consumption by force.

"The cause of Temperance was irresistible in the State of Maine, while it was upheld by reason and persuasion. It was broken down by legislation. The authors of the bill, in the narrowness of their intellect, could not see that truth was stronger than statutes. We are advised by commercial men, and by the missionary journals of China, that the attempt to put down the use of Opium by force, has been followed by the greatest social, moral, and political evils. There, as here, a dead law is like a dead limb upon a living man; it must be cut off, or it will carry decay and corruption into every part of the system. The mischiefs which we begin to feel, are there developed to their full extent, and he who will trace them there in all their influences, will be startled to find how great are the wrongs which grow out of mistaken principles of legislation, although prompted by good motives.

"The concealed currents of vice, like undercurrents of water, are most insidious and destructive. *At this time, the Maine law in several States converts a dangerous, and in many circumstances a destructive habit of drinking intoxicating liquors into one more dangerous and pernicious, for it superadds the meanness of concealment, and the demoralization of hypocrisy.* It also makes it more difficult to apply timely correctives to pernicious habits. You can not warn against the seductive habit, without first convicting of an unlawful and secret practice. In the mean time the taste has become irresistible. Prohibitory laws have not prevented drinking; they have made it more hurtful by introducing untruthful pretexts for its use.

"Let the advocates of temperance see what spirit this enactment has evoked. Is this the day of triumph for their cause? Persuasion requires virtue, ability and sincerity. Coercive laws are best enforced by the violent, vindictive and base. Hence these are now taking the lead. They even show a malignant hostility to those who have labored long and sacrificed much for the objects they claim to have in view if they refuse to become politically subservient. Men out of repair morally or politically in their struggles for party advantages throw the consistent advocates of temperance into the back-ground—a benevolent enterprise has fallen into the hands of those afflicted with a 'vindictive philanthropy,' which deranges them with the idea that they are virtuous, because they are denunciatory. The wise and the thoughtful are overruled by men raging with the delirium tremens of fanaticism, who assail the most sacred offices of religion, who see foul serpents coiling upon the Sacramental altar, infusing their venom into the sacred elements, and hissing amid the solemnities of the Last Supper.

"The terms of the law go beyond the sentiment of all classes, and cause a constant inconsistency of language and action. Public officers, judges, and clergymen, are compelled to denounce the use of wine as crime, when speaking with all the solemnities of official station, or invested with the sacredness of the pulpit. Yet they show by their constant intercourse with those who do not use intoxicating liquors, that this is a formal language, a mockery, a compliance with the terms of law which all feel to be untrue.

"The vital principle of the Christian religion is persuasion, in opposition to restraints. It makes temperance and all other virtues something positive. It aims to make men unwilling, not unable to do wrong. It educates alike the feelings and the understanding, the heart and the head. All experience shows that mere restraints from vice do not reform. Our prisons are the examples of the perfect system of restraint. Their inmates for a long series of years, are entirely prevented from indulging in intemperance or any kindred evil. They lead lives of perfect regularity, industry and propriety, because they are compelled to do so. Yet few are reformed by this. Our instincts teach us that forced propriety of conduct gives no assurance of future virtue, on the contrary, the very fact that they have been subjected to it, is by courts and communities regarded as evidence of depravity.

"The very condition of restraint is found to be a positive obstacle in the way of the influences of religious education, when brought to bear upon the inmates of our prisons. Are the advocates of the temperance law willing to place themselves upon the footing on which they strive to place others? Will they give up their convictions of duty and propriety—surrender every positive virtue, and become temperance men merely because they can not drink? They will shrink from the application of a principle to themselves which they try to apply to others. They know that virtues wither and die out under such systems. The law has and does lead away from the right remedy to the wrong one. I know that it is difficult to draw the line where persuasion should end and coercion begin. This has ever been the problem which has embarrassed legislatures: but this we do know, that the progress of civilization, morality and virtue, has been marked by the extension of education and religion and the contraction of coercive laws.

"Governments emanate from the people, and merely represent their morality or intelligence. The folly which looks to governments to evolve the virtues, is like the ignorance which regards the thermometer as a regulator of temperature, or the barometer as the controller of the weather.

"We object, then, to this law, because it demoralizes temperance men, making them vindictive and violent; because it arouses a spirit of resistance, increasing the evils of intemperance; because it is a step backward in civilization, substituting restraints for education. All admit that it is better to be temperate from choice, from thought and resolution, than from coercion. Who doubts that persuasion will win more than force?

" But it is said in a triumphant tone, if the law will increase intemperance, why do the sellers of intoxicating liquors object to it? Leaving out of view differences of opinion with regard to the propriety of their use as drink, this very law concedes their necessity for mechanical, medical, and sacred uses—but while it recognizes the legality and necessity of their manufacture and sale, it strives to make both odious, dangerous, and degrading, and this is naturally resisted by men whose objects are higher than mere gain, and who do not wish to see a business pursuit of conceded necessity, forced into the hands of those indifferent to their right of public sentiment.

" I do not assail the motives of its advocates, but good motives do not prevent the evil results of false principles. A good motive (to save men's soul's) originated the slave trade. The same good motives kindled the fires of the Inquisition. Good motives and wrong principles have lain at the root of almost every evil which has oppressed and afflicted mankind.

" It is gratifying that the great body of the clergy reject this union with the State. They continue to put their faith in the Christian and not in the Legislative dispensation. Their less sagacious brethren will soon find where their infidel alliances will lead them."

DEFENSE OF ADOPTED CITIZENS.

"While the coercionist is trying to limit the freedom of its neighbors, two other parties, actuated by the same sentiment of political meddling, are assailing different classes of our people. We have 'know-nothings' who wish to disfranchise those who come, and 'republicans' who are resolved to disfranchise those who go. The first, hold that those who come from the other side of the Atlantic, shall gain no political rights; the last assert that the citizens who go beyond the Missouri, should lose the rights of self-government they enjoy at home. Each party unite to place a class of persons in a condition of pupilage. They assume that men who have the vigor, energy, and enterprise, to leave their native land, are unfit to take care of themselves. They reverse every American sentiment. They believe that those who have hazarded their lives and fortunes, in their efforts to get homes and freedom for themselves and their families, have less interest in their own welfare than others have for them. These two parties hold in common, that men who emigrate will make better citizens if deprived of political right. What would our laborers say, if told they would make better workmen if they were not allowed to become their own employers? What would the apprentice think, if he was advised that he would be more faithful if he was not permitted to become a master mechanic? Or the lawyer if debarred from the Judge's seat, to make him a more trustworthy advocate? They would denounce such suggestions, they would demand encouragement for efforts, by the hopes of all the honors and advantages of their pursuits. The folly of trying to make good mechanics, lawyers, and doctors, by disfranchising them, is no greater than the folly which believes men can be made good citizens by taking from them the rights of citizenship.

"It is claimed that the original settlers of our country were endowed with all the cardinal virtues, and that they were the authors of our civil and religious liberty. Our forefathers committed more outrages upon personal rights than the most bigoted impute to those who now come to our shores. Under the influence of fanaticism, they drowned and hung their fellow-citizens. They were made wiser and better men by the enjoyment of full political rights in the land, and the modern emigrant must be allowed the full benefit of the same influences.

"Is the action of your legislators consistent upon the subject? They protest with justice against interference with the emigrants from this State to Kansas, when sent out by 'aid societies,' yet the border men of Missouri are only enforcing the laws which Massachusetts has passed against any foreigner who may be placed upon its shores by means of charitable assistance. He is called a pauper, and sent back across the ocean. Can that be wise and humane here, which is denounced as ruffianism and wrong in Kansas.

"Absurd efforts are made to trace all the virtues of the American character back to the early colonist; to find the germs of our institutions in their first acts after landing upon our shores, and thus to make a distinction between them and the modern emigrant. It is assumed that the former were models of virtue and wisdom, and that we get from them our ideas of civil and religious liberty. Nothing can be more fallacious. A contentious feeling was shown in the May Flower, for it is given as a reason for forming a government by its emigrants, that, 'observing some not well affected to unity and concord, but gave some appearance of faction, it was thought good to combine together in one body, and to submit to such government and governors as they should, by common consent, agree to make and choose.' The same considerations of religious freedom, or of personal advantage, which led the early colonists to the shores of this continent continue to draw hither the inhabitants of the old world. No one denounces the early emigration because there were criminals mingled among the good and wise.

"The know-nothing idea, that men will make better citizens if deprived of political privileges, is most undemocratic; that religious sentiments should be persecuted and denounced, is most un-American; and that homes should be denied to the poor and oppressed in our abundant unoccupied public domain, is most uncharitable and un-Christian.

"What is this emigration that is thus denounced? It is the victory of our country and its institutions. It is a mighty achievement in our contest for superiority with the old world. It is a triumph of peace. It is a glorious contrast with the devastations of war. It annually brings three hundred thousand 'pilgrims,' and transplants them into happy homes, making them prosperous, and our nation great, while, elsewhere, war sacrifices an equal number upon the battle field and by loathsome disease. It is the manifestation of the superior power of commerce over mere martial strength. While great nations exhaust their energies, embarrass their finances, and carry misery and desolation into the homes of their people, in transporting their armies to death and disease on distant shores, a few merchants of this city bring a greater host across the broad Atlantic, and never feel that it is more than an easy and familiar transaction. Compared with this great movement, the subjects of European diplomacy are trivial. This is the great combat which is to tell upon the destinies of the nation, and the history of the world. No Alexander or Cæsar in the height of their conquests, ever made such acquisitions of power as emigration brings to us.

"But those who are against the cause of their country in this contest, contend that emigration brings with it destitution, poverty and crime. Trace these bands of strong-limbed but poor foreigners until they plant themselves upon the hitherto useless land of the West, and see how wealth is evolved by their very contact with the soil. They were poor, and the fertile land was valueless, but combine these two kinds of poverty and the wealth which alchemists dreamed of, is the magical result. Whence the increase of the price of farms and lots, and broad, untilled lands, which has given to so many of our citizens wealth and prosperity? Whence comes this mighty volume of prosperity which rolls over our land? What gives employment to our cars and boats and ships, transporting armies of men, and retransporting the produce of their labor? Stop foreign emigration to this country, and thousands of those who ignorantly denounce the cause of the wealth they enjoy, would find their abundant prosperity wither and die away like Jonah's gourd.

"There is danger that this source of prosperity and power will be diverted elsewhere. It does not flow to our shores because we alone have fertile lands; there are broad, unoccupied plains, not owned by us, in South America and Australia. Emigration seeks here religious and political freedom and equality. Will it do so hereafter in view of late occurences? Recent outrages have been perpetrated aptly for the purpose of governments who are adopting active measures to turn elsewhere these living streams of population. British naturalization laws are changed in favor of emigration to the Canadas. Continental governments, under pretext of protecting the health of their subjects, impose vexatious and embarrassing restraints upon our vessels engaged in their transportation. The diminished number of emigrants during the past year shows that result.

"Divert emigration from our country, and you strike a deadly blow at its prosperity. Why are the farmers in the interior of our States able to send the fruits of their toil to foreign markets? Mainly because the cost of their transportation is lessened by emigration. When we trace out all its influences permeating every industrial purpose, we are amazed at the madness and folly that seeks to divert it elsewhere, and ashamed of the bigotry and ignorance which prompts the effort. The charges of pauperism and criminality made against our foreign citizens are unjust. Their violations of law, while they are not familiar with our institutions, and when placed under circumstances of great and novel temptations, are no more frequent than the commission of crimes by those of American birth, when removed from the conventional restraints of kindred and friends, in California, or on the shores of the Gulf of Mexico or the Caribbean Seas."

POLITICAL MEDDLING WITH THE RIGHTS OF SELF-GOVERNMENT IN STATES AND TERRITORIES.

"The spirit of political meddling with the affairs of others, and with the rights of man on account of birth or religion, has naturally given birth to a desire to interfere with distinct and distant communities. The idea of disfranchising those who go as well as those who come, inevitably grew up in the minds of those who wish to control the action of others. Such minds instinctively war against self-government by communities as well as by individuals.

"At this time a party powerful in numbers, resources and talents, in opposition to the warning and entreaties of the patriotic, whom the American people love and reverence, have entered into the pending political contest with· the determination of arraying one section of our common country against another. Its presses constantly urge upon the public attention every thing of past, present, or fancied occurrence which is calculated to excite the prejudices or arouse the passions of the North against the South. This treasonable conduct is called a necessary measure of defense against the aggressive power and political influences of the South.

"The people of the North are uniformly opposed to slavery, not from hostility to the South, but because it is repugnant to our sentiments. In conformity with our views we have abolished slavery here, and having exercised our rights in our own way, we should be willing to let other communities have the same rights and privileges we have enjoyed. We are bound to act upon our faith in the principles of self-government. * * *

"The republican organization proposes an assault upon the Southern States by a system of agitation and excitement, directly at war with the purposes of the Constitution. They constantly discuss questions belonging to other States, to the entire neglect of their own local affairs. They organize their party expressly on the ground that all and every difference of opinion about their own concerns are to be overlooked, provided they agree in their views about an institution which does not exist in their own States, and does exist in States where they admit they have no constitutional right to interfere. They give dispensation for all past offenses. Enrollment in their ranks expiates the most deadly heresies in doctrines and conduct, and exempts from the performance of all acts of charity, mercy or benevolence. The Union, among its members, is a libel upon their past professions and actions. They mock at consistency. They ask the foreign born citizen to unite with them in interfering with men afar off, and thus justify interference with their own religious and political rights at home. They invite the opponent of the Maine Law to unite with them to coerce those who live west of the Missouri, and thus justify coercion by their own neighbors. The pretext for this evasion of the Constitution, is the affairs of a single territory. The discussion, the appeals to passion and the influences of their actions, are not confined to that point; nor can they stop a that point, if they succeed in their present efforts. They must go to the extent of interfering with the sovereignties of the State. Their out-spoken allies, the abolitionists, declare that such are their intentions. The pretext for the war now waged against the South, is an alleged invasive policy on its part. Conscious of the wickedness of a sectional warfare, an attempt is made to show that their policy is defensive."

CONCLUSION.

"To charge upon the advocates of the let-alone policy the fruits of meddling, and thus attempt to justify interferences, is no new device. Tyrants always denounce liberty as anarchy; freedom of conscience as infidelity; reliance upon education and intelligence as immorality and disorder; and to the extent of their power they take care that all possible evils attend every effort to emancipate mind, action or conscience. This is the character of the warfare waged upon the democratic party. He who upholds the principle of interference, is responsible for interference. He who stands by the principle of local self-government, is not responsible for acts against which he protests in principle and practice. Every man knows that peace and good order will not be restored to this land while the press and political agitators urge sectional hatred and interference with local affairs.

"The evils of political meddling with morals, religion, and the rights of distinct communities are not only of a public nature, but they affect individual character. It causes the Pharisaic spirit which is prevalent in our country. It creates false standards of virtue. It misleads men in their estimates of themselves. How many men, harsh and hard in their dealings with their fellow-citizens, fancy themselves benevolent because they cherish a hatred of real or fancied wrong in remote parts of our country? How many who omit the charities and kindnesses of daily life, who forget to aid the poor in the next street, quiet their consciences by denunciations of those whom they charge with being wrongdoers a thousand miles away? How many bad men gain influence and power at home by occupying the public mind with alleged wrongs abroad? How many arrogate to themselves an exclusive Christianity because they reverse every principle of its teachings in their sentiments toward their fellowmen? How many have given rifles for Kansas who would not give aid to their suffering neighbors. The present practice of stirring up popular passions, threatens to destroy all freedom of opinion, and all individuality of action.

"The pulpit and the press are becoming unfaithful. They follow in the wake of popular excitement. They do not point out nor combat the faults of readers or hearers, but administer to the self-complacency by fierce denunciations of their distant fellow-citizens. They assume the bearing of courage while acting upon the principles of cowardice.

"Fanaticism gives its subjects no rest. It drives them on from one subject of excitement to another, from one hatred to another, from one persecution to another. We know that the political fanatic of to-day will be foremost in the religious persecutions of to-morrow.

"The leprosy of hypocrisy is spread over our land, giving us an outward whiteness because there is an internal corruption. Religion, charity and morals are hidden by 'vindictive piety' and 'malignant benevolence,' at war with every principle of Christianity. Unless the good and patriotic rebuke this spirit of cant and fanaticism, the sourness and hatred of the 'round head' will again, in its reaction, be followed by the gross licentiousness of the cavalier."

CHAPTER VIII.

FROM 1854 TO 1861.

CINCINNATI CONVENTION.

BETWEEN the close of the year 1854 and the Presidential canvass of 1856, Governor Seymour was indefatigable in his efforts to heal the breaches which threatened the integrity of the Democratic party; as well as to arouse the country to a true sense of the danger from the violent sectional agitations and conflicts then inaugurated for party purposes by the Northern Republican leaders. No public man was more outspoken and earnest in the discussion of public matters; and he, more than any other living Democratic politician, canvassed the State and nation. He was never a dumb or timid candidate; nor a time-serving politician. On all public questions he had well-matured and well-defined views, and convictions which he never sought to conceal from his fellow-citizens.

During this period also, he delivered several addresses before various literary and other societies; and received from Hamilton College and from the Norwich University the honorary degree of LL.D. He spent much time at the West, studying the characteristics and topography of the country, and the wants and necessities of its people.

The system of State commissions was instituted for party-purposes, at this period, with the intent of taking from the great city of New York control over their own affairs, and placing the same in the hands of the bold and bad men that came into power with the Republican party. Among the first of these partisan and aggressive schemes was the original organization of the metropolitan police, which, at the time, was generally looked upon as a glaring violation of the letter of the State Constitution, as well as of the true theory of popular government. After some resistance on the part of the local authorities, the legal question was presented to the Court of Appeals; and that body felt competent to decide that the evasion of the Constitution by the creation of the metropolitan district, was so complete, that the law must be sustained. Hiram Denio—an able jurist and prominent Democrat—delivered the opinion of the Court, which opinion was adverse to the views and sentiments of the great mass of the Democratic party, and particularly distasteful to the Democratic officials in the city.

Cotemporaneous with the publication of this decision, was held the nominating convention of 1857, when a successor to Judge Denio was to be selected. The party demanded a new candidate, and few deemed the re-nominating of the Judge either desirable or possible. At the very moment when the selection was about to be made, and after new names had been suggested, and speeches had been made denouncing the decision of the Court, Mr. Seymour, then a delegate from the county of Oneida, ascended the platform, and proposed the re-nomination of Judge Denio, advocating the same as the true mode of vindicating the sincerity of the party in its professions of respect for an independent judiciary. Although hostile to the system of commissions, and differing from Judge Denio in his views of the law, "Yet," said he, "let us nominate him, not because we approve his decision, but because we respect his office, have confidence in his motives, and are willing to accept and observe any statute legitimately passed and affirmed by the courts." "It is," said he, "the pride, the boast, and the strength of the Democratic party, that it is law-abiding. It is this that constitutes its conservatism, making it at the same time the party of progress and reform, and in its submission to lawful authority and observance of constitutional compacts, the guardian of the National Faith, the rights of the States, and the property and liberties of the citizens."

The occasion was one of great excitement; and the speech of Governor Seymour, the proudest of his whole life. The Convention at first listened in respectful silence, until convinced, when, catching the enthusiasm of the eloquent speaker, it broke into applause. The issue had been met, and the victory was complete. Judge Denio was promptly re-nominated by a convention that radically differed with him on this question; and he was triumphantly elected by the people. This attitude of the party carried the State, although a majority of the people were then in party sympathy with their opponents.

In the Cincinnati Convention, Governor Seymour

was its leading delegate. His friends inclined to the support of Judge Douglas, but cordially acquiesced in the selection of Buchanan and Breckinridge; in whose behalf he made strenuous exertions, speaking in almost every county in the State, in other States, and wherever requested by the committee directing the campaign. These valuable services were appreciated by President Buchanan, who, on his accession to power, tendered to Governor Seymour a position abroad—suggesting a first class mission to one of the European courts—a post for which Seymour was admirably qualified by nature and education; but flattering as was the offer, and desirable as was the position, Governor Seymour preferred to remain in private life.

When relieved from the duties of public office, Governor Seymour resumed his country life. It has been a desire with him to promote the substantial and permanent interests of agriculture; and the accomplishment of such a result would undoubtedly give him more satisfaction, and be the source of more unalloyed pleasure, than success in almost any other department of business.

This trait in the Governor's character is well understood by his neighbors, and by many agriculturists of other States. Soon after his nomination for the Presidency, the following appreciative article appeared in a leading paper published in Pennsylvania:—

"Horatio Seymour, although a man of the most brilliant parts—a profound scholar, a magnificent orator, a wise, sagacious and experienced statesman—is only a plain farmer after all. From the peaceful and pleasant occupations of rural life, he has been called by the unanimous voice of the great party of the people to become their standard-bearer in the mighty contest in which they are about to engage. He did not seek this office. The office—as all offices should—sought him, and he stands before the nation to-day as the proudest specimen of American yeomanry the world has ever looked upon. In the quiet retirement of his country home, he has, while earnestly devoting himself to the tilling of the soil, been giving the best energies of his comprehensive mind to national affairs. Familiar with all the details of government, thoroughly versed in national finances, accurately comprehending the wants of the nation at this imminent crisis in its history, he will bring to the office to which he will undoubtedly be elected in November next, a combination of qualifications such as have never been surpassed by any of the distinguished incumbents of the Presidential chair.

"We are proud to direct attention to the fact that our greatest statesman is a farmer. The great agricultural interest—the leading interest of the country—will receive at his hands the attention it so richly deserves—that attention which its vastness and importance imperatively demand, but which hitherto has not been given it. Our rural friends may point with just pride to the great farmer statesman—the finest representative of his class the world has ever looked upon. Under his administration the farmer may rest assured that the hitherto greatly neglected interests of agriculture will be properly attended to—that it will be made to occupy that position in our national industrial pursuits to which it is justly entitled. Let the yeomanry of the land rally to his support. His sympathies are in full accord with their interests. He understands in all their details the agricultural wants of the country. He comprehends the vital relation they hold to our national prosperity. His enlarged experience as a statesman, coupled with his extended practical experience as a farmer, render him of all other men the man to whom the farmer should extend his warmest support."

CHAPTER IX.

THE BREAKING OUT OF THE WAR.

Public events during Mr. Buchanan's administration excited alarm in the minds of all thoughtful men; they heard with dread, constant appeals to sectional passions and prejudices. The people of the North and South were taught to hate each other: the value of the Union was underrated. Statements were put forth to show that the Southern States cost more than they were worth to the North. When warned by the more thoughtful portion of the community of the impending danger of civil war, those who attempted to point out the dangers that lay in their pathway were treated with contempt and derision, and were sneered at as "Union Saviors." With others, Governor Seymour put forth his utmost efforts to avert the calamities which have been brought upon our country by sectional passions. He addressed meetings in his own and other States; and encountered the reproaches which were heaped upon all who attempted to keep alive the spirit which animated the founders of our constitutional form of government. It was said that the South could not be driven out of the Union. When, at length, the contest actually began, the same prejudices and passions which brought it on misled the public mind with respect to its nature and magnitude. It was treated by the leaders of the Republican party as a feeble and brief attempt to resist the Federal authority. It was still held that the South was incapable of supporting itself without northern aid ; and it was firmly believed if the Mississippi was closed, and the North witheld its supplies, the South would be reduced at once to abject submission. In vain did Governor Seymour and others point to official statistics and to the history of our country to dispel these fatal errors. They were denounced as traitors because they warned the people and Government against the inadequate measures of the adminstration, which were simply wasting the blood and treasures of the North. They were insulted because they uttered truths about the resources of the South, which should have been familiar to every school-boy. An effort was made to avert actual war by means of what was called the Peace Congress. A convention was also held at Albany of the leading men of the State of New York, and, among others, it was addressed by Governor Seymour. He showed the resources of the South and the horrors of the impending civil war, and urged some measures to prevent it. He contrasted two scenes in our history in the following eloquent language :—

' Threescore and ten years, the period allotted for the life of man, have rolled away since George Washington was inaugurated first President of the United States, in the city of New York. We were then among the feeblest people of the earth. The flag of Great Britain still waved over Oswego with insulting defiance of our national rights, and the treaty recognizing our independence. The powers of the world regarded us with indifference or treated us with contemptuous injustice. So swift has been our progress under the influence of our Union that but yesterday we could defy the world in arms, and none dared to insult our flag. When our Constitution was inaugurated the utmost enthusiasm pervaded our land. Stern warriors who had fought the battles of the Revolution wept for joy. Glad processions of men and women marched with triumphal pride along the streets of our cities—holy men of God prayed in His Temples that the spirit of fraternal love, which had shaped the compromises of the Constitution, might never fade away, and that sectional bigotry, hate and discord might never curse our land. Amid this wild enthusiasm there was no imagination so excited, nor piety with faith so strong, that it foresaw the full influence of the event then celebrated. Some yet live to see their numbers increased from four to thirty millions, our territories quadrupled and extended from the Atlantic to the Pacific, our power and progress the wonder of the world. Alas, sir, they also live to see the patriotism and fraternal love, which have wrought out these marvelous results die out, and the mighty fabric of our Government about to crumble and fall, because the virtues which reared and upheld it have departed from our councils.

"What a spectacle do we present to-day? Already six States have withdrawn from this Confederacy. Revolution has actually begun. The term 'secession' divests it of none of its terrors, nor do arguments to prove secession inconsistent with our Constitution, stay its progress or mitigate its evils. All virtue, patriotism, and intelligence seem to have fled from our national capital; it has been well likened to the conflagration of an asylum for madmen—some look on with idiotic imbecility, some in sullen silence, and some scatter the firebrands which consume the fabric above them, and bring upon all a common destruction. Is there one revolting aspect in this scene which has not its parallel at the Capital of your country? Do you not see there the senseless imbecility, the garrulous idiocy, the maddened rage displayed with regard to petty personal passions and party purposes, while the glory, the honor, and the safety of the country are all forgotten. The same pervading fanaticism has brought evil upon all the institutions of our land. Our churches are torn asunder and desecrated to partisan purposes. The wrongs of our local legislation, the growing burdens of debt and taxation, the gradual destruction of the African in the free States, which is marked by each recurring census, are all due to the neglect of our own duties, caused by the complete absorption of the public mind by a senseless, unreasoning fanaticism. The agitation of the question of slavery, has thus far brought greater social, moral, and legislative evils upon the people of the free States than it has upon the institutions of those against whom it has been excited. The wisdom of Franklin stamped upon the first coin issued by our Government the wise motto, 'mind your business!' The violations of the homely proverb, which lies at the foundation of local rights, has, thus far, proved more hurtful to the meddlers in the affairs of others than to those against whom this pragmatic action is directed."

When hostilities broke out and Fort Sumter was attacked, Governor Seymour was at the capital of the State of Wisconsin. Many of the democratic members of its Legislature consulted with him as to the course they should pursue. He advised them that it was their duty to uphold the administration in its efforts to enforce the laws; that they must accept the war as a fact, and there was but one side they could take in the contest; that in all matters where the administration had the right to decide, citizens were bound to obey.

While he remained in that State, he aided in the formation of companies, which were organized in pursuance of President Lincoln's first call. He also addressed meetings in the State of Wisconsin on the 4th of July, 1861, and on other occasions, urging upon all the duty of sustaining the Union. It is an honorable and pleasant fact, connected with his action in that State, than when he was assailed, while running for Governor in 1852, the charge that he had left New York for the purpose of being absent at the critical time when the war broke out, leading republicans holding high positions in the Western States, denounced this charge in writing as unjust and untrue, and bore witness to the services he had rendered to the Union cause.

Upon his return from the West he had an interview with Governor Morgan, and Adjutant-General Hillhouse, and at their request, was put at the head of the committee named to raise troops from the County of Oneida; and it is due to Governor Morgan and General Hillhouse to say, that at all times they have spoken in a just and honorable manner of the course of Governor Seymour, although they held political views at variance with his.

Governor Seymour has at all times felt the importance of a well regulated militia. He had urged this in his messages of 1853 and '54. The State military association was organized at that time by members of his staff. In 1862 he attended the meeting of this body at Albany, with a view of strengthening the military force of the State, and delivered an address from which we make the following brief extract:—

" *We denounce the rebellion as most wicked, because it wages war against the best government the world has ever seen.* Remember there is guilt in negligence as well as in disobedience; and there is danger, too. We complain that the arms of the General Government were, heretofore, unequally distributed. This is owing in part to the treasonable purpose of officials, but it is also due in part to our own neglect of our constitutional duties. Our enrolled militia should count more that five hundred thousand, but they do not exceed one-half of that number. Hence our quota of arms was diminished, and that of the Southern States increased. The want of these arms and a proper military organization, has added immensely to the cost of this war and to the burden of taxation. More than this, if we had respected our constitutional obligation, we might, at the outset, have placed in the field a force that would have put out this rebellion when it was first kindled."

At its conclusion Governor Morgan moved a vote of thanks; and the great services of Governor Seymour to the national cause were of them freely acknowledged.

CHAPTER X.

ELECTION OF 1862.

IN the course of the year 1862, the Government was falling into utter confusion; public confidence was weakened, and leading Republican papers proposed to push Mr. Lincoln from his place, and, by a revolutionary act, to place another person in the Executive Chair. The following extracts will show the length to which these conspirators were prepared to go. The *Times* of April 25, 1861, under the head of "Wanted—a Leader," said:—

> "In every great crisis the human heart demands a leader that incarnates its ideas, its emotions, and its aims. The moment he takes the helm, order, promptitude, and confidence follow as the necessary result. When we see such results, we know that a hero leads. No such hero at present directs affairs."
>
> *   *   *   *   *   *   *   *
>
> "A holy zeal inspires every loyal heart to sacrifice comfort, property, and life even is nothing, because if we fail, we must give up these for our children, for humanity, and for ourselves. '*Where is the leader of this sublime passion?*' Can the administration furnish him?"

From the *Times*, April 21, 1861:—

> "The President must direct the great national arm, which only waits his command to deliver a blow that will end the war at once, or that arm, fired with a public rage which will brook no control or guidance, will deal out, in its blind wrath, a destruction more terrible and complete than ever a people suffered before. *The interest of humanity will be forgotten, and that will prove a war of utter extermination, which the President has now the power to control.*"

From the *Times*, April 26, 1861 :—

"George Law only speaks the universal sentiments of the whole community, without reference to party or class, when he tells President Lincoln that the Government must clear the path to Washington, or the people will do it for them. If any man of position as a military leader, or as a strong resolute commander, would offer to lead a force through Baltimore, with or without orders, he could have 50,000 followers, as soon as they could rush to his standard."

From the *Times*, April 21, 1861 :—

"No one has observed carefully the development of public sentiment at the North, and especially in this city, during the last ten days, can doubt for a moment that our warning was perfectly justified by the condition of affairs, and absolutely demanded for the preservation of the public peace. We did not hesitate to say to the President that unless he acted with more vigor, with more courage, with a more thorough comprehension of public exigencies, and of public sentiment than had been displayed, he ran the risk of plunging the Government into embarrassments, from which it could only be rescued by *some one* who should more accurately represent the sentiments and purposes of the American people."

Further extracts of a similar character occur in the speech of 1862, which is given below.

Governor Seymour, while he felt the imbecility of the men in power—although he had opposed the election of Mr. Lincoln—denounced these treasonable purposes, in the Democratic Convention of Sept. 10, 1862. At this Convention he was again enthusiastically nominated for the office of Governor. He set forth, in the following terms, his views of the paramount duties of American citizens at that crisis :—

"Two years have not passed away since a Convention, remarkable for its numbers, patriotism, and intelligence, assembled at this place, to avert, if possible, the calamities which afflict our people. In respectful terms, it implored the leaders of the political party which had triumphed at a recent election to submit to the people of this country some measure of conciliation which would save them from civil war. It asked that before we should be involved in the evils and horrors of domestic bloodshed, those upon whom it would bring bankruptcy and ruin, and into whose homes it would carry desolation and death, should be allowed to speak. That prayer for the rights of our people was derided and denounced, and false assurances were given that there was no danger. The storm came upon us with all its fury —and the war, so constantly and clearly foretold, desolated our land. It is said no compromises would have satisfied the South. If we had tried them it would not now be a matter of discordant opinion. If these offers had not satisfied the South, they would have gratified loyal men at the North, and would have united us more perfectly.

"Animated by devotion to our Constitution and Union, our people rallied to the support of the Government, and one year since showed an armed strength that astonished the world. We again appealed to those who wielded this mighty material power, to use it for the restoration of the Union and to uphold the Constitution, and were told that he who clamored for his constitutional rights was a traitor!

"Congress assembled. Inexperienced in the conduct of public affairs, drunk with power, it began its course of agitation, outrage, and wrong. The defeat of our arms at Manassas, for a time, filled it with terror. Under this influence, it adopted the resolution of Mr. Crittenden, declaring,—

"'That the present deplorable civil war has been forced upon the country by the Disunionists of the Southern States, now in arms against the Constitutional Government, and in arms around the Capitol; that in this National emergency Congress, banishing all feelings of mere passion or resentment, will recollect only its duty to the whole country; that this war is not waged, on their part, in any spirit of oppression or for any purpose of conquest or subjugation, or purpose of overthrowing or interfering with the rights or established institutions of those States, but to defend and maintain the *supremacy* of the Constitution and to preserve the Union, with all the dignity, equality, and rights of the several States unimpaired, and that as soon as these objects are accomplished the war ought to cease.'

"Again the people rallied around the flag of the Union. But no sooner were their fears allayed than they began anew the factious intrigues—the violent discussions and the unconstitutional legislation which ever brings defeat and disgrace upon nations. In vain were they warned of the consequences of their follies. In vain did the President implore forbearance and moderation. No act was omitted which would give energy to the Secessionists, or which would humiliate and mortify the loyal men of the South. Every topic calculated to divide and distract the North was dragged into embittered debates. Proclamations of emancipation were urged upon the President, which could only confiscate the property of loyal citizens at the South; for none others could be reached by the power of the Government. The confiscation act had already forfeited the legal rights of all who were engaged in or who aided and upheld the rebellion. These were excited to desperate energy by laws which made their lives, their fortunes, the safety of their families and homes depend upon the success of their schemes. From the Dragon's teeth, sown broadcast by Congress, have sprung the armies which have driven back our forces, and which now beleaguer the Capital of our country. The acts of the National Legislature have given pleasure to the Abolitionists, victories to the Secessionists. But while treason rejoices and triumphs, defeat and disgrace have been brought upon the flag of our country and the defenders of our Constitution. Every man who visited Washington six months ago could see and feel we were upon the verge of disaster. Discord, jealousy, envy, and strife pervaded the atmosphere.

"I went to the camp of our soldiers. Amid the hardships of an exhausting campaign—amid sufferings from exposure and want—amid those languishing upon beds of sickness, or those struck down by the casualties of war, I heard and saw only devotion to our Constitution, and love for our country's flag. Each eye brightened as it looked upon the National standard with its glorious emblazonry of Stars and Stripes. From this scene of patriotic devotion I went into our National Capitol. I traversed its mosaic pavements; I gazed upon its walls of polished marble; I saw upon its ceilings all that wealth, lavishly poured out, could do to make them suggestive of our country's greatness and its wonderful wealth of varied productions. Art had exhausted itself in painting and sculpture, to make every aspect suggestive of high and noble thought and purpose. Full of the associations which cluster about this vast temple which should be dedicated to patriotism and truth, I entered its legislative halls; their gilded walls and gorgeous furniture did not contrast more strongly with the rude scenes of martial life than the glistening putrescence and thin lacquer of Congressional virtue contrast with the sterling loyalty and noble self-sacrifice of our country's defenders. I listened to debates full of bitterness and strife.

"I saw in the camp a heartfelt homage to our national flag—a stern defiance of those who dared to touch its sacred folds with hostile hands. I heard in the Capitol threats of mutilation of its emblazonry— by striking down the life of States. He who would rend our National standard by dividing our Union is a traitor. He who would put out one glittering star from its azure field, is a traitor, too."

THE PRESENT CONDITION OF OUR COUNTRY.

"Let us now confront the facts of our condition, and they shall be stated in the language of those who brought this administration into power, and who now are politically opposed to the members of this Convention. After the expenditure of nearly one thousand millions of dollars, and the sacrifice of more than one hundred thousand Northern lives, in the language of the *Evening Post*:—

"'What has been the result? Our armies of the West, the noble victors of Fort Donelson and Shiloh, are scattered so that no man knows their whereabout, while the foe they were sent to disperse is a hundred miles in their rear, threatening the cities of Tennessee and Kentucky, and even advancing toward one of the principal commercial cities of the Free States. There is no leadership, no unity of command, apparently no plan or concert of action in the entire region we have undertaken to hold and defend. At the same time, our army of the East, numbering 250,000 troops, fully armed and equipped and admirably disciplined, after investing the Capital of the enemy, has been driven back to its original position on the Potomac, decimated in numbers and unprepared to make a single vigorous movement in advance.'

"And it adds:—

"'Now it is useless to shut our eyes to the fact that this is a failure, disgraceful, humiliating, and awful.'

"The *Evening Journal*, the accredited organ of the Secretary of State, now admits the truths uttered in this hall when we assembled here in February, 1861, truths then denounced as absurd and treasonable. It says:—

"'The War has been a stern schoolmaster to the people of the loyal States. We have learned the folly of underrating our enemies. We have learned that they are equally brave, equally hardy, equally quick-witted, equally endowed with martial qualities with ourselves. We have learned that they are terribly in earnest in their efforts to achieve their ends,

"The New York *Tribune* declares that—

"'The country is in peril. Viewed from the standpoint of the public estimate of 'the situation,' it is in extreme peril. The Rebels seem to be pushing forward their forces all along the border line, from the Atlantic to the Missouri. They are threatening the Potomac and the Ohio. They are striking at Washington, Cincinnati, and Louisville. This simultaneous movement is both alarming and encouraging. It is alarming because, through the timidity, despondency or folly of the Federal Government, it may become temporarily successful, giving to the foe a lodgment in some portion of the Free States which may require weeks to break up.'

"But it is admitted by those who were opposed to us, that debt and defeat are not the heaviest calamities which weigh us down. A virtuous people and a pure government can bear up against any amount of outward pressure or physical calamity, but when rottenness and corruption pervade the legislative hall or executive department, the heart of the patriot faints and his arm withers. The organ of the Secretary of State admits:—

"'There have been mistakes. There have been speculations. Weak men have disgraced, and bad men have betrayed the Government. Contractors have fattened on fat jobs. Adventurers have found the war a source of private gain. Moral desperadoes have flocked about the National Capital and lain in wait for prey. The scum of the land has gathered about the sources of power and defiled them by its reek and offensive odor. There has been mismangement in the departments; mismanagement wherever great labor has been performed, and great responsibilties devolving. Men—even Presidents and Cabinet officers and Commanding Generals—have erred, because they could not grasp the full significance of the drama, and because they were compelled to strike out on untrodden paths.'—*Evening Journal.*

"Hear the voice of a leading Republican orator:—

"'I declare it upon my responsibitity as a Senator of the United States,' said John P. Hale, 'that the liberties of this country are in greater danger to-day from the corruptions and from the profligacy practiced in the various departments of the Government than they are from the open enemy in the field.'

"The New York *Times* demands a change in the administration, and in the conduct of affairs.

"I have thus carefully set forth the declarations and named the witnesses to this awful indictment against our rulers, for we mean to proceed with all the care and candor, and all the solemnity of a judicial tribunal.

"It is with a sorrowful heart I point to these dark pictures, not drawn by journals of the democratic party. God knows that as a member of that patriotic organization, as an American citizen, I would gladly efface them if I could. But, alas, they are grounded upon truths that can not be gainsaid. Once more, then, our republican fellow-citizens, in this day of our common humiliation and disgrace, we implore you as respectfully as in the hour of your political triumph listen to our suggestions. We do not come with reproaches, but with entreaties. Follow the pathways marked out by the Constitution and we shall be extricated from our perilous position. On the other hand, if you will still be governed by those who brought us into our present condition, you will learn too late that there are yet deeper depths of degradation before us, and greater miseries to be borne than those which now oppress us. Nay more, the President of the United States appeals to us all in his communication with the loyal men of the border States, when he says he is pressed to violate his duty, his oath of office, and the Constitution of the land—pressed by cowardly and heartless men, living far away from the scenes of war, fattening upon the wealth coined from the blood and misery of the land, and living in those localities where official investigation show that this people and Government have been robbed by fraudulent contracts. Such men demand that those who have suffered most in this contest, who have shown the highest and purest patriotism under the terrible trials of divided families, of desolated homes, of ruined fortunes and of blood-stained fields, should have a new and further evil inflicted upon them by the hands of a Government they are struggling to uphold. By the help of God and the people we will relieve the President from that pressure."

WHY THE REPUBLICAN PARTY CAN NOT SAVE THE COUNTRY.

"On the other hand, the very character of the republican organization, makes it incapable of conducting the affairs of the Government. For a series of years, it has practiced a system of coalitions, with men differing in principle, until it can have no distinctive policy. In such chaotic masses, the violent have most control. They have been educating their followers for years, through the press, not to obey laws which did not accord with their views. How can they demand submission from whole communities, while they contend that individuals may oppose laws opposed to their consciences? They are higher law men. They insist that the contest, in which we are engaged, is an irrepressible one, and that therefore the South could not avoid it, unless they were willing at the outset to surrender all that abolitionists demanded. To declare that this contest is irrepressible, declares that our fathers formed a government which could not stand. Are such men the proper guardians of this Government? Have not their speeches and acts given strength to the rebellion, and have they not also enabled its leaders to prove to their deluded followers, that the contest was an irrepressible one?

"But their leaders have not only asserted that this contest was irrepressible, unless the South will give up what extreme republicans demand (their local institution), but those in power have done much to justify this rebellion in the eyes of the world. The guilt of rebellion is determined by the character of the Government against which it is arrayed. The right of revolution, in the language of President Lincoln, is a sacred right when exerted against a bad Government.

"We charge that this rebellion is most wicked, because it is against the best Government that ever existed. It is the excellence of our Government that makes resistance a crime. Rebellion is not necessarily wrong. It might be an act of the highest virtue—it may be one of the deepest depravity. The rebellion of our fathers is our proudest boast—the rebellion of our brothers is the humiliation of our nation, is our national disgrace. To resist a bad Government is patriotism—to resist a good one is the greatest guilt. The first is patriotism, the last is treason. Legal tribunals can only regard resistance of laws as a crime but in the forum of public sentiment the character of the Government will decide if the act is treason or patriotism

"Our Government and its administration are different things; but in the eyes of the civilized world, abuses, weakness or folly in the conduct of affairs go far to justify resistance. I have read to you the testimony of Messrs. Greeley, Weed, Bryant, Raymond and Marble, charging fraud, corruption, outrage and incompetency upon those in power. Those who stand up to testify to the incompetency of these representatives of a discordant party to conduct the affairs of our Government are politically opposed to us. Bear in mind that the embarrassment of President Lincoln grows out of the conflicting views of his political friends, and their habits and principles of insubordination. His hands would be strengthened by a democratic victory. and if his private prayers are answered we will relieve him from the pressure of philanthropists who thirst for blood, and who call for the extermination of the men, women and children of the South. The brutal and bloody language of partisan editors and political preachers have lost us the sympathy of the civilized world in a contest where all mankind should be upon one side.

"Turning to the legislative departments of our Government, what do we see? In the history of the decline and fall of nations, there are no more striking displays of madness and folly. The assemblage of Congress throws gloom over the nation; its continuance in session is more disastrous than defeat upon the battle-field. It excites alike alarm and disgust.

"The public are disappointed in the results of the war This is owing to the differing objects of the people on the one hand, and of the fanatical agitators in and out of Congress on the other. In the army, the Union men of the North and South battle side by side, under one flag, to put down rebellion and uphold the Union and Constitution. In Congress a fanatical majority make war on the Union men of the South and strengthen the hands of secessionists by words and acts which enable them to keep alive the flames of civil war. What is done in the battle-field by the blood and treasure of the people, is undone by senators. Half of the time is spent in factious measures designed to destroy all confidence in the Government of the South, and the rest in annoying our army, in meddling with its operations, embarrassing our generals, and in publishing undigested and unfounded scandal. One party is seeking to bring about peace, the other to keep alive hatred and bitterness by interferences. They prove the wisdom of Solomon, when he said: 'It is an honor to a man to cease from strife, but every fool will be meddling.'

"This war can not be brought to a successful conclusion or our country restored to an honorable peace under the Republican leaders for another reason. Our disasters are mainly due to the fact that they have not dared to tell the truth to the community. A system of misrepresentation had been practised so long and so successfully that when the war burst upon us, they feared to let the people know its full proportions, and they persisted in assuring their friends it was but a passing excitement. They still asserted that the South was unable to maintain and carry on a war. They denounced as a traitor every man who tried to tell the truth, and to warn our people of the magnitude of the contest.

"Now, my Republican friends, you know that the misapprehensions of the North with regard to the South has drenched the land with blood. Was this ignorance accidental? I appeal to you, Republicans, if for years past, through the press and in publications which have been urged upon your attention by the leaders of your party, you have not been taught to despise the power and resources of the South? I appeal to you to say if this teaching has not been a part of the machinery by which power has been gained? I appeal to you to answer if those who tried to teach truths, now admitted, have not been denounced? I appeal to you if a book, beyond all others, false, bloody, and treasonable, was not sent out with the indorsement of all your managers; and is it not true that now, when men blush to own that they believed its statements, that its author is honored with an official station? It is now freely confessed by you all, that you have been deceived with respect to the South. Who deceived you? Who, by false teachings, instilled contempt and hate into the minds of our people? Who stained our land with blood? Who caused ruin and distress? All these things are within your own knowledge. Are their authors the leaders to rescue us from our calamities? They shrink back appalled from the mischief they have wrought, and tell you it is an irrepressible contest. That reason is as good for Jefferson Davis as for them. They attempt to drown reflections by new excitements and new appeals to our passions. Having already, in legislation, gone far beyond the limits at which, by their resolutions, they were pledged to stop, they now ask to adopt measures which they have heretofore denounced as unjust and unconstitutional. For this reason they can not save our country.

"The Republican party can not save the country, because through its powerful press it teaches contempt of the laws, Constitution, and constituted authorities. They are not only destroying the Union, but they are shaking and weakening the whole structures of State as well as of the National Government, by denunciations of every law and of all authority that stands in the way of their passions or their purposes. They have not only carried discord into our churches and legislative halls, but into our armies. Every general who agrees with them upon the subject of slavery is upheld in every act of insubordination, and sustained against the clearest proofs of incompetence, if not of corruption. On the other hand every commander who differs from their views upon the single point of slavery, is denounced, not only for incompetency, but constantly depreciated in every act. No man is allowed to be a Christian; no man is regarded as a statesman; no man is suffered, unmolested, to do his duty as a soldier unless he supports measures which no one dared to urge eighteen months since. They insist that martial law is superior to constitutional law; that the wills of generals in the field are above all restraints; but they demand for themselves the right to direct and control these generals. They claim an influence higher than they will allow to the laws of the land. Are these displays of insubordination and violence safe at this time?

"The weight of annual taxation will test severely the loyalty of the people of the North. Repudiation of our financial obligations would cause disorder and endless moral evils. Pecuniary rights will never be held more sacred than personal rights. Repudiation of the Constitution involves repudiation of national debts; of its guaranties of rights of property, of person, and of conscience.

"The moment we show the world that we do not hold the Constitution to be a sacred compact, we not only destroy all sense of security, but we turn away from our shores the vast tide of foreign emigration. It comes here now, not because there are not other skies as bright and other lands as productive as ours; it seeks here security for freedom—for rights of conscience—for immunity from tyrannical interferences, and from meddling impertinence. The home and fireside rights heretofore enjoyed by the American people—enjoyed under protection of written Constitution, have made us great and prosperous. I entreat you again, touch them not with sacrilegious hands! We are threatened with the breaking up of our social system, with the overthrow of State and National Governments. If we begin a war upon the compromises of the Constitution we must go through with it. It contains many restraints upon our natural rights. It may be asked by what right do the six small New England States, with a population less than that of New York, have six times its power in the Senate, which has become the controlling branch of Government? By what natural right do these States, with their small united populations and limited territories, balance the power of New York, Pennsylvania, Ohio, Illinois, Indiana and Michigan? The vast debt growing out of this war will give rise to new and angry discussions. It will be held almost exclusively in a few Atlantic States. Look upon the map of the Union and see how small is the territory in which it will be owned. We are to be divided into creditor and debtor States, and the last will have a vast preponderance of power and strength. Unfortunately there is no taxation upon this national debt, and its share is thrown off upon other property. It is held where many of the Government contracts have been executed, and where in some instances, gross frauds have been practiced. It is held largely where the Constitution gives a disproportional share of political power. With all these elements of discord, is it wise to assail constitutional law, or bring authority into contempt. Is it safe to encourage the formation of irresponsible committees, made up of impertinent men, who thrust themselves into the conduct of public affairs and try to dictate to legal rulers? or will you tolerate the enrollment of armies which are not constituted or organized by proper authorities? Are such things just toward those who have placed their fortunes in the hands of the Government at this crisis?

"We implore you do not be deceived again with this syren song of no danger. There is danger, great and imminent, of the destruction of all government, of safety for life and property, unless the duty of obedience to law and respect for authorities and the honest support of those in the public service both military and civil, are taught and enforced, by all means within our control.

"With us there is no excuse for revolutionary action. Our system of government gives peaceful remedies for all evils in legislation."

WHAT THE DEMOCRATIC PARTY PROPOSE TO DO.

'Mr. President: It will be asked what do we propose to do? We mean, with all our powers of mind and person to support the Constitution and uphold the Union; to maintain the laws, to preserve the public faith. We insist upon obedience to laws and respect for Constitutional authority; we will defend the rights of citizens; we mean that rulers and subjects shall respect the laws; we will put down all revolutionary committees; we will resist all unauthorized organizations of armed men; we will spurn officious meddlers who are impudently pushing themselves into the councils of our Government. Politically opposed to those in authority, we demand they shall be treated with the respect due to their positions as the representatives of the dignity and honor of the American people. We do not try to save our country by abandoning its Government. In these times of trial and danger we cling more closely to the great principles of civil and religious liberty and of personal right; we will man the defenses and barriers which the Constitution throws around them; we will revive the courage and strengthen the arms of loyal men by showing them they have a living Government about which to rally; we will proclaim amidst the confusion and uproar of civil war, with louder tones and firmer voices the great maxims and principles of civil liberty, order and obedience. What has perpetuated the greatness of that nation from which we derive so many of our maxims? Not its victories upon land nor its triumphs upon the seas, but its firm adherence to its traditional policy.

"The words of Coke, of Camden and Iansfield, have for long periods of time given strength and vitality and honor to its social system, while battles have lost their significance. When England was agitated by the throes of violence,—when the person of the king was insulted; when Parliament was besieged by mobs maddened by bigotry; when the life of Lord Mansfield was sought by infuriated fanatics, and his house was burned by incendiary fires, then he uttered those words which checked at once unlawful power and lawless violence. He declared that every citizen was entitled to his rights according to the known procedures of the land. He showed to the world the calm and awful majesty of the law, unshaken amidst convulsions. Self-reliant in its strength and purity, it was driven to no acts which destroy the spirit of law. Violence was rebuked; the heart of the nation was reassured; a sense of security grew up, and the storm was stilled. Listen to his words:—

"'Miserable is the condition of individuals; dangerous is the condition of the State where there is no certain law, or what is the same thing, no certain administration of law by which individuals may be protected and the State made secure.'

"Thus, too, will we stand calmly up amidst present disasters. We have warned the public that every act of disobedience weakened their claims to protection. We have admonished our rulers that every violation of right destroyed sentiments of loyalty and duty. That obedience and protection were reciprocal obligations. He who withholds his earnest and cheerful support to any legal demand of his Government, invites oppression and usurpation on the part of those in authority. The public servant who oversteps his jurisdiction or tramples upon the rights, person, property or procedure of the governed, instigates resistance and revolt.

"Under abuse and detraction we have faithfully acted upon these precepts. If our purposes were factious, the elements of disorder are everywhere within our reach. If we were as disobedient to this Government and as denunciatory of its officials as those who placed them in power, we could make them tremble in their seats of power. We have been obedient, loyal, and patient. We shall continue to be so under all circumstances. But let no man mistake this devotion to our country and its Constitution for unworthy fear. We have no greater stake in good order than other men. Our arms are as strong, our endurance as great, our fortitude as unwavering as that of our political opponents. But we seek the blessings of peace, of law, of order. We ask the public to mark our policy and our position. Opposed to the election of Mr. Lincoln, we have loyally sustained him. Differing from the administration as to the course and the conduct of the war, we have cheerfully responded to every demand made upon us. To-day we are putting forth our utmost efforts to re-enforce our armies in the field. Without conditions or threats we are exerting our energies to strengthen the hands of Government and to replace it in the commanding position it held in the eyes of the world before recent disasters. We are pouring out our blood, our treasures and our men, to rescue it from a position in which it can neither propose peace nor conduct successful war. And this support is freely and generously accorded. We wish to see our Union saved, our laws vindicated, and peace once more restored to our land. We do not claim more virtue or intelligence than we award to our opponents, but we now have the sad and bloody proof that we act upon sounder principles of government. Animated by the motto we have placed upon our banner—"The Union, the Constitution and the Laws"—we go into the political contest confident of the support of a people who can not be deaf or blind to the teachings of the last two years."

CHAPTER XI.

MESSAGE OF 1863 AND INVASION OF PENNSYLVANIA.

Upon his nomination Gov. Seymour resolved upon a course unusual in the political history of New York, which was to traverse the State, and address meetings. This involved a vast amount of labor, and he was obliged to speak mainly to outdoor meetings nine times each week, in addition to the toil of travel, and of his intercourse with the throngs which came to hear him. The Republicans were confident of victory. They were supported by the full force of the power and patronage of the State and National Governments. They were arrogant and threatening; but they were met by a firm defiance and a fixed purpose on the part of the Democratic party to exercise their rights of speaking and of voting. The result of this canvass, which is unparalleled in the political history of New York, was a signal triumph, which saved its citizens from outrages and insults, which in all human probabilities would have led to dangerous disturbances.

The inauguration of Governor Seymour on the first of January, 1863, excited the liveliest interest throughout the country. It took place in the Assembly Chamber, in the presence of a large and enthusiastic audience; Gov. Seymour was introduced by the retiring Governor Morgan, and said:—

"Fellow-citizens: In your presence I have solemnly sworn to support the Constitution of the United States, with all its grants, restrictions and guarantees, and shall support it. (Cheers.) I have also sworn to support another Constitution, the Constitution of the State of New York, with all its powers and rights. I shall uphold it (Great applause.) I have sworn faithfully to perform the duties of the office of Governor of this State, and with your aid they shall be faithfully performed. These constitutions and laws are meant for the guidance of official conduct, and for your protection and welfare. * * * * This occasion, fellow-citizens, when official power is so courteously transferred from the hands of one political organization to those of another, holding opposite sentiments upon public affairs, is not only a striking exemplification of the spirit of our institutions, but highly honorable to the minority party. Had our misguided fellow-citizens of the South acted as the minority of the citizens of our own State (a minority but little inferior in numbers to the majority) are now acting in this surrender of power, the nation would not now be involved in civil war.—(Applause.)"

He closed as follows:—

"Under no circumstance can the division of the Union be conceded. We will put forth every exertion of power; we will use every policy of conciliation; we will hold out every inducement to the people of the South, to return to their allegiance, consistent with honor; we will guaranty them every right, every consideration demanded by the Constitution, and by that fraternal regard which must prevail in a common country; but we can never voluntarily consent to the breaking up of the Union of these States, or the destruction of the Constitution."

On the 7th he transmitted his message to the Senate. This document contained an able review of the public affairs.

We are only able to quote from it very briefly. In view of the denunciations of the administration, in which the radical press were then indulging, the following passage is interesting:—

"In order to uphold our Government, it is also necessary that we should show respect to the authority of our rulers. While acting within the limits of their jurisdictions, and representing the interests, the honor, and the dignity of our people, they are entitled to deference. Where it is their right to decide upon measures and policy, it is our duty to obey and to give a ready support to their decisions. This is a vital maxim of liberty. Without this loyalty, no Government can conduct public affairs with success, no people can be safe in the enjoyment of their rights. This duty is peculiarly strong under our system, which gives the people the right at their elections to sit in judgment upon their rulers, to commend or condemn them to keep them in, or expel them from official stations."

In reference to arbitrary arrests, he said :—

"Our people have viewed with alarm, practices and pretensions on the part of officials, which violate every principle of good order, of civil liberty, and of constitutional law. It is claimed that in time of war the President has powers, as Commander-in-Chief of our armies, which authorize him to declare martial law, not only within the sphere of hostile movements, where other law can not be enforced, but also over our whole land. That at his pleasure he can disregard not only the statutes of Congress, but the decisions of the National judiciary. That in loyal States the least intelligent class of officials may be clothed with power not only to act as spies and informers, but, also, without due process of law, to seize and imprison our citizens, and carry them beyond the limits of the State, to hold them in prisons without a hearing or a knowledge of the offenses with which they are charged. Not only the passions and prejudices of these inferior agents lead them to acts of tyranny, but their interests are advanced and their positions secured by promoting discontent and discord. Even to ask the aid of counsel has been held to be an offense. It has been well said that 'to be arrested for one knows not what; to be confined, no one entitled to ask where; to be tried, no one can say when, by a law nowhere known or established; or to linger out life in a cell without trial, presents a body of tyranny which can not be enlarged.'

"The suppression of journals and the imprisonment of persons have been glaringly partisan, allowing to some the utmost licentiousness of criticism, and punishing others for a fair exercise of the right of discussion. Conscious of these gross abuses, an attempt has been made to shield the violators of law and suppress inquiry into their motives and conduct. This attempt will fail. Unconstitutional acts can not be shielded by unconstitutional laws. Such attempts will not save the guilty, while they will bring a just condemnation upon those who try to pervert the powers of legislation to the purposes of oppression. To justify such action by precedents drawn from the practice of governments where there is no restraint upon legislative power, will be of no avail under our system, which restrains the Government and protects the citizen by written constitutions.

"I shall not inquire what rights States in rebellion have forfeited, but I deny that this rebellion can suspend a single right of the citizens of loyal States. I denounce the doctrine that civil war in the South takes away from the loyal North the benefits of one principle of civil liberty.

"It is a high crime to abduct a citizen of this State. It is made my duty by the Constitution to see that the laws are enforced. I shall investigate every alleged violation of our statutes, and see that offenders are brought to justice. Sheriffs and district attorneys are admonished that it is their duty to take care that no person within their respective counties is imprisoned, or carried by force beyond their limits, without due process of legal authority. The removal to England of persons charged with offense, away from their friends, their witnesses and means of defense, was one of the acts of tyranny for which we asserted our independence. The abduction of citizens from this State, for offenses charged to have been done here, and carrying them many hundred miles to distant prisons in other States or Territories, is an outrage of the same character upon every principle of right and justice.

"The General Government has ample powers to establish courts, to appoint officers to arrest, and commissioners to hear complaints, and to imprison upon reasonable grounds of suspicion. It has a judicial system, in full and undisturbed operation. Its own courts, held at convenient points in this and other loyal States, are open for the hearing of all complaints. If its laws are not ample for the punishment of offenses, it is due to the neglect of those in power.

"Government is not strengthened by the exercise of doubtful powers, but by a wise and energetic exertion of those which are incontestable. The former course never fails to produce discord, suspicion and distrust, while the latter inspires respect and confidence.

"This loyal State, whose laws, whose courts, and whose officers have thus been treated with marked and public contempt, and whose social order and sacred rights have been violated, was at the very time sending forth great armies to protect the National Capital, and to save the national officials from flight or capture. It was while the arms of New York thus sheltered them against rebellion, that, without consultation with its chief magistrate, a subordinate department at Washington insulted our people and invaded our rights. Against these wrongs and outrages the people of the State of New York, at its late election, solemnly protested.

"The submission of our people to these abuses, for a time only was mistaken at home and abroad for an indifference to their liberties. But it was only in a spirit of respect for our institutions, that they waited until they could express their will in the manner pointed out by our laws. At the late election they vindicated at once their regard for law and their love of liberty. Amidst all the confusion of civil war, they calmly sat in judgment upon the administration, voting against its candidates. Nor was this the only striking proof of respect for the Constitution. The minority, of nearly equal numbers, yielded to this decision without resistance, although the canvass was animated by strong partisan excitements. This calm assertion of rights, and this honorable submission to the verdict of the ballot-box, vindicated at once the character of our people and the stability of our institutions. Had the secessionists of the South thus yielded to constitutional decisions, they would have saved themselves and our country from the horrors of this war, and they would have found the same remedy for every wrong and danger."

While Governor Seymour had declared his purpose to maintain the rights of the people of the State of New York, he also declared in equally plain terms his purpose to respect the rights of the administration, and to yield a prompt obedience to any demand they had a right to make upon him. His sincerity upon the latter point was soon tested. The Confederate army, under Gen. Lee, invaded Pennsylvania, and threatened not only the national capital but the city of Philadelphia. There was the utmost alarm and confusion at Washington. They had been taught to distrust Gov. Seymour; they had denounced him as an enemy to the cause of the Union. They were now forced to call upon him for help. The Republican

Governor of Pennsylvania appealed to him to save the cities of his State from the invading army. How promptly these appeals from the National and State authorities were met, is best shown by the following official documents, and telegrams:—

STANTON CALLS ON GOVERNOR SEYMOUR FOR HELP.

BY TELEGRAPH FROM WASHINGTON, June 15, 1863.

To His Excellency, GOVERNOR SEYMOUR :—

The movements of the rebel forces in Virginia are now sufficiently developed to show that General Lee, with his whole army, is moving forward to invade the States of Maryland, Pennsylvania, and other States.

The President, to repel this invasion promptly, has called upon Ohio, Pennsylvania, Maryland, Western Virginia, for one hundred thousand (100,000) militia for six (6) months, unless sooner discharged. It is important to have the largest possible force in the least time, and if other States would furnish militia for a short term, to be allowed on the draft, it would greatly advance the object. Will you please inform me immediately if, in answer to a special call of the President, you can raise and forward, say twenty thousand (20,000) militia, as volunteers without bounty, to be credited on the draft of your State, or what number you can probably raise?

E. M. STANTON, Secretary of War.

THE PROMPT RESPONSE.

ALBANY, June 15, 1863.

Hon. E. M. STANTON, *Secretary of War, Washington:*—

I will spare no efforts to send you troops at once. I have sent orders to the militia officers of the State.

HORATIO SEYMOUR.

ALBANY, June 15, 1863.

Hon. E. M. STANTON, *Secretary of War, Washington:*—

I will order the New York and Brooklyn troops to Philadelphia at once. Where can they get arms, if they are needed?

HORATIO SEYMOUR.

DOCUMENTS AND TELEGRAMS.

PRESIDENT LINCOLN THANKS GOVERNOR SEYMOUR.

BY TELEGRAPH FROM WASHINGTON, June 16, 1863.

To GOVERNOR SEYMOUR:—

The President desires me to return his thanks with those of the Department for your prompt response. A strong movement of your city regiments to Philadelphia would be a very encouraging movement, and do great good in giving strength to the State. The call had to be for six months unless sooner discharged in order to comply with the law. It is not likely that more than thirty days' service—perhaps not so long—would be required. Can you forward your city regiments speedily? Please reply early.

EDWIN M. STANTON, Secretary of War.

ALBANY, June 15, 1863.

Hon. E. M. STANTON, *Secretary of War, Washington:*—

We have about two thousand enlisted volunteers in this State. I will have them consolidated into companies and regiments, and sent on at once. You must provide them with arms.

HORATIO SEYMOUR.

ALBANY, June 19, 1863.

Hon. E. M. STANTON, *Secretary of War, Washington:*—

Four returned volunteer regiments can be put in the field at once, for three months' service. Can arms and accouterments be supplied in New York? Old arms not fit for the field.

J. T. SPRAGUE, Adjutant-General.

BY TELEGRAPH FROM WASHINGTON, June 16, 1863.

To ADJUTANT-GENERAL SPRAGUE:—

Upon your requisition, any troops you may send to Pennsylvania will be armed and equipped in New York, with new arms.

Orders have been given to the Bureau of Ordnance.

EDWIN M. STANTON.

GOV. SEYMOUR PUSHING ON TROOPS.

ALBANY, June 16, 1863.

Hon. E. M. STANTON, *Secretary of War, Washington, D. C.:*—

Officers of old organizations here will take the field with their men, and can march to-morrow, if they can be paid irrespective of ordnance accounts. The Government would still have a hold upon them to refund for losses.

JOHN T. SPRAGUE, Adjutant-General.

ALBANY, June 15, 1863.

Hon. E. M. STANTON, *Secretary of War, Washington:*—

By request of Governor Seymour, who has called me here, I write to say that the New York city regiments can go with full ranks for any time not over three months—say from eight to ten thousand men. The shorter the period the larger will be the force. For what time will they be required? Please answer immediately.

C. W. SANFORD, Major-General.

BY TELEGRAPH FROM WASHINGTON, June 16, 1863.

To MAJOR-GENERAL SANFORD:—

The Government will be glad to have your city regiments hasten to Pennsylvania for any term of service; it is not possible to say how long they might be useful, but it is not expected that they would be detained more than three (3) months, possibly not longer than twenty (20) or thirty (30) days.

They would be accepted for (3) months, and discharged as soon as the present exigency is over. If aided at the present by your troops, the people of that State might soon be able to raise a sufficient force to relieve your city regiments.

EDWIN M. STANTOM, Secretary of War.

ALBANY, June 18, 1863.

To Hon. E. M. STANTON, *Secretary of War, Washington, D. C.:*—

About twelve thousand (12,000) men are now on the move for Harrisburg, in good spirits and well equipped.

The Governor says: "Shall troops continue to be forwarded?" Please answer.

Nothing from Washington since first telegrams.

JOHN T. SPRAGUE, Adjutant-General

ALBANY, June 18, 1863.

To GOVERNOR CURTIN, *Harrisburg, Pa.:*—

About twelve thousand men are now moving nd are under orders for Harrisburg, in good spirits and well equipped.

Governor Seymour desires to know if he shall continue to send men. He is ignorant of your real condition.

JOHN T. SPRAGUE, Adjutant-General.

MR. LINCOLN AGAIN THANKS SEYMOUR FOR HIS "ENERGETIC AND PROMPT ACTION."

BY TELEGRAPH FROM WASHINGTON, June 19, 1863.

TO ADJUTANT-GENERAL SPRAGUE:—

The President directs me to return his thanks to his Excellency, Governor Seymour and his staff, for their energetic and prompt action. Whether any further force is likely to be required will be communicated to you to-morrow, by which time it is expected the movements of the enemy will be more fully developed.

EDWIN M. STANTON, Secretary of War.

DO YOU WANT MORE MEN?

ALBANY, June 20, 1863.

Hon. E. M. STANTON, *Secretary of War, Washington* :—

The Governor desires to be informed if he shall continue sending on the militia regiments from this State. If so, to what extent and to what point?

J. B. STONEHOUSE, A. A. Adj.-Gen.

BY TELEGRAPH FROM WASHINGTON, June 21, 1863.

TO ACTING ASS'T ADJUTANT-GENERAL STONEHOUSE:—

The President desires Governor Seymour to forward to Baltimore all the militia regiments that he can raise.

EDWIN M. STANTON, Secretary of War.

A REPUBLICAN GOVERNOR CRYING FOR HELP AND GETTING IT.

BY TELEGRAPH FROM HARRISBURG, July 2, 1863.

TO HIS EXCELLENCY GOVERNOR SEYMOUR:—

Send forward more troops as rapidly as possible. Every hour increases the necessity for large forces to protect Pennsylvania. The battles of yesterday were not decisive, and if Meade should be defeated, unless we have a large army, this State will be overrun by the rebels.

A. G. CURTIN, Governor of Pennsylvania.

NEW YORK, July 2, 1863.
To GOVERNOR CURTIN, *Harrisburg, Pa.:* —

Your telegram is received. Troops will continue to be sent. One regiment leaves to-day, another to-morrow, all in good pluck.

JOHN T. SPRAGUE, Adjutant-General.

CHAPTER XII.

THE CONSPIRACY AGAINST NEW YORK.

WHEN the future historian shall tell the story of our late civil war, among other facts which will arrest his attention will be the circumstance that the city of New York was for a long time left in a defenseless condition. The destruction of this city would have been a fatal blow to the Union cause. It was not only filled with a vast amount of stores and materials of war which were essential to our armies, but it was the great financial center which supplied the money, without which the Government would have been paralyzed. Upon his entrance into office, Governor Seymour learned that the fortifications of the harbor of New York, inadequately manned, were a peril, and not a protection, to that great commercial point. A few men entering the harbor from the sea could have seized them, have turned their guns against the city; and, before they could be dislodged, could have wrought vast injury, or have extorted large sums of money to induce them to stop their work of destruction. It is well known that hostile cruisers destroyed our shipping at no great distance from the coast. Fortunately they did not know the condition of affairs in the harbor itself. Every effort was made by Mr. Seymour to have these fortifications properly manned. He offered to raise soldiers for the purpose, who should be placed under the command of the General Government, or to make arrangements with the different regiments of the National Guards to hold in turn these important strongholds. The administration at Washington gave no heed to his warnings and showed no respect to his wishes. In the month of July, 1863, he visited the city and harbor of New York with Senator Morgan and Comptroller Robinson, to learn the condition of its defenses. They were under the control of General Wool, who then commanded the Department of the East. This able and distinguished soldier showed the deepest anxiety to have a sufficient force placed under his command to repel any attacks which should be made. He advised the Governor that he had only 500 men available for the defense of the city, and that but one-half of them could be relied upon as artillerists. He also stated that every vessel of war in the harbor of New York or at the depot had been ordered to Hampton Roads, whence, in case of need, no one could be made available in less then ten days. On the 10th of July, the following letter was received by the Governor from General Wool:—

HEAD-QUARTERS, DEPARTMENT OF THE EAST, }
NEW YORK CITY, July 9, 1863. }

HIS EXCELLENCY, H. SEYMOUR,
Governor of New York:—

SIR—For want of troops, this city is in a defenseless condition. I require, including a regiment of heavy artillery, expected from General Couch, at Harrisburg, reported by Brigadier General Miller, Inspector-General of New York, to be about four hundred strong, eight companies of artillery, of volunteers or militia, to be placed in the nine forts of this harbor. These ought to be furnished with as little delay as practicable.

If you have a capable major of artillery, I should be gratified if you would send him with the companies.

Yesterday, I received an order from the War Department, directing me "to organize immediately, by detachment or otherwise, four companies of infantry for service at the draft rendezvous established in the State of New York, two of the companies to be sent to report to the commanding officer at Riker's Island, one company to the commanding officer at Buffalo, and one company to the commanding officer at Elmira, N. Y."

As I have no infantry companies in the State of New York for this service, I would respectfully ask your Excellency to order the four companies to be furnished as soon as practicable.

I have the honor to be,
Very respectfully,
Your ob't servant,
JOHN E. WOOL,
Major-General.

To which the following reply was immediately made :—

STATE OF NEW YORK:
INSPECTOR-GENERAL'S OFFICE,
NEW YORK, July 10, 1863.

MAJOR-GENERAL JOHN E. WOOL, *Com'dg Dep't of the East, N. Y.* :—

GENERAL—Your communication addressed to his Excellency, Governor Seymour, under date of July 9th, inst., received yesterday, stating that for the want of troops this city was in a defenseless condition ; and further stating that you require, in addition to a regiment of heavy artillery, expected from General Couch, reported to be about four hundred strong. (but since reported to me as about five hundred strong), eight companies of artillery, of volunteers or militia, to be placed in the nine forts of this harbor, and that these ought to be furnished with as little delay as practicable.

His Excellency, the Governor, directs me to say in reply, that, referring to the conversations had by you with him and myself, and to the communications on this subject I had the honor to address to you on the 8th inst., you will observe that State troops in excess of the number now required by you, are in readiness for the service specified, only waiting orders from the Governor, conveying the assurance that they will be received on reporting at your headquarters as State militia, temporarily placed under your orders by the commander-in-chief for service in the forts of this harbor, and that they will be subsisted by the Government on reporting for duty.

As soon as the Governor is notified that you concur in these views, the troops will be ordered to report to you; they will be furnished with clothing for sixty days from the Quartermaster-General's department, and the subject of pay, &c., will hereafter, be submitted for the consideration of the General Government.

Awaiting a reply upon these points, at your very earliest convenience,

I remain, general, very respectfully,

Your obedient servant,

JOSIAH T. MILLER,

Inspector-General.

As the National Guard of the city of New York were in Pennsylvania, orders were at once issued to regiments in the interior to report to Gen. Wool. Several regiments were on their way, and had reached Albany and Binghamton, when the Governor received the following dispatch from Gen Wool, and was at the same moment advised by telegraph of a riot in the city, growing out of the enforcement of the draft:

NEW YORK, July 13, 1863.

To Hon. H. SEYMOUR:—

SIR—Orders just received from the War Department superseded the necessity of the two companies I required of those now recruiting at New Dorp, and, until further advices, *please countermand any militia that is ordered to this place.*

J. E. WOOL, Major-General.

Thus, through the refusal of the Administration to allow troops to be placed in the city, under the command of Gen. Wool, it was laid open to the double peril of invasion from the sea and from riot within its own limits. The enrolling officers of the General Government have never given any explanation for their conduct in making the draft while the National Guards were all absent from the city, and without giving either to Gen. Wool, to the Governor of the State, or the Mayor of the city any notice of what they were about to do. The draft was commenced on Saturday, in a district where the quota was so excessive that the General Government was afterward forced to correct it; the names of those drawn were published in the Sunday papers, on a day when the cessation of all labor was calculated to draw together in discussion large bodies of men, who were surprised and excited by learning for the first time what had been done, and what was going on. It appears from a letter of Gen. Wool that he heard of these disturbances on Monday morning, and that he called the attention of the Provost Marshal of the city to the subject. That officer told the general he required no assistance, and through this untrue statement the disturbance gathered headway.

When Gov. Seymour reached the city, he found that he had not only to deal with an excited populace, but that the Republican journals, and some of the political leaders of that party, were intent upon embarrassing his action, and were doing what they could to incite the mob to lawlessness and crime. Gen. Wool and Mr. Opdyke, the Mayor of the city, were exerting themselves to uphold the supremacy of the laws. But the Republican papers, and more particularly Mr. Greeley, the editor of the *Tribune*, influenced, in part, by constitutional timidity, and in part by political purposes, were determined to have New York placed under martial law. Gov. Seymour had foreseen this scheme, and in an address which he delivered on the 4th of July, had made an appeal to the Republican leaders, imploring them to refrain from all measures of unjust and illegal violence against the rights of their political opponents. At the same time he invoked his own political friends at all times to render a prompt obedience to those in authority, and to submit to their laws, where they had the right to make them, whether such laws were agreeable or not. He had just received, from the Administration at Washington, and from the leading members of the Republican party, such expressions of their gratitude for his prompt response to the calls of the President and Secretary of War for help, that he hoped that this respectful appeal would be listened to. It was made to them on a day full of sacred memories; it was made to them at a time of great solemnity, when the men that New York and other States had sent to support the flag of the country were engaged in the actual conflict, and were then dying and bleeding upon the battle-field of Gettysburg.

But these appeals were received by the Republican journals in the most malignant spirit. He found then that in putting down the riots, he had not only to deal with open violators of the law, but with the intrigues of those who hoped violence would go on until the General Government could be induced to declare martial law, and to take away the political rights of the people of the State of New York. Gen. Wool was urged to declare martial law; because he refused to do so, he was removed and another General put in his place. Despite the difficulties with which he was surrounded, by firmness on the one hand, and prudent measures to allay excitement on the other, the riots were put down before the Administration could get a pretext for interference.

It is due to the War Department to state that when false statements were sent on to Washington with regard to the conduct of the Governor, that it refused to act, until he had sent a high official to learn the facts, and this official reported that these accusations were groundless.

The following are Governor Seymour's two proclamations during the riot:—

To the People of the City of New York: A riotous demonstration in your city, originating in opposition to the conscription of soldiers for the military service of the United States, had swelled into vast proportions, directing its fury against the property and lives of peaceful citizens. I know that many of those who have participated in these proceedings would not have allowed themselves to be carried to such extremes of violence and wrong, except under an apprehension of injustice: but such persons are reminded that the only opposition to the conscription which can be allowed is an appeal to the courts. The right of every citizen to make such an appeal will be maintained, and the decision of the court must be respected and obeyed by rulers and people alike. No other course is consistent with the maintenance of the laws, the peace and order of the city, and the safety of its inhabitants. Riotous proceedings must and shall be put down. The laws of the State must be enforced, its peace and order maintained, and the lives and property of all citizens protected at any and every hazard. The rights of every citizen will be properly guarded and defended by the chief magistrate of the State. I do therefore call upon all persons engaged in these riotous proceedings to retire to their homes and employments, declaring to them that unless they do so at once I shall use all the power necessary to restore the peace and order of the city. I also call upon all well-disposed persons, not enrolled for the preservation of order, to pursue their ordinary avocations. Let all citizens stand firmly by the constitutional authorities, sustaining law and order in the city, and ready to answer any such demand as circumstances may render necessary for me to make upon their services; and they may rely upon a rigid enforcement of the laws of this State against all who violate them.

HORATIO SEYMOUR, Governor.

Whereas, It is manifest that combinations for forcible resistance to the laws of the State of New York, and the execution of civil and criminal process, exists in the city and county of New York, whereby the peace and safety of the city and the lives and property of its inhabitants are endangered; and whereas, the power of the said city and county has been exerted, and it is not sufficient to enable the officers of the said city and county to maintain the laws of the State and execute the legal process of its officers; and whereas application has been made to me by the Sheriff of the city and county of New York to declare the said city and county to be in a state of insurrection: now, therefore, I, Horatio Seymour, Governor of the State of New York, and Commander-in-Chief of the force of the same, do, in its name and by its authority, issue a proclamation in accordance with the statute in such cases made and provided, and do hereby declare the city and county of New York to be in a state of insurrection, and give notice to all persons that the means provided by the laws of this State for the maintenance of law and order will be employed to whatever degree may be necessary, and that all persons who shall, after the publication of this proclamation, resist, or aid or assist in resisting, any force ordered out by the Governor to quell or suppress such insurrection, will render themselves liable to the penalty prescribed by law. HORATIO SEYMOUR."

The Republican press indulged in the most inflammatory appeals to exasperate the mob and to keep up the disorder. The *Tribune* denounced the Irish, demanded that they should be shot down, spoke of the "indecision" and imbecility of the mayor of the city and of the incapacity of General Wool, because they would not order wholesale murder, would not demand martial law, and were willing to accept the co-operation of Governor Seymour. It said during the riot:

"The incapacity of the military head of this department, and the fatal indecision of the chief magistrate of the city are permitting power to lapse into the hands of the Governor."

The cause of their rage was, not the disorder in the city, but the fact that the Governor was taking the power in his own hands, and suppressing the riot before they could frighten the administration into declaring martial law. Again the *Tribune* said:—

"Nor did the Governor and his advisers adopt any other policy than that of *controlling* —not *subduing*—the riot till they saw that such a task was hopeless. He attempted to restrain General Brown from the use of ball-cartridge, while his partisans urged military commander to retire and leave the mob to their sweet persuasions, and lest martial law should be declared, he was induced to declare the city in a state of insurrection—a proclamation written for him by a Copperhead editor—that he might hold control over the military, and preclude all interference on the part of the Federal Government."

On July 15th, the *Tribune* said:—

"We do not know how far the Government has been made acquainted with the state of affairs in this city, or whether they know any thing about it further than is to be learned from the public press. But if they depend upon that source of information, we beg to assure them of one fact of vital moment, that is, that this district is in lamentable want of a military commander. We yield to none in respect for the past services of General Wool, but these are not times to sacrifice present interests to a respect for a reputation earned in years that are past. General Wool is now a very old man, and has neither the physical ability nor the mental resources to meet the fearful emergency into which we have been precipitated by the machinations of the treacherous 'Copperheads' and their organs. He clearly does not comprehend either the magnitude or the character of the crisis, and failing to do this, he as necessarily fails to delegate the proper authority and responsibility to younger and more active men, who, if left to themselves even, might prove quite equal to the demands of the moment. That moment demands wisdom, energy, promptness, and above all, the courage of a true soldier, who, recognizing that a real battle is before him, with a desperate and savage, though undisciplined force, hesitates not an instant to use the means at his command to defeat and exterminate it."

It denied Governor Seymour's statement, which was subsequently proved to be true, that the draft had been suspended, and raved after this fashion:—

"Traitors at the North will begin to comprehend that this Government means to crush treason wherever it dares to lift its head, and they will soon be made to believe, if they do not already know, that the people will stand by the Government spite of the efforts of Copperhead presses, of murderous mobs, and of Governors who openly proclaim their friendship and affiliation with the scoundrels composing them, and who seek to conciliate favor with insurgents by professing to have extorted from the President a cowardly concession which he publicly denies having made."

Again, calling for martial law, July 18, it said:—

"The military power of the National Government must enforce the draft. We tell the President plainly, if it is possible he can need to be told, that unless vigorous measures are adopted in season, he must expect to witness another, and beyond doubt a better organized, more extensive, and infinitely more dangerous insurrection than has yet occurred. Martial law and the means of enforcing it, soldiers, and a general of courage and capacity, will secure the execution of the draft, and they only will secure it. Will the Government be warned in time?"

The *Times* said, "give them grape, and a plenty of it!" The *Post* called for the removal of an officer who fired blank cartridges from a battery at a crowd of men, women, and children, instead of solid shot, and it said July 14th:—

"It did not require pacificatory speeches from Mr. Kennedy, or any other person; there was demanded a light battery, with a supply of grape and canister, half a regiment of cavalry, and two or three officers with pluck to use these means."

When peace and quiet was restored, those who had been engaged in open and flagrant crime,—the destruction of life and property,—showed less malignant rage and vindictive hate when they were defeated and beaten down than was exhibited by the editors of the leading Republican journals and some of the active managers of that party. Governor Seymour had foiled their scheme for putting New York under martial law. It was renewed at a later day with a view of depriving the city of its votes at the Presidential election. Their rage knew no bounds when they were checkmated at every point. It is just to say, that many prominent Republicans expressed their detestation of the conduct of these men, and gave efficient aid to the Governor, the Mayor, and Gen. Wool, in their efforts to uphold the laws.

During the riots, the non-partisan journals acknowledged the fact tha the effect of Gov. Seymour's presence and actions was to show a marked improvement in the order of the city. The *Herald* said:—

"The surrender of the management of the city by Mayor Opdyke into the hands of Gov. Seymour seemed calculated to allay the excitement for a time."

The *Journal of Commerce* of July 16, said:—

"From the moment that Governor Seymour arrived in the city, it became manifest that a cool and determined, as well as a judicious mind was at the head of affairs, and the riot, which had gained to terrible force during the weak management of the Mayor, began to lose ground. The Governor proceeded with great calmness and energy. He went in person during the day to all parts of the city, exhibiting himself to the excited populace as the controlling spirit of the movements to suppress the mob. Unmoved by the furious insanity of the radical politicians, who besought him to exterminate the mob with cannon and musketry without attempting to talk or to save their lives, he issued his proclamation, and at once the effect began to be visible. The people who were aiding the mob by silent acquiescence began to desert them, and rally to the side of law and order. A very wise speech, most excellent in its effect, was delivered by the Governor to a large mass of this class of persons, who had been standing around the *Tribune* office and the Park, expecting another riotous demonstration there, and the effect proved the Governor's keen and thoughtful appreciation of affairs. The crowds at once dispersed, and from that time there has been no larger gathering than is daily seen in that locality. This speech undoubtedly restored the quiet of the lower part of the city, and prevented any further demonstrations against the *Tribune*."

But the Governor received still higher praise from his political opponents. The Albany *Evening Journal*, immediately after the riot, said:—

"Governor Seymour, in so PROMPTLY 'DECLARING THE CITY IN A STATE OF INSURRECTION,' contributed largely to the suppression of the mob. It gave immediate legal efficiency to the military arm, and enabled the civil authorities to use that power with terrible effect. IT SHOWED ALSO, THAT IT WAS GOVERNOR SEYMOUR'S PURPOSE TO GIVE 'NO QUARTER' TO THE RUFFIANS who seized upon the occasion of a popular excitement to rob and murder. The exercise of the power thus called into service was effective. The 'insurrection' has been quelled. THE MOB HAS BEEN OVERPOWERED. Law and order have TRIUMPHED, and the RIOTOUSLY DISPOSED everywhere have RECEIVED A LESSON WHICH THEY WILL NOT SOON FORGET."

Mayor Opdyke, on several subsequent occasions, publicly expressed his approval and commendation of Governor Seymour's course during the riots, stating that all co-operated to restore the peace of the city. He did not hesitate to say in the Constitutional Convention, "Everything that it was possible for him to do was done to aid in the suppression of the riots."

But the most undeniable and conclusive proof of the effect of Governor Seymour's presence in the city is shown in the course of the price of gold in Wall Street. The *Times* of July 16, notes the fact that after the issue of the proclamation of Seymour, gold fell four per cent. The following table shows its course:—

July 14, Monday, ...	131¼
July 15, Wednesday, ...	127
July 16, Thursday, ...	126

Beyond the fact that the draft was ordered while the military of the city was in Pennsylvania, and that it was conducted under circumstances showing sinister purposes, other facts soon came to light, proving that a cruel and wicked outrage was attempted against the laboring classes of New York and Brooklyn. It was found that the districts in which they lived were charged with nearly thrice the number of conscripts demanded in other districts with equal population. Thus, the fifth district, with a population of 129,983, was required to furnish 5,887 conscripts, while it was afterward admitted that it ought to furnish only 1,771, and seven Democratic districts in New York City were required to furnish two-fifths of the conscripts, and twenty-one Republican districts in the county only three-fifths. Undeterred by the clamor which was raised against him, Governor Seymour resolved that these wrongs should be righted. While President Lincoln appeared to be willing to look into the charges brought by the Governor against his officials, there were many leading Republicans, wealthy men of the city, mindless of their duty to protect the poor and the helpless, who demanded that the draft should go on. A sharp correspondence took place between Mr. Seymour and the President. The proofs of fraud and corruption were made so strong, that at length even partisan malice was forced to give way. A commission of three was appointed, two named by the war department and one by the governor, to look into the facts. They unanimously found that the quotas were unequally and unjustly assigned. They made a deduction of 14,000, and found that all the excesses were in democratic districts. Their report was approved by the Secretary of War. The city was saved from a direct outrage and a heavy tax; and at the end of the controversy, and of events so exciting and embittered, Governor Seymour enjoyed a triumph which few men have ever tasted. A Republican Assembly, honorably rising above not only partisan feelings, but their own commitments, on April 16, 1864, unanimously passed a resolution, thanking him for his course about the quota, and thus more than vindicating his actions during all the violence, and excitements, and conspiracies against the rights of the people of the State of New York, which occurred during the summer of 1863.

We give these resolutions, for but few of the Republican papers have been fair enough to let their readers know they were ever passed :—

"*Resolved*, That the thanks of this House be, and are hereby, tendered to his Excellency, Governor Seymour, for calling the attention of the General Government at Washington to the errors in the apportionment of the quota of this State, under the enrollment act of March 3, 1863, and for his prompt and efficient efforts in procuring a correction of the same.

"*Resolved*, That the Clerk of this House transmit to the Governor a copy of this report and resolutions."

The Board of Supervisors of New York, equally divided between Democrats and Republicans, also unanimously passed a similar resolution.

If the public has at times been surprised at the malignant attacks upon Governor Seymour, made by Mr. Greeley and others, they must bear in mind that no men are so unyielding in their hate, as those who have been detected and foiled in base, dishonorable and criminal purposes.

Such was the rage of these men against all who sought to restore order to the city, that when Archbishop Hughes, in the performance of his duties as a minister of Christ's religion, sought to persuade erring men to return to their duties, he was bitterly assailed by these partisan journals. The following touching letter from him shows how keenly he felt these attacks upon his person and his sacred office :—

NEW YORK, July 14, 1863.

His Excellency, HORATIO SEYMOUR,
    Governor State of New York:—

MY DEAR GOVERNOR:—I have just received yours of this date; I shall leave nothing undone by means of direct and indirect influence to correspond with your wishes in regard to our present calamities. Once before, I prevented a riot; but some of our local newspapers warned me off, intimating that if the civil authorities could not protect the peace of the community, better allow the streets to run with blood than that such consequences should be prevented by ecclesiastical influence or authority.

At present, there does not appear any fair opportunity of addressing the unfortunate people who are now disturbing the tranquillity of the city, since it is stated to me that their boldest leader is a man from Virginia, named Andrews, and that most of his subordinates in leadership are from the State of Connecticut, having recruited additional force in the city of Brooklyn.

It is not surprising that they should find many dupes, along the wharves and in the workshops of New York.

I shall have a letter in the New York *Herald* to-morrow, and in the postscript thereto I shall make an appeal to the Catholics, who may be unfortunately engaged in this sad business, to retire from their connection with it in as brief a time as possible.

I am, with great respect,
Your Excellency's sincere and humble servant,
†JOHN, Archbishop of New York.

The following is the postscript referred to :—

"In spite of Mr. Greeley's assault upon the Irish, in the present disturbed condition of the city, I will appeal not only to them, but to all persons who love God and revere the holy Catholic religion which they profess, to respect also the laws of man and the peace of society, to retire to their homes with as little delay as possible, and disconnect themselves from the seemingly deliberate intention to disturb the peace and social rights of the citizens of New York. If they are Catholics, or of such of them as are Catholics, I ask, for God's sake —for the sake of their holy religion—for my own sake, if they have any respect for the Episcopal authority—to dissolve their bad associations with reckless men, who have little regard either for Divine or human laws.

"† JOHN," &c., &c

It is due to the leading capitalists of the city of New York, who were consenting witnesses to these outrages upon their poorer neighbors whom it was their duty to protect, that, at length, shamed into a sense of their own unmanly course during these difficulties, they came forward and expressed to the commission whose decision had lifted such a load of taxation from the city, and to the Governor who had prevented so much outrage and wrong, their sense of the obligations under which he had placed all classes of men in the great cities of New York and Brooklyn.

CHAPTER XIII.

MEASURES FOR THE RELIEF OF SOLDIERS.—NEGRO RECRUITING.

During this term, Governor Seymour omitted no opportunity to render practical service to the New York soldiers in the field. On March 30, 1863, he transmitted to the Legislature a special message recommending "an ample appropriation by this State for its sick and wounded troops." The Legislature acceded to his request, and, having made an appropriation, the Governor appointed his brother, Colonel John F. Seymour, as general agent for the relief of sick and wounded soldiers. He devoted his whole time and energies to this noble work until the close of the Governor's term. The State agency at Washington was opened upon an ample basis, together with agencies at Baltimore, Philadelphia, Harrisburg, and Louisville, and a soldiers' depot, with ample accommodations for sick or returning soldiers, in the city of New York. The whole work was placed under the control of a board of managers, and was conducted with great economy and efficiency.

Governor Seymour was present at the dedication of the Gettysburg Cemetery, November 19, 1863. In the afternoon, after the formal ceremonies, the

Fifth New York Regiment, Colonel Murray, marched to his temporary residence, and passed in review before him. Upon the conclusion of this ceremony, Governor Seymour presented a handsome silk regimental standard to the regiment, and spoke briefly to the soldiers. He concluded by saying:—

"When you return from your fields of dangerous duty, you will bring back this standard to place among the archives of our State. I do not doubt that although it may perhaps, be returned torn and stained, yet that it will be still more glorious with the recollections clustering around it. In concluding these remarks, I ask in return of the men of New York, to give three cheers for the 'Union of our country, and three cheers for the flag of our land.'"

It is unnecessary to say that they were heartily given.

During Governor Seymour's term, through his brother, the State agent, he purchased lots in the cemeteries at Gettysburg and Antietam for the burial of New York soldiers who fell at those points.

At the commencement of his term, Governor Seymour desired to adopt a rule to make promotions in the volunteer service according to seniority, and the recommendations of field officers. In order to obtain appropriations from those politically opposed to him, he was sometimes compelled, against his judgment, to depart from it, but always did so reluctantly. During the height of the canvass of 1864, a friend of the governor, traveling between Washington and Albany, overheard a conversation, in which a New York officer indulged in the most violent abuse of Governor Seymour, designating him as a Copperhead, traitor, &c. On entering the executive department at

Albany, Governor Seymour's friend was surprised to find this officer an applicant for promotion. He took opportunity to mention to his Excellency the conversation referred to, and remonstrated against the promotion. The Governor merely smiled, and on examining the papers and finding that the officer was in regular line of promotion, and well recommended, granted the recommendation. The officer was very much mortified afterward, to learn that the Governor had granted it with a full knowledge of what he had said.

The Governor always promptly responded when called upon to aid in any measures for the relief of the soldiers. On the 22d of February, 1864, he was present and inaugurated the Albany Relief Bazaar, the fair and exhibition connected with which was kept open for some weeks, and from which a large sum was realized.

All the veteran regiments which returned by way of the State capital were warmly received and welcomed by him. During the session of the Legislature of 1863, a formal presentation of war-worn flags of veteran regiments to the State, took place at the Assembly Chamber, and were received by the Governor on behalf of the Bureau of Military Record. A like presentation was made during the session of 1864. We quote a passage from Governor Seymour's speech on the last occasion:—

"It has required no stretch of imagination to picture to ourselves the scene when these brave, bold and stalwart men went forth from the hills and valleys and cities of our land to battle for our flag. You have seen them from time to time, returning here shattered and broken, the mere remnants of those glorious bands, which excited our admiration and our enthusiasm on their departure. And in their history you have an epitome of the whole war. The banners that have been presented to you this night have been fanned by the breezes of Carolina, have been dampened with the dews that have fallen in the swamps of Virginia, have drooped under the almost tropical sun of Louisiana, have floated high in the heavens 'in the battle above the clouds,' at Lookout Mountain, where, under their folds, we won an honorable victory. It is well that our State on this occasion has shown its ancient fidelity to the flag of our country, to the Union of these States, and to the Constitution of our land."

Upon the repeal of the three hundred dollar commutation clause of the United Enrolment Act, passed July 4, 1864, provision was made by Congress for the enlistment of negroes in certain of the Southern States.

Competition between localities for the early filling of the quotas assigned under the call of the President of July 18, 1864, ran high, large bounties were demanded and paid to volunteers in the military or naval service, and great hopes of relief from negro recruits, were entertained in some quarters.

Numerous applications were accordingly made to Governor Seymour by local authorities, for commissions to proceed to the South as agents of the State, to procure negro recruits.

The Governor, foreseeing that this was a scheme to plunder the people while it would not aid the army, refused to grant these applications, or to commit the State to this scheme of evasion of duty and fraud.

In cases where supervisors of counties deputed agents for this purpose, he merely gave a certificate of the fact of such desigations by local boards, "subject at all times to revocation or modification," and with the provision that it was to be "expressly understood, that the State of New York is in no way to be held responsible for the acts of such agents."

While Governor Blair, of Michigan, adopted a similar course of action, the decision of Governor Seymour was coarsely assailed by many of the Republican journals of the State.

The New York *Tribune*, in speaking of the course of the Governor, charged that "he will be held responsible for the draft of just so many men as might, by proper diligence, have been obtained elsewhere."

The persons who were sent forward by towns and cities, as was anticipated, met with but indifferent success, and only a few hundred recruits were thus obtained. Many of the agents returned home in disgust without accomplishing any thing.

A system of fraud was inaugurated through complicity of United States authorities, whereby some "credits upon paper" were secured, while but few actual accessions were made to the army by the whole scheme, rendering new and additional calls for troops necessary in December, 1864.

So gross were these frauds, that while the quotas were apparently filled, the War Department has declared that although the records show that eight hundred thousand men had been enrolled, and bounties paid for them, not one-third of the number ever reached the army.

A Congressional investigation was at once entered upon, but the frauds were so wide-spread, they involved so many leading Republicans, and were so gross in their character, that the Committee did not dare to proceed with their investigations. To get rid of the subject, the late Provost-Marshal-General was hastily thrown overboard, and as far as possible public attention turned away from the subject; but there is not a county in the State, which was not cheated and robbed under this system against which the Governor protested.

Since the close of the war, some of these bounty frauds have been unearthed and exposed and the Attorney-General of New York has instituted legal proceedings to try and determine charges of frauds against several "loyal" Republicans of the State.

CHAPTER XIV.

GOV. SEYMOUR'S EFFORTS TO PROCURE THE SOLDIERS THE RIGHT OF VOTING, AND TO PROTECT THEM AGAINST FRAUD.

On the 13th of April, 1863, Gov. Seymour sent to the Legislature a message upon the subject of taking the votes of soldiers and sailors absent at the seat of war. It commenced as follows:—

"*To the Senate:* The question of a method by which those of our fellow-citizens who are absent in the military and naval service of the nation may be enabled to enjoy their right of suffrage, is one of great interest to the people of this State, and has justly excited their attention. I do not doubt that the members of the Legislature participate in the general desire that those who so nobly endure fatigue and suffering, and peril life in the hope that by such sacrifices our National Union may be preserved and our Constitution upheld, shall, if possible, be secured an opportunity for the free and intelligent exercise of all their political rights and privileges. The Constitution of this State requires the elector to vote in the election district in which he resides; but it is claimed by some that a law can be passed whereby the vote of an absent citizen may be given by his authorized representative. It is clear to me that the Constitution intends that the right to vote shall only be exercised by the elector in person. It would be an insult and an injury to the soldier to place the exercise of this right upon a doubtful or unconstitutional law, when it can be readily secured to him by a constitutional amendment."

In view of these considerations, Gov. Seymour submitted the following recommendations and suggestions to the Legislature:—

"It is not necessary that the effort to secure to our gallant soldiers and seamen a just participation in the choice of the next administration of the National Government, should be subjected to such dangers. A proposed amendment of the Constitution, giving to the Legislature the needful power upon this subject, can be adopted at the present session, and if concurred in by the next Legislature, can be submitted to the people in such season, that, if their decision is favorable, the action which would be afterward necessary, could be taken by that legislature. I respectfully recommend that this course be taken, rather than the passage of an unconstitutional law or one of questionable validity.

"Great care should be taken to prevent, by the most efficient checks, the abuses and frauds to which the exercise of the rights of suffrage by absentees would be liable. These safeguards would properly be a matter of legislation after the adoption of a constitutional amendment. Measures should be taken for securing perfect independence to absent soldiers and seamen in giving their votes, which shall be so comprehensive and efficient, as to relieve any reasonable apprehension upon this point."

Notwithstanding this message, the Republican Legislature passed a law which they knew to be unconstitutional, and which they knew Gov. Seymour would be compelled to veto, apparently for the sole purpose of being able to pervert his action into an argument that he was opposed to soldiers voting.

Gov. Seymour promptly vetoed this bill, giving, as follows, the primary reason for so doing:—

"It is so clearly in violation of the Constitution, in the judgment of men of all parties, that it is needless to dwell upon that objection to the bill. While it only received, in the Assembly, the number of votes necessary to its passage, some of those who voted for it openly stated their opposition to the measure. After its passage, that branch of the Legislature, with great unanimity and without regard to political differences, adopted the resolution for an amendment to the Constitution, to secure the objects of this bill, in accordance with the recommendations of the message which I lately sent to the Legislature on this subject."

Gov. Seymour also referred to other fatal defects in the bill, and continued:—

"The bill is in conflict with vital principles of electoral purity and independence. It is well said by Dr. Lieber, in his work on 'Civil Liberty and Self-Government,' that 'All elections must be superintended by election judges and officers, *independent* of the executive, or any other organized or unorganized power of the Government. The indecency, as well as the absurdity and immorality, of the Government recommending what is to be voted, ought never to be permitted.' This bill not only fails to guard against abuses and frauds, but it offers every inducement and temptation to perpetrate them by those who are under the immediate and particular control of the General Government. That Government has not hesitated to interfere, directly with the local elections, by permitting officers of high rank to engage in them in States of which they are not citizens. In marked instances, high and profitable military commissions have been given to those who have never rendered one day of military duty, who have never been upon a battle-field, but who have been in the receipt of military pay and military honors, to support them in their interference, in behalf of the Administration, with the elective franchises of different sovereign and loyal States.

"Not only have some been thus rewarded for going beyond the bounds of military propriety, but other and subordinate officers have been punished and degraded for the fair and independent exercise of their political rights, at their own homes, and in the performance of their civil duties. I call the attention of the Legislature and of the public to the following order:

"'WAR DEPARTMENT—ADJUTANT GENERAL'S OFFICE,
WASHINGTON, March 13, 1863.

[SPECIAL ORDERS—No. 119.]

(*Extract.*

'34. By direction of the President, the following officer is hereby dismissed from the service of the United States:—

'Lieut. A. J. Edgerly, Fourth New Hampshire Volunteers, for circulating Copperhead tickets—doing all in his power to promote the success of the rebel cause in his State.

'By order of the Secretary of War,

'L. THOMAS, Adjutant General.'

'*To the Governor of New Hampshire.*'

"I regret to say, that I have ample evidence that this order was issued in the terms above recited. This order, unjust and unworthy in its purposes, and most offensive in its terms, punishes a citizen and a soldier for supporting a candidate for the office of Governor, in his own State, who received many thousand more of the votes of its electors than any other candidate for the station, including the one who represented, more particularly, the views and purposes of the National Administration. Such acts are more disastrous to the cause of our Union than the loss of battles. Such violent measures of partisanship weaken, divide, and distract the people of the North, at the very moment they are called upon, without distinction of party, to make vast sacrifices of blood and treasure to uphold the Government. Notwithstanding the notoriety of these acts, the bill I return throws no guard around the rights and independence of our soldiers in the field. An amendment, designed to protect them against coercion and fraud, was rejected in one branch of the Legislature."

The principles of this veto, for which Gov. Seymour, as for every other public act, was violently assailed with epithets and with charges of treason, were subsequently sustained by the veto by Gov. Gilmore, the Republican Executive of New Hampshire, of a bill of precisely the same character in which he insisted that the same end should be accomplished by an amendment to, rather than by a violation of, the State Constitution. He advised the course pursued in New York. Gov. Gilmore added, "The next step after the violation of the Constitution of the State of New Hampshire, and of the United States, is anarchy."

At an early period of the subsequent session of the Legislature, an act was passed to submit an amendment of the Constitution, enabling soldiers to vote, which was signed by Gov. Seymour. In March, 1864, the amendment was submitted under this act, and received the almost unanimous sanction of the people of the State, the Democratic party generally supporting it. At a later stage in the session, an act was passed to provide for soldiers and sailors voting by power of attorney. That bill was signed by the Governor, and he, in the following autumn after the National and State nominations had been made, proceeded to carry out its provisions. Thus, it will be seen that the plan of the Republicans to cheat the soldiers by an invalid law, was thwarted by Gov. Seymour. The soldiers understood this and therefore, in large numbers, voted for him against all the threats and other influences brought to bear by the General Government. They felt that they owed the privilege of voting to him.

Under date of September 30, 1864, Gov. Seymour issued a circular to the commandants and surgeons of New York regiments in the field, from which the following is a quotation:—

"You can do much toward securing to your officers and men a fair expression of their political preferences, if you will detail one or more officers of your command of each political party, to distribute the ballots and to aid the soldiers and commissioners in filling up the requisite powers of attorney. You are also requested to use every effort, to send forward the envelopes containing the powers of attorney and ballots, to the electors in the several election districts of this State, named on the back thereof—either by express or mail, or through such reliable Commissioners as may visit your command. I feel confident that every officer from New York will feel an honorable pride in seeing that the laws of his State are carried out according to their letter and spirit, and that they will protect all under their care, in the full and free exercise of their personal and political rights."

Under the same date, the Governor addressed the

following letter to Hon. Chauncey M. Depew, then Secretary of State, the highest Republican State officer then in office, and who by law was charged with the distribution of blanks under the Soldiers' Voting Act:—

"I shall send a set of ballots to every regiment from New York. I will send them for both political parties, if you or any other person will furnish me those for the candidates of the Republican party— or if you prefer to send them I will give you any facility in my power."

Gov. Seymour called on Mr. Depew, and suggested to him that commisioners, of whose high character there would be no question, should be appointed to represent each party, so that there should be entire fairness in taking the votes of the soldiers. To the propriety of this Mr. Depew assented, but did not take further action, and Gov. Seymour therefore made the appointment on his own responsibility, notifying Mr. Depew of the proceeding in the following letter:

"Some days since I spoke with you concerning the appointment by you and myself of joint commissioners to proceed to the several United States Hospitals, and to visit the armies in the field, for the purpose of distributing ballots to our New York soldiers, now in the United States service, and to carry out the purposes of the law for soldiers voting.

"As the day for the election approaches, every delay becomes injurious to our soldiers—and as I have heard nothing from you, with reference to a co-operation in making such appointments, I have selected several commissioners to proceed to Washington and the army of the Potomac to this end.

"I shall be happy to add others if you will name them. I have directed them to carry ballots for any parties, that may see fit to put them into their hands."

Among the agents so appointed to furnish and receive votes, where the agents of the State, for the relief of sick and wounded soldiers at Washington and Baltimore, who were directed to receive the votes of New York soldiers at the hospitals. Hon. John F. Seymour, the General Agent, issued orders that they should provide themselves with Republican as well as Democratic ballots, and furnish them to all soldiers who wished them. A delay of ten or twelve days occurred on account of the refusal to furnish the agents with passes and other obstacles placed in their way by administration officials. Notwithstanding these, however, it was found that a very large vote was being given by the soldiers for McClellan and Seymour.

CHAPTER XV.

THE OUTRAGE ON THE NEW YORK STATE AGENTS.—THEIR ARREST AND LONG INCARCERATION AND SUBSEQUENT ACQUITTAL AND VINDICATION.

THE National Administration became alarmed for their success in the Empire State, and for the purpose of furnishing a pretext to seize the votes and also to create a revulsion of public sentiment in New York, a scheme was concocted to arrest the State agents on the charge of fraud, and bring them before a secret tribunal for trial, while false and malicious stories and alleged confessions were industriously circulated through the press. The outrage perpetrated in carrying out this plot was one of the most flagrant and inexcusable in the long list of violations of personal rights which form a part of the history of the civil war.

On the 27th of October, 1864, about a week prior to the election, Col. Samuel North, Major Levi Cohn, and M. M. Jones, citizens of the State, were arrested and incarcerated in the Old Capitol Prison. The ballots deposited for transmission by the State agents were seized and detained. Thousands of ballots, which had been deposited in the mails, were detained in the post-offices of New York City and elsewhere until after the election. To prevent detection of this fraud, the post-marks were changed. In some instances also where the sick soldiers returned home in time to vote in person, they discovered that the democratic ballots which they had placed in the envelope had been taken out and republican ballots substituted. It was clearly shown by those who investigated the matter that enough votes were detained and changed to have carried the New York election for McClellan and Seymour. Immediately upon the arrest, Gov. Seymour sent on a commission of three eminent gentlemen from New York, two of whom had been candidates for governor and the third the present state comptroller and a judge of the highest court in the State—Hon. Amasa J. Parker, Hon. Wm. F. Allen, and Hon. William Kelley—to demand the speedy trial and release of Col. North and his associates. They procured some mitigation of the rigor of their confinement, but the administration refused to listen to any further demands on their part.

Their report will make the face of every American tingle with shame to think that such atrocities could be perpetrated against innocent citizens at the National Capital—acts which would disgrace a barbarous people.

We can give only the following extract:—

"The undersigned availed themselves of the permit granted them to visit Col. North, Marvin M. Jones, and Levi Cohn. They found them in the 'Carrol Prison,' in close confinement. They then learned that Messrs. North and Cohn had been confined together in one room, and had not been permitted to leave it for a moment during the four days they had been prisoners, even for the purpose of answering the calls of nature. They had been supplied with meager and coarse prison rations, to be eaten in the room, where they constantly breathed the foul atmosphere arising from the standing ordure. They had no vessel out of which to drink water except the one furnished them for the purpose of urination. They had but one chair, and slept three of the nights of their confinement upon a sack of straw on the floor. They had not been permitted to see a newspaper, and were ignorant of the cause of their arrest. All communication between them and the outer world had been denied them, and no friend had been allowed to see them."

By such brutal appliances it was sought to break down the spirit of these men and mold them to the purposes of the administration. It had been communicated to them, and was well understood, that in case they would make false confessions, implicating Governor Seymour in frauds upon the elective franchise, they could thereby secure an early release.

It having been determined to proceed to the trial of the agents by a Military Commission, in violation of the law under which they were appointed, Gov. Seymour selected and sent to Washington as counsel and to attend to their interests Hon. William A. Beach and Hon. Ransom H. Gillett.

From the day of the arrest till the day of the election the Republican press teemed with false accounts of the alleged frauds, and it was boldly charged, in order to cover their own frauds upon the soldiers, that a gigantic conspiracy was headed by Gov. Seymour to divert the whole soldiers' vote to the Democratic ticket.

The correspondent of the N. Y. *Tribune* wrote from Penn Yan, N. Y., October 28, 1864, stating that Gov. Seymour had just closed a speech which was " one tissue of the basest sophistry ; a low appeal to the fears, the selfishness, and the passions of the uneducated masses. He alluded to the arrest of the agent whom he sent to obtain the soldiers' vote in the following cheeky, brassy, unprincipled and false manner." The correspondent then quotes a passage in which Gov. Seymour spoke merely of the fact of the arrest of the agents, and remarks: "The impression flashed over many a mind that the apologist for this criminal was not only his MASTER but his INSTRUCTOR and ACCOMPLICE in this nefarious, undemocratic crime against our brave soldiers." The capitals are the *Tribune's*.

On November 1, 1864, the *Tribune* said:—

"That agents appointed by Gov. Seymour to obtain the votes of soldiers in the field, for the opposition ticket, have been engaged in wholesale forgeries of the names of voters and officers, with intent to poll tens of thousands of bogus votes for McClellan and Seymour, is well established, as any fact can be, by a concurrence of positive and circumstantial testimony. Seymour *knows* this to be so."

The trial commenced on the 3d of November, 1864, and was protracted to January 6, 1865, but even then neither the public nor the accused were allowed to know the findings of the court, and the prisoners were kept in the Old Capitol for several weeks after the finding was made. To quote from an able speech by Hon. John C. Jacobs, at the last session of the Legislature:—

"These citizens and agents of the State, though released, were told by one man that they were convicted, and by another that they were acquitted, all the while resting under stigma, regarded by some as forgers, and by many treated with contempt. Finally, sir, when years have passed, we are permitted to look upon the official records.

"Col. North first learns of his acquittal by being released upon the following order:—

WASHINGTON, D. C., Jan. 30, 1865.

MY DEAR SIR—I inclose you a certified copy directing your release, saying you are acquitted.

The others are convicted and sentenced to imprisonment for life. *So says the Secretary of War.*

Very truly yours,
JOHN GANSON.

Col. *Samuel North*, Unadilla, N. Y.

(Copy.)

WAR DEPARTMENT,
ADJUTANT-GENERAL'S OFFICE,
WASHINGTON, January 26, 1865.

MR. WM. P. WOOD, *Superintendent Old Capitol Prison:—*

SIR—Col. North having been acquitted by the Military Commission before which he was tried, the Secretary of War directs that he be immediately released from confinement.

Report receipt and execution of this order.

(Signed) Very respectfully,

Your obedient servant,
E. D. TOWNSEND, Asst. Adj.-Gen.

(A true copy.)
E. D. TOWNSEND, Asst. Adj.-General.

"It will be noticed that the Secretary of War stated that Cohn and Jones had been convicted and sentenced to imprisonment for life. He repeated this to Col. North and others, and insisted upon it. The statement was published in the papers and generally believed. Then comes another letter from John Ganson, as follows:

WASHINGTON, D. C., Feb. 15, 1865.

MY DEAR SIR—Cohn and Jones were acquitted and discharged accordingly, on my application to the Secretary of War.

The statements made in regard to them *were for the purpose of letting the party in power down easy.*

I hope your freedom has restored you to good health.

Very truly yours,
JOHN GANSON.

Col. *Samuel North*, Unadilla, N. Y.

"Edwin M. Stanton deliberately lied, in saying that Cohn and Jones were convicted, as this letter shows, and as the records, then in Stanton's possession, establish. Though these general statements were made, and the agents were released, yet the War Secretary refused to allow any official verdict of the Military Commission to be published. Why, I do not care to presume, unless it was to prevent further publicity of his atrocious falsehood. It was not till last year that the records were furnished the accused, and then by order of Andrew Johnson, upon the application of Congressman Goodyear."

Here follows official record of proceedings of the Military Commission, dated February 12, 1867, showing that North, Cohn, and Jones were found "not guilty" on all the charges, "and do therefore acquit said Samuel North, Levi Cohn, and Marvin M. Jones." Signed, John A. Foster, Col. and Judge Advocate, and Abner Doubleday, Maj. Gen. of Vol. and President of Military Commission.

The *Tribune* having just before the election charged that Mr. Jones made a confession, and afterward claming that the three persons named had been convicted, but released through the leniency of the President, was obliged through fear of legal proceedings to publish two denials of its former statement, of which the following, from the issue of February 3, 1868, is one:—

"The New York Daily *Tribune*, on the 2d day of November, 1864, in an article in relation to the arrest of Messrs. North, Jones, and Cohn, at Washington, upon a charge of fraud in connection with soldiers' votes, published the following referring to M. M. Jones, Esq., of Utica, N. Y.:—

"'Marvin Jones, Colonel North's Chief Assistant, confined with him at Old Capitol, has thrown gravel and ashes into the teeth of Governor Seymour's Special Commission to-day, by making a full confession of his complicity in the forging of votes, and that the business has been carried on at Colonel North's Agency, much more extensively than any thing done at Baltimore. It is understood that the Commissioners are further staggered by his complete implication of Colonel North in the frauds. The end is not yet reached.

"'It appears that injustice was done Mr. Jones by this article, although, at the time, we supposed it to be true, having received it from a Washington correspondent. Mr. Jones was, after a long imprisonment, discharged by the Military Commission, and we are satisfied that there was no evidence that he made any confession of, or that he was guilty of any forgery by himself, or at the New York Soldiers' Agency, as we charged in the above extract, and his discharge is satisfactory proof to us that no evidence of forgery existed.'"

Similar falsehoods were circulated in regard to the Baltimore arrests, and it is sufficient to say that not a single person appointed by Governor Seymour was convicted of fraud, although tried by secret and partisan military tribunals. The whole affair was characterized by Hon. William C. Bently, in the Assembly last winter, as follows:—

"If gentlemen knew the degrading character of that imprisonment, and the means used to insult and persecute the accused, it seems to me that they must unanimously condemn the affair as the most outrageous and abhorrent acts of a bold, wanton, and unscrupulous administration, *inasmuch as the proof is irrefragable that Stanton and his accomplices knew the innocence of the accused at the time they arrested and incarcerated them like condemned felons, in the strong cells of a dungeon.*"

And it is honorable to the Republican party, when these facts were laid before them, and their eyes for the first time were opened to the crimes thus perpetrated against the soldiers of New York, and the agents who were engaged in taking care of the sick and wounded, that they aided to pass a bill which appropriated an ample sum to pay the counsel engaged in their defense, and thus to show their abhorrence of the shameful acts of the administration at Washington. Thus in another instance Governor Seymour stands vindicated by the official votes of his opponents from the charges persistently made against him.

CHAPTER XVI.

PROCLAMATIONS DURING THE WAR.

Governor Seymour's Proclamations during his gubernatorial terms were invariably models of elegant and vigorous writing, and were remarkable for touching and patriotic sentiments. Yet for every one that he issued as for every other act or expression of his life, however wise and pure it might be, he was unscrupulously abused. The reader may be pleased to judge for himself of their character by some extracts from proclamations issued during the war.

The proclamation of a thanksgiving on the last Thursday of April, 1863, said:—

"Acknowledging our dependence upon His power, let us put away pride and ingratitude, malice and uncharitableness, and implore Him to deliver our land from sedition, privy conspiracy, and rebellion, and to restore the blessings of peace, concord, and union to the several States of our distracted and afflicted country."

The following is the proclamation of August 3, 1863:—

"Whereas, The President of the United States has set apart Thursday, the sixth day of August, to be observed as a day of National thanksgiving and praise, for the signal victories recently gained by our armies and navies; I, Horatio Seymour, Governor of New York, do hereby request the people of this State to observe that day in the manner and for the purposes recommended by the Chief Magistrate of the Union.

"Humbly acknowledging our dependence upon Almighty God, let us assemble in our respective places of public worship, and with heartfelt gratitude thank Him for our National successes. Let us pour forth the fervent prayer for His blessings upon those who have periled their lives in desperate conflicts, to uphold the Constitution of our country, and to maintain that Union of these States which is essential to the peace and happiness of our people. In the midst of our rejoicings, let us remember those whose homes have been made desolate by the ravages of war. Let us offer up our petitions that our people may be animated by virtue, intelligence, and patriotism, and that our rulers may be endowed with wisdom to put down rebellion, to uphold the liberties and rights of our people, and to restore the blessings of peace, order, and prosperity to our afflicted country."

The Thanksgiving Proclamation for November, 1863, read:—

"Let us offer our fervent prayers that rebellion may be put down, our Union saved, our liberties preserved, and our Constitution and Government upheld. As a becoming proof of thankfulness to God, and as a proper evidence of our gratitude to the armies and navy, I urge our citizens to make contributions on that day, for the comfort and support of the destitute families of those who have lost their lives, or have become disabled in the service of their country."

The following appointed a day of fasting:—

STATE OF NEW YORK,
EXECUTIVE DEPARTMENT, ALBANY.

PROCLAMATION BY THE GOVERNOR.

The President of the United States, having set apart Thursday, the 4th inst., for national fasting, humiliation, and prayer; I, Horatio Seymour, Governor of the State of New York, do recommend that the day be observed thoughout the State with suitable religious solemnities. Let us repent of our manifold sins and offenses, and humbly pray that Almighty God will put down all rebellious resistance to rightful authority, all sectional hatred, all bigotry and malice, all hurtful ambition or partisan purposes which tend to discord and strife. That he will restore the Union of our States, and fraternal affection between the inhabitants thereof, and give peace to our land. Acknowledging the justice of his punishments upon us for our national and personal sins, let us entreat him to have mercy upon us, to turn away his wrath, to stop the shedding of blood, to return our soldiers to their homes, to relieve the sick, wounded, and suffering, to comfort those in mourning, to reward the industry of our people, to relieve them from heavy burdens, to make them safe in their persons and homes from all violence and oppression, and to give the protection of law to all conditions of men. To these ends let us pray that God will give wisdom to our rulers, purity to our legislators, uprightness and boldness to our judges, meekness and charity to our clergy, and virtue, intelligence, and godliness to our people.

In witness whereof, I have hereunto signed my name, and affixed the Privy Seal of the State, at the City of Albany, this first day of August, in the year of our Lord one thousand eight hundred and sixty-four.

By the Governor.   HORATIO SEYMOUR.
   D. WILLERS, JR.,
      Private Secretary.

That appointing Thursday, November 26, 1864, contained the following:—

"Gratitude to God is best shown by mercy and charity to our fellow-men. I therefore exhort the citizens of this State to help the poor, relieve the sick, and to comfort those who are in affliction. Many living in our large towns are threatened with a want of labor, and the means to buy food and fuel, while the withdrawal of great numbers of able-bodied men from our State into our armies, leaves thousands of helpless persons without support.

"I specially invoke the public to make contributions for the comfort and assistance of the families of those who are in the service of the armies and navies of our country."

CHAPTER XVII.

PRISON DISCIPLINE.

ONE of the most trying and perplexing duties devolving upon the executive of a great State like New York, grows out of the exercise of the pardoning power.

In the several State prisons and penitentiaries of the State, many thousand convicts are constantly incarcerated—under sentences ranging from three months to a lifetime.

It becomes the painful duty of the Governor annually to examine and pass often nearly or quite one thousand applications for pardons or commutations of sentence.

These applications are made at all hours, in season and out of season—by strong men, and by mothers, wives, and sisters.

The following incident, related by an eye-witness, will suffice to give an idea of scenes daily enacted at the Executive Chamber:—

"A few days ago, after a hard day's ride, I went in the evening to the Executive Chamber of the chief magistrate of the State. I found that I had been preceded by a woman and five young children. At a glance I saw that a pardon case was awaiting the arrival of the Governor, who soon came in, greeted me in his usual bland manner, turned to the woman, and said: 'My good woman, you were here with your children last summer, and I then told you that I could do nothing to relieve your husband; and future efforts on your part would prove fruitless. Should I pardon him, the doors of all the State prisons of the State might as well be opened and let every prisoner go forth.'

"The woman sobbed and prayed, that 'his Honor would relent, and put her husband, as honest a man as ever lived, out of prison.'

"The Governor, although much annoyed, remembering the case so well, and knowing the poverty of the family, asked the woman how she was enabled to travel so far with all her children. She replied:—

"'Your Honor, I worked until I earned eight dollars.'

"He said: 'My good woman, that small sum would hardly have brought you so far with all your children.'

"'Your Honor,' she said, 'I paid five dollars for myself, and the railroad men charged me nothing for the children, and I have three dollars left.'

"'Have your children eaten to-day?'

"'No, your Honor.'

"The Governor then asked her how she expected to go back with only three dollars.

"Touching the bell (for a different purpose than the one which one of his predecessors now uses it), he said to his messenger, after giving her some money: 'Take this woman with her children to my house; see that they are well fed, and then take them to the cars.'

"After the woman with her five children had left the room, he said: 'Judge, this is only one case among many; do you wonder that I begged our friends, last September, to give me rest.'

"After a pleasant chat with him, I retired with the idea that the position of Governor of this State was no sinecure."

During his first term, Governor Seymour was struck with the defects of our criminal code, and the want of some principle in the management of our prisons, which was calculated to reform their inmates. He found that our courts were forced in many cases by the letter of the law to impose unreasonable terms of punishment, which led to numerous applications for pardon. He was also satisfied that no criminal could be made a better man unless some inducement was held out which would encourage and strengthen him in his efforts to overcome his evil propensities. He held that Hope was the great reformer. He, therefore, made exertions to introduce a new principal into our criminal code. Something had been done in that direction before, but the obscurity of the law made it a dead letter. He urged upon the Legislature as a measure of relief to the pardoning power and as a measure of mercy to the convict, that the latter should be allowed to shorten his term by his own good conduct. This would be attended by a double advantage. It would not only tend to make him conduct himself with propriety, but when he went out of prison with the proofs that his good behavior had shortened his term, it would give him a sense of his own worth, which must be felt before he would have self-confidence to enter upon a course of virtue and of industry. This mode of ending his imprisonment would also give to the world proof of his reformation. By the provisions of this law, if the sentence is for two years, good conduct would strike off a month in each year; if it was for a longer term, up to five years, it would strike off two months in each year; if for a longer period than five years, up to ten years, it would strike out three months in each year; for all terms beyond ten years, good conduct would strike out four months of imprisonment in each year.

By this system of graduation hope was given to all. It is believed that this plan of rewards is the beginning of a reform in our prisons which will hold out every encouragement to their unfortunate inmates, while it will not interfere with that certainty of punishment so necessary to restrain vice. This measure has been hailed with satisfaction by those who have given thought to prison discipline; but it was only by persistent and personal appeals that the governor was able to secure its adoption by the Legislature. Indeed, it was once rejected by one branch. All who have any thing to do with the management of our prisons testify to the great good which this method has wrought out.

It has been charged as a matter of reproach to Governor Seymour that he called bad men his " friends," but he has reason to feel a just pride in the fact that, in this matter, he has proved himself to be the true friend of the unfortunate and unhappy, although guilty inmates of our prisons. We warn the modern Pharisee that our Saviour was reproached with being the friend to publicans and sinners, and that He even saluted him as " friend" who came at the head of armed men to betray him to a cruel death.

During the past year, a convention to revise the State Constitution, which met at the city of Albany, and was composed of a decided majority of Republicans, through one of its Standing Committees, solicited the views of Governor Seymour upon the exercise of the pardoning power. He at once responded to their call and appeared and was heard before the Committee, who in their report referred at length to the experience and views of the Governor upon this branch of executive duty.

CHAPTER XVIII.

PUBLIC FAITH.

It is remarkable at this time, when financial questions are so much discussed, and when the Democrats are charged with bad faith to the public creditors, that certain facts of history have been overlooked. When Government has agreed to pay in gold, the Democratic party has demanded payment in gold. When bonds are payable in legal tender paper, popularly called "greenbacks," they demand they shall be paid in legal tender notes, and they declare that the true interpretation of the contract is that when it does not provide that bonds shall be paid in coin, they ought, in justice, to be paid in lawful money of the United States. Many of the leading Republicans hold this to be the true construction. Their Convention passed an equivocal resolution on the subject, and their candidates can not be made to say what their views are. On the Democratic side there is frankness, on the Republican side there are evasions. The Republicans mean, to cheat either the bondholder or the tax-payer. Yet a clamor is raised that the Democrats are repudiators, while the only cases of direct, open violation of contracts to pay in coin are those made by Republican action, or by virtue of Republican laws. It is admitted that the legal tenders which will be given in payment of the bonds are worth much more than the money given to the Government for these bonds when they were sold. When the bonds of New York, which were to be paid in gold, and for which the creditor had given gold, were due, the Republicans refused to pay even the interest in any thing but "greenbacks," which were then worth only forty cents on the dollar. Yet the specie borrowed of the creditors of the State was used to build canals which are paying great revenues to the treasury of New York. In vain Governor Seymour appealed to a Republican Legislature not to break the contract. Every Democrat voted to keep faith with the men who had loaned specie funds. Every Republican Senator voted in favor of repudiation. We give an extract from Governor Seymour's appeal:—

"Principle and policy unite to urge the action I recommend to you. It is the only way in which the State can in truth fulfill its contracts. It is the only way in which the State can keep itself in a position to go into the market hereafter decently as a borrower. The State is even now in the market for money to pay its bounties and volunteers. The whole amount of the appropriation I urge upon you will be more than repaid in the first negotiation the State may make, by the enhanced price of its securities. Not only our future credit, but our immediate gain will be served by adhering now to the strictest letter of our contracts. The saving proposed by not paying in coin is small and temporary, while the dishonor is lasting, and the pecuniary loss consequent upon this dishonor will be in the end enormous.

"Bad faith on the part of New York, the leading member of our confederacy, must inevitably weaken very greatly, if it do not destroy, the credit of our Government securities in foreign markets. Compared with the importance of this State's action in its effects upon the credit of the Government, the cost of paying our interest in coin is insignificant.

"Aside from all considerations of interest or policy, our duty, in my judgment, is plain; it is to pay the debts of the State; to pay them in precisely the mode in which they were promised to be paid; to keep the honor of the State unsullied; and to this plain duty we should be true, cost what it may.

"HORATIO SEYMOUR."

The refusal of the Republican members of the Legislature to respond to these appeals was the heaviest blow given during the war to the credit of our country. In the end it cost both the State and nation a hundredfold more than the expense which would have been caused by the payment of the interest in specie.

This act, which so dishonored New York, and sunk the credit of the country, is one of the chief causes of the vast sum of our national indebtedness. It is due to the Democratic members of the Legislature to state, that to a man they voted to uphold the policy urged by the Governor. So anxious was he to save the hitherto unstained honor of New York, that he made an appeal to the banks and to the capitalists of the State to step forward and furnish the specie, relying upon a returning sense of good faith to repay them for such advances. Some of these were willing to do their share; but it is a sad proof of the selfishness and shortsightedness of the banks and capitalists of the commercial emporium, that they turned a deaf ear to the appeals of Governor Seymour, and refused to uphold him in his efforts to check repudiation at the outset.

We can now see why it was that at one period of the war our bonds sold for forty cents on the dollar, and had less credit in the markets of the world than those put forth by the Confederate States.

There is not a Democrat in the United States who will not say that this was an indecent, dishonest act of repudiation, but it was never rebuked by a Republican paper or preacher. Again, if a man borrows coin of his neighbors to any amount, say $1,000, and gives the solemn promise to repay it in coin, a Republican Congress steps in and by its laws advises the debtor to cheat his creditor. It tells him he may force his creditor to take $1,000 in greenbacks, and thus give him $250 less in value than the debtor borrowed. How is it, in the face of such facts, and the fact that the Republican party has sunk the national credit below that of the Turk, that it is claimed that the national honor is only safe in their hands? One year of an honest, economical, Democratic administration would do more to build up the national credit and honor, than can ever be done by those who take the money collected to pay the public creditor, and use it for partisan purposes and corrupt schemes.

CHAPTER XIX.

GOVERNOR SEYMOUR AND THE WESTERN STATES.

At an early day Governor Seymour became impressed with the importance of cherishing the commercial relationship between New York and the great West. As Chairman of the Canal Committee in the Legislature, as early as 1844, he made a report urging the importance of building up the prosperity of the new States in the valley of the Mississippi. He at all times protested against that narrow policy that looked at the returns which our canals should give in the form of tolls, rather than at their influence in giving life to the commerce of our country, growth to our cities, markets for our mechanics, and activity to the internal carrying trade of the State. In his message to the Legislature in 1863, he called public attention to the fact that the estimated tonnage on our canals, for the year 1862, was nearly five millions of tons, and that about eighty per cent. of the value of the canal freights moved from West to East. He added:—

"These facts should induce us to give every possible facility to the vast and growing commerce of the Western States, mainly dependent upon them as we are for the immense through traffic which constitutes so large a share of our carrying trade, and forms a most important source of our commercial greatness, affording at the same time one of the many reasons for cultivating the most enduring relationship with that section."

In his message of 1864, he recurred to these subjects in these words:—

"A deep interest is felt with regard to our commerce with the Western States. Its growing value and the loss of our trade with the Southern States make us dependent for commercial prosperity upon that section of our country which sustains our domestic and foreign commerce, and which adds so largely to the imports and business prosperity of the city of New York. This State will be untrue to itself if it fails to control this great source of wealth by a vigorous and generous policy. Rather than suffer its diversion or depression, we should strike off all tolls upon Western produce.

"New York should exhibit that degree of interest in all measures designed to benefit the West which shall show our purpose to keep up the most intimate commercial relationship with that portion of our Union."

As the cost of transportation was at that time a serious injury to the West, and as, at an early period in the war, produce brought only nominal prices, and at one time corn was actually used for fuel in Southern Illinois, he urged that such discriminations should be made in favor of the West as would revive its industry. But he urged in vain, for the Republican party controlled the Legislature of the State. He has devoted much time and effort in favor of water communications between the Mississippi River and the Lakes, which would not only cheapen transportation, but, as they would be open to the use of all, would regulate the prices of railroad transportation for the Western States, as the Erie canal checks unreasonable charges within the limits of the State of New York.

When our present National Banking Law was established, and a bill was passed through the Legislature of New York allowing its banks to organize under its provisions, he refused to sign the bill. He withheld his assent not only because he saw that the system involved a great loss of interest to the people of the country, but that it was doing a flagrant wrong to the Western States. The scheme limited the amount of bank circulation to three hundred millions of dollars. Those who had money were allowed to come in and take up these privileges without regard to the rights, or wants of the country at large. The privileges thus granted were of great value, and were completely sectionalized. The country was not only divided by our bonds into debtor and creditor States, but the entire control of bank currency was given to those States which made money out of the war, and which had been enriched by profitable contracts. The Western States were not then in a condition to enter into the struggle for their share of this banking privilege, and they are now, by its limitations, cut off from its benefits. Governor Seymour felt, that what was injurious to the West was injurious to the great interests of trade and commerce. He foresaw that this system would fasten upon the West rates of interest which, beyond even the enormous taxation of Government, would paralyze its industry; and that a system which would prove so baleful could not be lasting. The States which hold an undue share of this currency need but little of it in their business affairs. Manufacturing and commercial communities have less need for the use of currency than agricultural States, as they conduct their business, to a large degree, by means of bank checks and bank credits. But to buy the wheat and the corn of the great Northwestern States, currency is essential. No State in the Union needs as much as the State of Illinois, and yet, in common with the other Western States, it has but a trifling amount. This is not merely a matter of inconvenience, but it is also an enormous tax. When currency is wanted to buy up the wheat and corn, and other products of the West, Western bankers are obliged to come to the Eastern States to borrow bank bills which have been given to these Eastern States by the Government, in excess of their business wants. The Western banker has to pay an interest for the use of these bills, and thus he is compelled to charge the produce-buyer two interests: one for himself, and the other for the Eastern banker. While the commercial paper of the Western cities, for its purposes, its short dates, its places of payment at the East, and the security given by a bill of sale of the property that is sent forward, is made the best commercial paper of the country, it is charged with enormous discounts, ranging from eight to twelve per cent.—the like paper in the Eastern States would be discounted for five or six per cent. All of this, as well as the other costs of purchase and of transportation, is taken out of the pockets of the farmers of the West. The West complains of the want of currency: but it will be seen that the great difficulty is that the Government gave the share of currency due the West to a few of the Eastern States.

Foreseeing this wrong, Gov. Seymour did what he could to prevent the establishment of the system, and he refused to remain a director of a bank with which he had been connected nearly thirty years, when it was reorganized under the national banking law. And while he has at all times firmly upheld the public faith, *he has never allowed himself to be the owner of a single Government bond,* for the reason that they were issued under a financial system which he opposed from the outset, and which he denounced as unwise and dangerous, as it was dividing our Union into debtor and creditor States, and engendered sectional controversies which were perilous to the peace of our country. He has always carefully abstained from any investment under a policy which he could not approve. While Gov. Seymour never had an interest in Government bonds, and while his property consists of real estate, a large share of which lies in the West, he has ever been so firm an advocate of the National faith, that the public was led to suppose that he was interested in Government securities. This, as has been explained, is untrue; he has no other interest in them than that of a tax-payer, no anxiety about them save that which springs from his desire to maintain the honor of our Government, the interests of the laborer, and the welfare of all classes of society.

7*

CHAPTER XX.

GOV. SEYMOUR AND THE INTERESTS OF LABOR.

Gov. SEYMOUR has always shown an active interest in favor of the mechanical, industrial, and laboring classes. He did what he could in the town where he lived to cherish all kinds of industry, by the erection of buildings, and by aiding its various enterprises. He was one of the first members of the Mechanics' Association of the city of Utica, and tried to give interest to its fairs and its system of lectures. His sympathy with the wants and interests of our mechanics and laborers gave him his strength with that class, as well as with the mass of the farmers of the State.

It was his deep feeling in behalf of labor that prompted him, in the face of the most violent denunciation, to take his stand against the waste and corruption of the administration. He pointed out where, in the end, the whole weight of taxation would rest. Years ago, he warned the people of this country that the policy of hate, of military despotism, and of political meddling would come home to our citizens, and that they would find the costs in the tax-gatherer's bill. He analyzed the cost of living to those who work for the support of themselves or their families. He showed that six hours of toil would give a man more than he now gains by ten, if it was not for the taxation which, in its endless forms, direct and indirect, swells up the cost of all he buys. He clearly proved that one hour of toil ought to pay a laborer's share of the cost of good government—that another hour was his full share toward the payment of the national debt—that the time which he was forced to labor, beyond eight hours, measured the waste and corruptions of government. He told of the swarms of idle and useless officials who are clothed and fed by his exertions. He pointed out the mockery of declaring that eight hours made a legal day's labor, if, at the same time, Congress piled up a load of taxation that forced him to work ten hours or starve; that this whole question of the labor movement resolved itself into a question of taxation; that to-day the tax-gatherer was the taskmaster; that men should see that if, beyond feeding and clothing themselves and their families, they had to feed and clothe great armies of armed men, and still greater and more voracious armies of hungry officials, that the laborer must toil on, for these armies must be fed and clothed before himself or his family. The cost of this would be found in the price of the flour, meat, tea, sugar which he consumed, and of the clothing which he wore.

CHAPTER XXI.

THE ELECTION OF 1864.

Mr. Seymour was averse to be nominated for the office of Governor in 1864. He only yielded a partial assent to this act when it was urged that his refusal to run might be looked upon as showing a lack of confidence in the strength of General McClellan as a candidate. He had not favored the general at the Chicago convention, although he held him in the highest regard. Their relationships were of the most confidential and friendly character, but he thought the day had not come when the general's conduct and claims would be fairly considered, and that he ought not to be damaged by a premature trial. For these reasons he was embarrassed in making a direct refusal of a nomination which was unanimously tendered to him. Being thus placed upon the ticket, he was forced to make great sacrifices of time and exertions in a way not only injurious to his health and comfort, but in one that imperiled his liberty. He went forth in the face of the fact that his agents were locked up in prison; that he was threatened with arrest, and that an army was sent to keep by terror the voters from the polls of the city of New York. The fact that this armed force was commanded by General Butler was deemed proof that the property as well as the political rights of the people of the State of New York was in danger. The Governor at once issued a proclamation, assuring the voters that they should be protected if need be, by the armed power of the State. The city of New York gave an enormous majority in favor of the Democratic ticket, and the unlucky general was forced to withdraw discomfited in his political efforts, and shorn of any spoils of victory. Although every appeal was made to the passions and prejudices of the soldiers, a majority of those from New York voted in favor of the Democratic nominees. While they were robbed of their votes by officials and at the post-offices throughout the States, yet the Democrats would have carried the State of New York had there been a sufficient number of voting places to enable all to deposit their ballots. Let those who think that gross and shameless abuse will harm the character of a nominee, compare the vote given to Governor Seymour in 1862, when he was elected, with that given in 1864, when he was declared defeated, and they will find that under all this storm of detraction and falsehood he gained 54,615 voters over those which were given him in 1862. His vote was 200,000 more than in 1854, when he came within 309 votes of an election, and nearly 100,000 more votes than in 1852, when he was elected by 22,000 majority. His vote in 1864 was much larger than that cast for any democratic candidate at any prior election.

The ceremony of the retirement of Governor Seymour, and the inauguration of Governor Fenton, took place in the Assembly Chamber, at 12 M., Monday, January 2d. The chamber was crowded by members of the Legislature, citizens and strangers. Governor Seymour, as is usual, made a short address. He invoked the consideration of the people of the State for the incoming executive in the performance of onerous duties. He remarked:—

> "The present war has added to these duties, until the position of Chief Magistrate of this State calls for every energy of body and of mind. Within the past four years, New York has sent nearly 440,000 men to the armies and navies of the country. More than 30,000 military commissions have been given out by the Executive Department during the same period."

He then addressed Governor Fenton. The following is an extract from his remarks:—

> "To you, sir, who now enter upon the duties of Chief Magistrate of this great State, I tender my sincere wishes for your successful administration. You and I look upon public affairs from different stand-points, and we have held conflicting views and reached different conclusions with regard to the methods by which our country can best be saved from the perils which overhang it, but none the less, sir, have you my best wishes for your personal welfare and success in all the affairs of public and private life. In these days when we are called upon to confront problems so great, so vital, and so far-reaching in their effects, he who does not speak out his honest convictions lacks manhood, *and he who can not treat with respect and forbearance the convictions of others lacks sense and patriotism.* It is a source of pleasure to me that during the sharp political conflicts of the day, and the distinct antagonisms of our parties, our relationships have been those of friendly courtesy."

Governor Seymour's relations with the executive officers of other States, and with his predecessors, successors, and opponents in his own State, have always been very cordial. In the contest against Governor Fenton, certain criminal proceedings were brought to light in the records in the Albany courts, but Governor Seymour objected to their use in the campaign, and so far as they have been published, it has been done by Governor Fenton's enemies in his own party.

On May 10, 1864, Governor Seymour issued a general order of condolence and respect on the death of General James S. Wadsworth, who had been the opposing candidate in the contest of '62; speaking of him as " from the outset an ardent supporter of the war, to whom belongs the merit of freely periling his own person in upholding the opinions which he vindicated."

CHAPTER XXII.

GOVERNOR SEYMOUR'S COOPER INSTITUTE SPEECH OF 1866.

In October, 1866, Governor Seymour spoke at New York on the questions which now agitate the public mind. We give the following extracts from his remarks, made at the Cooper Institute in that year, as they could not have in view the action of the National Convention in 1868. He showed the failure of the Republicans to keep the promises made in the election of 1864:—

"In the election of 1864 we were told that the war which then raged in our land must be settled by force of arms; that when armed rebellion was put down our Union would be restored; that fraternal relationship between the North and South would be firmly based on mutual respect, wrought out on the battle-field, where both parties had shown courage worthy of the American name.

"We urged that our soldiers had won victories that enabled statesmanship to put an end to the contest that was filling our land with mourning, and loading down our industry with debt and taxation. That prolonged war made new questions, and that it was unsafe to leave the fruits of triumph ungathered.

"In answer it was said that the sword would soonest hew out the road to peace, to union, and concord; that Grant and Sherman were the only negotiators they would trust. When they had done their work there would be no questions left to perplex the public mind. We then warned the people that when every Southern army was driven from the field, and resistance was given up, it would be found that obstacles would be put in the way of the return of the Southern States to their duties. But the people trusted those who said force alone should be used.

"It is nearly two years since the surrender of the Southern armies. Within that time an European statesman has waged a victorious war against greater numbers, has built up a nation from scattered and jarring principalities, and has settled perplexing problems that disturbed the peace of Europe. And this was done by vigor and use of statesmanship within a period of six months. Nearly six years have rolled away since this Government began the work of putting down resistance to its authority on the part of a minority of the American people, and yet we are vexed to-day with more doubts and difficulties than at any other period since the war broke out.

"During the four years of active warfare, it was the policy of those who wished to throw off from themselves the disgrace of unfitness and imbecility, to say that it was simply a military problem, and thus to cast upon our armies the discredit of a lingering, indecisive struggle between forces so unequal. This was unjust and untrue. The historian will tell of victories won by heroic valor which would have ended the contest, if there had been an honest purpose on the part of those who controlled the administrative and legislative departments of government. But the Southern armies were crushed out two years ago. No longer can those who wield power shield themselves by throwing upon the soldiers the discredit of our disorganized condition.

"What has been done since our final victory to unite our people, to bind the States together by bonds of common interest, of fraternal regard, and by measures of wise statesmanship? Nothing; worse than nothing. We have drifted farther than ever from a restored Union. Two years ago we were battling to bring back seceded States to their duties; to-day we are haggling over terms of reunion; and the interests of party and not the safety of the Republic directs the political action. At the end of the battle the people of the North were in favor of a generous use of their victories, and the South was ready to accept results and return to their duties. But now all is changed. Men in power find their advantage in discord; hatred of the South is taught by the press, by a class of men in the pulpit whose vindictive piety was never drawn from our Saviour's teachings; by public speakers and by pictorial papers, they strive to stir up malignant passions. The questions growing out of this state of affairs have been discussed mainly with regard to their effects upon the rights, duties, and conditions of the South.

"I ask you now to look at the perils they cause to the rights, the interests, and well-being of the North. The people of the South were divided during the war. Some opposed the rebellion; some were hurried into it without thought, and were glad when it was over; all yielded to the result. They are now settling down into the belief that we are their unrelenting foes, that there can be no hearty Union. Unless there is a change of policy, in a little while they will accept the theory that they are a conquered people, with the rights as well as the liabilities of that condition. A military government will be forced upon us by making a military government necessary for their subjection. They will have every thing to gain and nothing to lose by revolutions. We have more to fear from the South if it accepts the doctrine of subjugation than we ever had to fear from its armed rebellion; we can not enslave them without enslaving ourselves. We can not have a government whose northern face shall smile devotion to the popular will, and whose southern aspect shall frown contempt, defiance, and hate to the people of eleven States.

"The South has comparatively little to fear from misgovernment; its lands already have been laid waste; its system of labor broken up; its homes impoverished; and its families thinned by the sword. It has seen and felt the worst. To-day the power of Great Britain is paralyzed by its harsh, unjust, and contemptuous treatment of Ireland. We are taught that if a people are to be treated as outlaws, they can bide their time; they can wait for domestic strife or foreign invasion. It is not wise or safe to trample upon those who for years, with desperate courage, held their ground against the millions we sent to the field, and the thousands of millions of treasure we spent in the contest—a contest which filled our homes with mourning, loaded us down with debt and taxation, and wrought great and lasting changes in the policy, the maxims, and structure of our Government. A wise settlement of pending questions will do much to build up the prosperity of the South; an unwise policy will do more to break down the wealth and prosperity of the North."

He also set forth the curses brought upon the laboring man by constant interference with the affairs of the South, and the consequent increase of taxation:

"The wisdom of Solomon has admonished the world that 'a wise man seeks peace, but a fool will be meddling.' I approve the purposes of President Johnson, because he seeks peace and concord. I oppose the policy of Congress, because it is one that is meddling and dangerous.

"I shall show why the policy of meddling and strife is hurtful to the capital, the labor, and the home-rights of the people of the North. The debt of the Government is about $3,000,000,000.

* * * * * * * * *

"The chief peril to the public faith is the wastefulness of Government, growing out of the violence of factions. Until the Union is saved, the cost of armies and of hordes of officers must be kept up. Beyond the direct cost of an honest and careful use of public money for these purposes, there is the danger from the growing corruption which always festers, when far-off States are put under the control of agents with unusual and undefined powers, meddling not only with public concerns, but private business and family affairs. These agents, mostly adventurers and men unknown to the people, and beyond the reach of the eye of those who pay the cost of keeping them, are tempted by love of power—lust for money—to act corruptly. This form of government for the South, at once base and debasing, lives only by keeping up the passions and hates of the people of this country. It is an ingenious and costly plan to keep the country in disorder; to unsettle all ideas of law, justice, and rights of persons and property. It is teaching the people of the North that power may rightfully do its will, trampling upon all the written laws and unwritten maxims which have heretofore governed our country and guarded the public faith, the personal safety, and the home-rights of our people.

"The meddling and disorganizing policy of Congress, if carried out, will be hurtful to the working men of the North. It calls for large armies. If the South is to be held in subjection until, in the language of Mr. Phillips, it gravitates toward the ideas of Massachusetts, at least one hundred thousand men must be kept in arms, at a cost of more than one hundred millions each year. The South will have the benefit of the money thus spent, and in time may look with as much satisfaction upon the arrival of troops as is shown by our Canadian friends when regiments are quartered in their towns. Great armies are to be kept up by Congressional legislation—the usual evils will follow.

"Our general and State Governments are fast getting to be corrupt and wasteful. The cost of them must be borne by labor. Government bonds pay no taxes; the disorganized South, instead of helping to bear these burdens, will add to their weight.

"Meetings are now held in all parts of our country to shorten the hours of toil. Men claim they should have more time for rest and mental culture. All agree that this is right; all promise to support them in their movement, Republicans and Democrats alike. But promises are cheap, and sympathy is of little value if it stops with the mere sentiment. I ask the workingmen to think of this. You must pay your taxes, and you must work to do so. It matters not if these taxes are paid into the hands of the tax-gatherers, or to the merchant, who puts them into the price you pay for his goods, of course. If you could buy your food, fuel, clothes, and other necessaries and comforts of life at the cost of production, adding a reasonable profit, free from the taxation which enter into prices at this time, you could live with your present wages by laboring four hours each day.

"Taxation in its varied forms more than doubles the cost of life in this country. Each man in the shop and field works a part of the day for himself and family, and part of the day to meet the cost of Government.

"Taxation means toil. And more taxation means more hours of toil.

"The Congressional policy of hate, of discord, of meddling, of large armies, and of corrupt patronage, will lengthen out your hours of labor—for you must pay for these things.

"In a little time you will feel that the questions of the day do not merely concern the South. They are agitated at your cost, and you will find them all in the tax-gatherer's bill. You will then learn that the number of hours you are to work is not a question between you and your employers, but between you and the tax-gatherer."

He also showed at that early day that the Western States were suffering from a want of currency, because their share of banking capital and of bank notes had been given to a few of the Eastern States.

"Another evil to the North growing out of the system of firing the minds of our people with hatred of the South, is that public attention is turned away from great questions of our financial policy which concern every class of our citizens. All admit that our inflated currency and its shifting value is a cause of business confusion, of wild speculation, and of demoralizing waste and extravagance. We have reason to fear these evils will grow until they bring us to financial ruin.

"Not only is the public debt, which pays nothing to support Government, held mainly in one corner of our country, but the banks, which have a right to make the currency for all the States, are placed and owned in a large degree by the Eastern and Middle States. Not only our debt, but our currency is sectionalized. In the report of the Secretary of the Treasury on this subject, made last session to Congress, it was shown that of the national bank notes then issued, Massachusetts had $52 for every person within her borders; Connecticut, $42; and Rhode Island, $77; while in the great commercial States of the West, Ohio, Illinois, Wisconsin and Michigan, the proportion is in Ohio only $8 per head; in Illinois, $6; in Michigan, $3; and in Wisconsin, $3 per head of the population. So that whatever profits are made out of bank circulation, by far the largest proportion thereof goes to these three New England States. The number and wealth of the people of the great States thus left with little or no means of getting currency except as borrowed from more favored sections, makes this a glaring evil. As they grow in commerce, wealth, and power, they will demand, with a strong show of reason, that they shall be put upon an equal footing with the Northern section of the Union."

More than two years ago it was seen that the baser men of the Republican party were getting control of its organization, and that it was no longer under the lead of its ablest minds. Since that time those who cherish any regard for decency, justice, political or personal rights, have been driven from its ranks, or forced to yield in blind obedience to the clamors and passions of the unthinking or unscrupulous. Governor Seymour, in common with all patriotic men, regretted this demoralization of a great party. He then said:—

"Let us look at the moral evils which this gospel of hate has brought upon all forms of public action in party, church or literature. I do not speak now of the abuse and untruth uttered against us. We have learned to bear those unmoved, and to go on unswerved in those pathways which we think lead to the right ends. The day of our triumph will be when truth triumphs, and that day will surely come.

I speak of the sad spectacle which we have seen in the discomfiture of those who built up the party of bigotry and hate, and who are now the very victims of the passion they have stirred up, but which they cannot quiet. Each of the men of mind who have led in the revolution which has changed the whole aspect of our country, has tried to check its violence or to direct his course into better channels; and each has been trampled down as ruthlessly as a herd of maddened buffaloes tread out the lives of their leaders if they stop in their speed or swerve from their course. Each of these men of brains, who thought they were guiding events, have had to pick themselves out of the dust into which they were tumbled because they dared to speak out an honest opinion which did not chime with the coarse passions and narrow views of the mass of their party. The rough-hewn, vigorous editor of the *Tribune*, who, beyond other men, had pushed on the political fight against the South until he may partly claim to have done most of all to kindle the flames of civil war, saw, in his bloody course, that wise statesmanship could save the Union and stop the waste of life and treasure. He made the attempt, and the wild herd behind him trod him down. An eloquent clergyman, who prided himself upon boldness and daring, felt that he owed something to religion as well as to party; he tried to teach men that as our Saviour came to save us while we were in open rebellion to Divine authority, we who prayed each night God's forgiveness of our daily sin, should at least have pity upon our brethren who had laid down their arms; but the bellowing crowds drowned the words of charity, and the frightened divine dare not to-day preach words of love and peace from our Saviour's Sermon on the Mount. The poets and philosophers, whose journal is read by the educated and thinking portion of society, once ventured to say that Congress was corrupt, its legislation destructive to the interests of the country, that its tariff suppressed honest industry, and filled with dishonest gains the pockets of speculators and swindlers; but they never dared to face the threatening crowd. They know that the Southern States are kept out of the Union because, as agricultural States, they would be represented by those who would act for the interest of commerce here, and for the interests of agriculture in the Northwest. There was meaning in Mr. Wendell Phillips's statement in this hall, when he said South Carolina would have representation in Congress when it acted in accord with Massachusetts. Another editor, who trusted in his dexterity to ride upon many animals at once, tried to turn the brutal throng by the bait of an office, and he has been so tossed upon their horns that neither he nor we can tell upon what spot he will fall. I might speak of others as well as these, who have learned the humiliating truth that their abilities govern less than the blind rage and stentorian lungs of men they despise in their hearts, and that they only keep their leadership by outrunning in an ignorant race brutal and stupid bigots. While I feel no friendship for these men, and while they think ill of me, I know they are men of ability; and it is a public evil when those most fitted to guide a great party become the mere slaves of the meaner passions of their associates.

"The public safety is endangered when the ablest men of a governing party dare not speak out their honest thoughts or act out their clear convictions. But there are republicans who admit that Congress is too violent; that it is dangerous to leave open the great break in the circle of our national unity, and who see that there is a class of men who make their zeal and fanaticism pay by stealthily and steadily fastening upon the country a system of taxation which will enrich them at the cost of the general welfare.

"I do not say nor believe that the body of the republicans want violence or discord; but the violent of all party govern in the end. A party which is unchecked in its power loses control of its own action. The vigorous, excited minority within its own ranks, by the machinery of organization, governs the larger number, as was done in the last Congress. In every instance those in power have from year to year gone beyond their own purpose, because there has not been enough opposing force to keep them within the bounds which their own sober judgment feels to be right."

CHAPTER XXIII.

THE SPEECH OF THE CONVENTION OF 1867.

WHEN the Democratic Convention of the State of New York was held in 1867, Governor Seymour was called to the Chair as the permanent President. The Convention was exceedingly enthusiastic, and nominated the ticket headed by Homer J. Nelson, for Secretary of State. Under the principles which were marked out in the speech of Gov. Seymour on that occasion, the party went into the contest, and carried the State by nearly fifty thousand majority.

At the afternoon session of the Convention, Mr. Smith M. Weed, from the Committee on Permanent Organization, reported the name of Gov. Seymour for President, and, amid rounds of cheers, Messrs. Danforth, of Schoharie, and DeWitt, of Ulster, escorted him to the Chair. He spoke as follows:—

"*Gentlemen of the Convention:*—

"We are startled by the cry of the leaders of the party holding political power that our country is in great peril. After wading through the bloodshed of civil war that peace which we hailed with joy, and which they told us was to give strength and prosperity to our land, brings new danger to the Republic. We can not, if we would, escape from confronting the problems of the day. Neither safety, honor, nor patriotism will suffer us to stand dumb or inactive in the dark hour of danger. We have put down rebellion, we are now struggling with revolution. The first was sectional; the last is universal. The first sought to divide our country; the last threatens to destroy it.

"At the National Capital we see that the party that placed in power the present Chief Magistrate, now charges him with treason, and many of its leaders have instilled into the public mind the horrible suspicion that he was in league with the murderers who struck down the life that stood between him and the Executive Chair. The world is aghast while it hears so foul an accusation uttered in the halls of the Legislature without rebuke. In the House of Representatives members make against each other charges of judicial murder, robbery, theft, and corruption. A military member alleges his legal associate plotted the death and carried to the gallows an innocent woman for partisan purposes. The accuser is charged in return with the fact of going to the war a poor man and coming back a poor general and a rich man; laden, not with the spoils of victory, but plunder stolen from those placed under his protection. The Congressman who stands up as the accuser of the President is confronted by his own letter, showing his utter rottenness. We are saved from the hateful task of laying bare the frauds and crimes of those who are administering our Government. God's law for punishing the guilty makes them become mutual accusers. In the hate and rage which ever springs up among criminals all are anxious to turn upon and convict their fellows.

"While the Senate has done less to shock the world and bring our Government into contempt, it has been the forum where principles have been asserted and a policy pursued revolutionary in tendency, and far-reaching in their influences to keep alive disorder and political convulsions. In its blindness it is striking suicidal blows against its own existence. Its members have become the ruling power in our Government. Vested with equal rights of law-making with the popular branch, they can also decide upon all treaties, which, within their scope, rise above the statutes. They control the appointing power; for the vast patronage of Government can only be exercised with their consent. They can, as a judicial body, depose the President or Vice-President, elected by the people, and put one of their own members into the Executive Chair. They hold their places by terms longer than those of any other elective branch of Government, yet they do not in the nature of their organization represent the people in form or fact. They are chosen by Legislatures not by the people. States having, by the census of 1860, less than one-quarter of the population of our country, appoint a majority of its members.

Nine States, whose citizens are more than one half of this people, are represented by only one-fourth of its members. Thus made up, and wielding a power over-topping that of all other branches, they should pause and ponder well before opening the flood-gates of revolution. Yet, if these members sought to have the Senate rubbed out of the constitutional scheme, they could not do acts more hateful to the people, or give reasons more powerful for its overthrow than their own teaching with regard to the rights of impartial suffrage, and by their action in the face of their teachings.

"But a bolder act is in view unless this dangerous game to get power over the majority by a rotten borough system is stopped. Twenty Senators are to be admitted from ten States lately in rebellion, not as representatives of the white people, for they are disfranchised; not of the blacks, for it is indecent to claim that a race who are declared by Congress to be unable to take care of themselves, and are placed under the guardianship of the Freedmen's Bureau, and military chiefs, would, as a body, know of the existence of such representatives—but they are to be admitted because they hold the views of the majority of the Senators, and because they are sent to Washington—by their agents. These Senators mean to be their own constituents, to become a close corporation, and to have more representatives of their own selection than the majority of the people of the country living in nine States. About sixty Republican Senators will, beyond their own votes, have in the twenty members sent by the Freedmen's Bureau, more representatives than sixteen millions of American people living in New York, Pennsylvania, Kentucky, Tennessee, Illinois, Indiana, Wisconsin, Ohio, and Missouri. Not content with holding in subjection the people of the South, they mean to extend in the name of the negro their domination over the North and South alike. It would seem that this madness was enough to make their destruction sure. But after acts like these they solemnly declare they are in favor of what they call manhood suffrage. Be it so, but with it must go manhood representation. Manhood suffrage must not be used to destroy the right of the majority of the people of this country. If it is the natural right of a negro in Florida to have a vote, it is not his right to have it count forty-fold, in the Senate of the United States, that of a man in New York. If it is the natural right of a man in New York to have a vote, it is also his natural right to have it count as much in the controlling branch of the Government as that of a man in Rhode Island. If this revolution is begun it must go on to its logical, just end. It must not roll on the necks of the majority of the American people and stop there but numbers must be represented, not rotten boroughs or sham States. We implore Senators not to begin revolution. Be content with your vast powers. Your organization is at war with impartial suffrage and impartial representation. If you continue your usurpation the country may not be content with driving you back within constitutional limits. It may go farther, and acting upon doctrines you assert it may crush you out and make another Senate based in truth upon manhood suffrage. The country needs peace, but if you will have revolution it can not stop at any chalk-lines you may mark out. The nine States, with a majority of the people, all of which are now virtually disfranchised in your body, for they are controlled by the representatives of a quarter of our population, if our Government is to be reshaped, will have their full rights. They are not suffering merely from theoretical wrongs. The destruction of the carrying trade of New York and the over-taxation of the Northwest, show how unequal distribution of power makes unequal burdens. During the war of the rebellion we felt the exertion of the Senatorial power upon the weak-head of the Enrolling Bureau in fixing the quotas of States. While their purposes were to save their own constituents from the sacrifices of war; by so doing they threw upon other States the cost of life and blood. In New York this grew into abuses so flagrant that even partisan passions could not be blind to the outrages. But the Northwestern States suffered the most severely from this injustice. I have the official proof that while the average quotas in the Congressional Districts of Massachusetts and New Hampshire were 2,167,

In Illinois they were	4,004
In Indiana they were	3,248
In Wisconsin they were	3,172
In Michigan they were	3,047

'We ask the people of New England if it is not time for them to stop the stupid malice of their Senators; to put a stop to the teaching that New England Senatorial power is in violation of natural rights. We suffer in New York by the present constitutional law, but we seek peace. We wish to uphold the constitutional powers of all the States. We remember the glorious part they bore in the revolutionary contest. If time has changed their comparative population, we do not wish to strip them of any political power. We implore them not to teach doctrines which must, in their ends be destructive to them and hurtful to the peace of the country.

"But I will pass by the question growing out of administrative crimes and follies, to speak of that which is uppermost in men's minds, our financial condition. Upon this we should be outspoken and true. It burdens and harasses labor. It hinders and perplexes business. It carries taxation and curse into every home. We owe a vast debt, made by the consent of the people of this country. In the details of heaping it up, there was much of fraud and more of folly. But at the time and since its creation, the citizens of the United States have in their elections approved of these acts of their representatives. The fabric of our Government has been already fearfully shaken by the violation of personal and political rights; we must not add repudiation to the list of crimes which destroy confidence in Republican Governments. The first step to uphold the public faith, is to put forth an honest statement of our affairs. The credit of our Government is lower in the markets of the world than that of any Christian nation in Europe. It has sunk to the level of that of the Turk, the "sick man of the East." When you look at the list of prices of national stocks, you will find that our bonds, taking into account the great interest we pay, are selling for about half the price given for those of Great Britain. When we lay them side by side upon the counter of the capitalist, he takes the British bond at a rate which will give him back in the course of twenty years, only $1,700, while we pay him $2,700 during the same time. That is to say, when the United States borrows $1,000 in gold, it pays the lender principal and interest in twenty years $2,700; England pays only $1,700. When we borrow $1,000,000 we pay on a twenty year loan $2,700,000; England pays only $1,700,000. But leaving the markets of the world, and coming to our own shores, we find our citizens will not trust our Government upon the same terms which they give to their neighbors.

"The bonds of the United States pay an interest to those who buy them of about eight per cent. They also give an exemption from taxation, worth one or two per cent. more. Yet men eagerly seek safe securities which, with the drawback of taxation, pay about half the interest given by our Government. Every day's report from Europe that flashes along the electric line, tells that the nation's credit is lower than that of the bonds put forth by a corporation of its own creation. Our shame is proclaimed in the markets of the world once in twenty-four hours. This is a position of danger and disgrace. At any moment foreign war or civil commotion may topple over this feeble credit and leave us helpless, despite all our resources and our boastful sense of national power. Why does the world—why do our own citizens distrust the faith of the Government? Why, when this question presses itself upon the public mind, do those who hold political power in our land, strive to turn public attention away from the subject? Constant efforts to keep alive the passions of the North, do not spring so much from hatred of the South, as from the fear that the people may look into the financial condition of the country. When taxation presses heavily upon labor, a new committee is at once ordered by Congress, to look up or invent Southern outrages. A series of telescopic views of far off and irritating subjects are constantly held up to the public eye, lest these things which most concern us at home, should get a share of our scrutiny. They are anxious at the pending election, to keep men's thoughts intent upon the squabble between military and civil members of their party. They would have these bubbles of the hour take up the attention of our people. This through all time has been the device of those unable to face their creditors, or who seek public tor private plunder. I believe wise statesmanship can save our honor can pay our debts, and lift the load of taxation from our people. Let us then confront these financial problems. Why is our national credit so low? Because ours is the only Government in the world that seeks to keep alive hatred and discord within its borders; because it is revolutionary in its tendencies; because it tramples upon all those rights of person, of property, of freedom of thought, and opinion, which had heretofore been the living principles of our political fabric, and which alone gives it strength and value; because it has violated all the pledges which it gave from time to time, in the course of the rebellion; because it influenced the different States making up the Union, to repudiate their sacred obligations. They say with truth, that to pay a man with debased paper money when he has had the promise of coin, is bad faith. Yet in New York, the great commercial State of the Union, when we were about to pay the public creditor, who had given us not a depreciated currency, but sterling coin, the interest money that was due him, he was forced to take a debased paper, at times worth less than one-half its face. As Governor of this State, I implored a Republican Legislature not to do this great wrong. I pointed out the cost of repudiation to our State and nation; I reminded them that we could not disgrace the chief—the commercial State of this Union, the most popular and wealthy of all, without bringing shame upon our land. The appeal was made in vain. Every Democratic Senator voted in favor of keeping up the faith of the State, while each Republican placed himself upon the record in favor of repudiation. This one base act has cost our State tenfold in coin the price of an honest payment of our debts. It has thrown upon us a shame which no words can tell. Another cause for the law and at this time waning credit of the Government, is that the business men of the world see that the statements put forth by the Treasury, are used to mislead the people. I do not charge that they are untrue; they give the amount of bond and currency debt, and such claims as appear upon the books of the department, but they are used to make the false impression upon the minds of the people, that the burdens of taxation will soon grow lighter, and that the public securities are gaining in real strength and value. Perhaps it is not the fault of the Secretary that they do not set forth other facts which fill with alarm every thoughtful man. We are in truth making in this country another form of indebtedness, which does not appear upon his books, but which are a prior lien to that held by the public creditor. When a Government by its policy, fastens upon a people new and lasting expenses, it makes obligations which are as burdensome to the tax-payers, as if they were annual interest upon its bonds.

"When our Government entered upon the plan of governing the South by military power, when it resolved to upturn the whole political structure in one-third of the Union, by disfranchising the intelligent white man, and giving to the ignorant negro political control, it increased the permanent cost of this Government to about two hundred millions every year. The man does not live who will see the day when this military power and its fearful cost can be cut down under the policy that now directs our public affairs. Our public expenses, apart from interest on the debt, have gone up from $58,000,000 in 1860, to about $185,000,000. In 1866, if we add the interest on the debt, it foots up $322,000,000. Our rulers are making beyond the cost of the last democratic administration, and beyond the interest on any debt, extra charges upon the Treasury of $127,000,000, or what would be the interest of five per cent. on $2,500,000,000. But this is not all, as these new charges are counted among the expenses of Government they are prior liens, and must be first paid.

"If the pledges of the party in power had been kept, to-day there would have been but a narrow margin between the claims of the bond-holder and the sum paid by revenue into the national Treasury. But the world now sees an army with banners, a host of officials, and vast and corrupting expenditure wedging in between the public Treasury and the public creditor. The latter is constantly pushed back in the order of payment. He finds his demand rapidly sinking toward the bottom of a lengthening list of claims. Yet the bond-holders are called upon by the Republican leaders to act as a rear guard to the hosts who are emptying the Treasury and putting into their own pockets the money that should go to the public creditor. There is another peril to the holders of our securities; the odium of taxation is thrown upon them. The people are taught that the money wrung from them by the tax-gatherer all goes to the holder of bonds, yet in truth, while $137,000,000 was paid for interest in 1866, $185,000,000 was given to uphold armies and military power to officials, to Freedmen's Bureau to feed and clothe the negro, and other expenses growing out of the policy of crushing out the Southern States. Men of the North, you will soon find that the fetters forged for the hands of the South are light indeed compared with the yokes which are placed upon your necks. The annual increase of the cost of our Government, beyond its expenses in 1860, is equal to the interest at six per cent., upon a debt of $2,100,000,000. It is due to the Secretary of the Treasury to say that any warning he has given against waste and corruption has been unheeded by Congress. Are we then lessening our national obligations? Again, while the Republican journals use the reports of the Secretary of the Treasury to encourage their followers with hope of relief, they do not point out to them the startling fact that if the volume of bonded debt is diminished, the interest to be paid upon that debt is growing greater. The policy of our rulers is to turn non-interest paying obligations into a tax-exacting form, so that the Treasury reports show that the taxation demanded to pay the national interest is growing greater each day.

* * * * * * *

"Those who now hold the power have not only hewed up to the line of repudiation, but they have done the public creditor wrong in other respects; they have turned away the public mind from all scrutiny into our financial condition; they have not tried to give value to the public credit; they have, in that boastful spirit which made the late civil war so wasteful in blood and treasure, by understating the difficulties and dangers of the public position, tried to deaden the public sense with regard to impending danger. If we put the value of our bonds upon a level with those of Great Britain, we add more than two thousand millions to the value of the securities held by our citizens. This simple act would give a vast amount of wealth to the holder, greater security to the laboring men and women who have put their earnings into savings banks which are secured by these stocks, and would place the paper money of the country upon a basis above distrust. This one act, like a magic wand, would change the aspect of our affairs, and would give us vast wealth and resources. Yet it would not cost the tax-payer one cent! It would, in fact, lessen his burden. The measures which would do this would lift off from the labor of the country the burdens which now crush down so many industrial pursuits. The policy which must give character to our bonds, must, in the nature of things, give prosperity to our country and profits to labor. These must rise and fall together. I do not own a Government bond; I have deplored the waste and corruption which piled up the national debt; I have protested against the criminal folly which exempted them from taxation; but these were acts of the American people, through their lawful representatives, and have been sanctioned by them in their subsequent elections, and they should pay the penalty. I would keep the public faith. While we condemn the errors of the past, let us, with zeal, seek to make the future prosperous by patient, patriotic efforts to bring back again our Government to its former wisdom, honesty, and simplicity. Why should not our credit be made as good as that of Britain's? We owe less, our means are greater. Why is not our credit better than that of the Turk, whose wealth and power does not compare with ours? Simply because these powers are seeking to uphold the integrity of their domain, the peace and well-being of their people, and to keep down the cost of their Government. In no other Government in the world than ours are military officers wielding despotic powers told that they will be deposed when peace and order exists within their domains. In no other country than ours are agents, like those of the Freedmen's Bureau, bribed by the love of power and by the love of gain to keep up discord and instigate sectional hate. If the expense of our Government had been put down at an expense twice as great as that spent by the last democratic administration, and the balance of our income had been used to pay the public debt, our bonds would have been worth as much as those of Britain, or nearly twice their present value. It is not the bond-holder, it is the office-holder who most taxes our people and wrings from labor the fruits of its toil. These are the vampires that suck the blood of the people. It is not the task-master, but the Government agents and officials who force the mechanic to lengthened hours of toil, for he must support these as well as his family, before he can take rest for his wearied limbs. If the money collected by Government, after letting the Republicans spend twice as much as was ever used by a democratic administration, was paid to lessen our debt, not only would we give wealth to the bond-holder and relief to the tax-payer, but we should lessen the cost of all that our country buys. It would go into market with a better credit. We could then command the specie of the world;

we could gain it in exchange for our securities as the governments of Europe do. Now they are peddled out all over Europe at half price in exchange for dry-goods and groceries. They are taken cautiously and slowly, although the European buyer gets an interest of about eight per cent. in coin, while the rate of interest paid for money in London to-day is barely two per cent. Does not every man see and know that this monstrous disgrace would not stain the honor of our country if there was a wise, honest, and patriotic administration of its affairs? Do not the reports of the Secretary of the Treasury show that we could swiftly wipe out our debt if our income was not perverted to partisan purposes? Do not the columns of the press teem with statements of official plunder and frauds in every quarter of our land, while public virtue rots under this wasteful expenditure of the public fund? It is said it is repudiation to force our legal tender upon the bond-holder. What makes it so? The low credit of the country. Build that up; make your paper as good as gold, and this question can not come up. Then the bond-holder will not care which you give him. This controversy grows out of the fact that men do not believe our legal tenders are, or ever will be as good as gold. If it is repudiation to pay such money it was repudiation to make it, and it is repudiation to keep it debased by waste and by partisan plans to keep our country in disorder and danger. Give a decent credit to our bonds and we can make new loans. We can pay off those which are exempt from taxation, and make the burdens of the Government rest equally easy upon all.

* * * * * * *

"Another measure is needed to restore our credit and our honor. Give us back our commerce. A few years since we were a great maritime power—our ships whitened every ocean. Where are they now? Official reports show that the carrying trade, once a source of wealth and power, has been nearly lost. The ships which bear our products abroad or bring the emigrant to our shores sail under foreign flags. Our commerce was swept from the sea, not by Southern corsairs, but by Northern Congressmen. Britain will pay for the few vessels burned by privateers fitted out in her ports, not from a sense of justice, but from a feeling of gratitude toward an administration that has done so much to build up her power and greatness. She has reaped all the fruits of our civil war. She is now indeed the mistress of the sea. We no longer vex her with our rivalry. We once stood in the way of her ambition; we built better and cheaper vessels. Our skill upon the seas was unrivaled; our untaxed artisans were driving her out of her best markets. Her looms could not move unless we gave her cotton. All is now changed. Our shipyards are idle. American imports and American exports are borne over the ocean under British or foreign flags. Our manufacturers call upon Congress to help them live against foreign competition upon our own soil. We pile up tariffs to fence out cheap products and then load down labor with taxation until the burdens of our Government overtop the protection we give by duties upon foreign imports, and so a leaden pall weighs upon our industry. Beyond all this we have given Britain that for which she has heretofore planned and schemed in vain—cotton producing colonies. Her India possessions, which were of doubtful value, are now made by Republican stupidity, the source of enormous wealth and the successful rivals of American industry. In five years before the rebellion the annual value of the cotton sent from India was about $17,000,000. In the five following, the annual average was about $113,000,000. In 1866 it rose to nearly the sum of $150,000,000. More effectually to foster this branch of British industry, Congress gives it a bonus in the markets of the world by putting an export duty on American cotton. While her production grows great ours falls off. Never in all her history has she had such allies as the Republican party. Her people can well afford to give marked honors to those who have brought our country upon the verge of ruin.

"The great and crowning measure to lessen the taxation of the North; to shorten the hours of labor for our mechanics; to raise the credit of our securities; to insure the peace and safety of our land, is to give us back our Union. We can no longer bear the cost of armies; of spendthrift agents, of corrupt officials, of food and clothing to vagrant idlers, of meddling with the concerns of far-off States, and of neglecting our own affairs. It is at this point that the antagonisms of party show themselves in principles as well as policy. Talk as we may about the rise and fall of parties there are sentiments in the minds of our people which will always make one party favoring centralization and meddling. It may in the future, as in the past, change its name and pretext, as the result of its policy makes it odious. It has filled our land with bloodshed and strife. It has loaded us down with debt and taxation. It has put back religion, temperance, and virtue, by dragging them into political strife, and by the passage of laws, which tend to make them odious in the minds of the people. It is ever on the lookout for some pretext to meddle with the rights of men, upon some ground of birth, of lineage, of religious belief, of social custom. These, more than positive crimes, excite its passions. While our German citizens, a people marked for their frugality, industry, good order and freedom from intemperance, have been arrested and imprisoned because their social habits differ from our own, not one of our public officers who are charged and convicted by their own friends of fraud and public robberies have ever been brought to the bar of justice.

* * * * * * *

"If any man doubts the influence of a change of the men in power, let him look at the effect of the victories we have gained. Since the result in Maine, California, and Connecticut, a Republican Convention has discovered that foreign-born citizens have rights; that there ought to be freedom enough in the land to let the German have the social customs endeared to him by the associations of home, and that he was not bound to give up all his rights of opinion, and all his freedom of action, when he becomes an American citizen. As the shadow of coming defeat falls upon the Republicans, they even promise to become honest; and in their zeal they have pitched overboard all of their officials who have not robbed the treasury. We will end the good work they begun, by throwing the rogues after them. Let us lift up the Democratic standard, and lift it high. Let us fight for fireside rights, for freedom of opinion, for an honest management of public affairs. Above all, let us battle for the restoration of the Union, and may God defend the right."

At the close of the Convention, Governor Seymour bid his colleagues good-bye in an affecting speech, some portions of which were prophetic. In the same connection he referred to the death of Dean Richmond: said he,—

"We have seen the close of days of defeat. We are now about to see the opening of days of triumph. * * * *
Other men will take our places; younger men will take the stage of action. Therefore it is, I say, that while to-day I congratulate you, because I feel that the hour of triumph has advanced upon us, I would give one thought to the memory of days that are past, and to those who have been taken away so recently, and whom we miss so much on this occasion."

CHAPTER XXIV.

THE NATIONAL DEMOCRATIC CONVENTION.

The National Democratic Convention met in Tammany Hall, New York City, on Saturday, July 4, 1868. Mr. August Belmont, Chairman of the National Executive Committee, called the Convention to order promptly at 12 o'clock, M., and after a few pertinent remarks, which frequently were interrupted with cheers, nominated Hon. Henry L. Palmer, of Wisconsin, as temporary President. Mr. Palmer, being unanimously chosen to preside, made a brief, well-timed speech before taking the chair, and called upon Rev. Dr. Morgan, Rector of St. Thomas's Church, New York, to offer prayer, which that clergyman accordingly did. The usual committees on permanent organization and resolutions were then appointed, and the convention adjourned until Monday morning.

On Monday morning the committee on permanent organization reported the name of Horatio Seymour for President of the Convention, the announcement of which was received with rapturous cheers. Mr. Seymour then took the chair, and acknowledged the honor thus conferred upon him in most suitable terms, closing his remarks with the following words:—

"We meet to-day to see what measures can be taken to arrest the dangers which threaten our country, and to retrieve it from the evils and burdens resulting from bad government and unwise counsels. I thank God that the strife of arms has ceased, and that once more in the great conventions of our party we can call through the whole roll of States and find men to answer for each. (Tremendous and continued cheering.) Time and events in their great cycles have brought us to this spot to renew and invigorate that Constitutional Government which nearly eighty years ago was inaugurated in this city, (Loud cheers.) It was here that George Washington, the first President, swore to 'preserve, protect, and defend,' the Constitution of these United States. (Cheers.) And here, this day, we as solemnly pledge ourselves to uphold the rights and liberties of the American people Then, as now, a great war which had desolated our land had ceased. Then, as now, there was in every patriotic breast a longing for the blessings of a good government, for the protection of laws, and for sentiments of fraternal regard and affection among the inhabitants of all the States of this Union. When our Government, in 1789, was inaugurated in this city, there were glad processions of men and those manifestations of great joy which a people show when they feel that an event has happened which is to give lasting blessings to the land. (Cheers.) To-day in this same spirit this vast assemblage meets, and the streets are thronged with men who have come from the utmost borders of our continent. They are filled with the hope that we are about, by our actions and our policy, to bring back the blessings of good government. It is among the happiest omens which inspire us now that those who fought bravely in our late civil war are foremost in their demands that there shall be peace in our land. The passions of hate and malice may linger in meaner breasts, but we find ourselves upheld in our generous purposes by those who showed true courage and manhood on the field of battle. (Cheers.) In the spirit, then, of George Washington and of the patriots of the Revolution, let us take the steps to reinaugurate our Government, to start it once again on its course to greatness and prosperity. (Loud cheers.) May Almighty God give us the wisdom to carry out our purposes, to give to every State of our Union the blessings of peace, good order, and fraternal affection."

A delegation from the convention of the conservative soldiers and sailors of the Union army, headed by Major-General Franklin, then appeared and presented an address announcing the determination of the Union soldiers and sailors to oppose radicalism to the last, and stand by the action of the Democratic Convention. The address, as well as those who presented it, was received with great enthusiasm, and in response to repeated calls, General Thomas Ewing, Jr., made a brief speech.

Hon. Henry C. Murphy, of New York, on behalf of the committee on resolutions, presented the following platform of principles, the reading of which was frequently interrupted with enthusiastic cheering:—

THE PLATFORM.

The Democratic party in National Convention assembled, reposing its trust in the intelligence, patriotism, and discriminating justice of the people, standing upon the Constitution as the foundation and limitation of the powers of the Government, and the guaranty of the liberties of the citizen; and recognizing the questions of slavery and secession as having been settled for all time to come—(tremendous cheering)—by the war or the voluntary action of the Southern States in Constitutional Convention assembled, and never to be renewed or re-agitated, do with the return of peace demand:

First—Immediate restoration of all the States to their rights in the Union under the Constitution, and of civil government to the American people. (Cheers.)

Second—Amnesty for all past political offenses, and the regulation of the elective franchise in the States by their citizens. (Cheers.)

Third—Payment of the public debt of the United States as rapidly as practicable; all moneys drawn from the people by taxation, except so much as is requisite for the necessities of the Government, economically administered, being honestly applied as such payment; and where the obligations of the Government do not expressly state upon their face, or the law under which they were issued does not provide, that they shall be paid in coin, they ought, in right and in justice, to be paid in the lawful money of the United States. (Thunders of applause.)

Fourth—Equal taxation of every species of property according to its real value, including Government bonds and other public securities. (Renewed cheering and cries of "Read it again.")

Fifth—One currency for the Government and the people, the laborer and the office-holder, the pensioner and the soldier, the producer and the bond-holder. (Great cheering and cries of "Read it again.") The fifth resolution was again read and again cheered.

Sixth—Economy in the administration of the Government; the reduction of the standing army and the navy; the abolition of the Freedmen's Bureau—(great cheering)—and all political instrumentalities designed to secure negro supremacy; simplification of the system, and the discontinuance of inquisitorial modes of assessing and collecting Internal Revenue, so that the burden of taxation may be equalized and lessened; the credit of the Government, and the currency made good; the repeal of all enactments for enrolling the State militia into national forces in time of peace; and a tariff for revenue upon foreign imports, and such equal taxation under the Internal Revenue laws as will afford incidental protection to domestic manufactures, and as will, without impairing the revenue, impose the least burden upon, and yet promote and encourage, the great industrial interests of the country.

Seventh—Reform of abuses in the administration, the expulsion of corrupt men from office, the abrogation of useless offices, the restoration of rightful authority to, and the independence of, the executive and judicial departments of the Government, the subordination of the military to the civil power, to the end that the usurpation of Congress and the despotism of the sword may cease. (Cheers.)

Eighth—Equal rights and protection for naturalized and native born citizens at home and abroad, the assertion of American nationality which shall command the respect of foreign powers, and furnish an example and encouragement to people struggling for national integrity, constitutional liberty and individual rights, and the maintenance of the rights of naturalized citizens against the absolute doctrine of immutable allegiance, and the claims of foreign powers to punish them for alleged crime committed beyond their jurisdiction. (Loud applause.)

In demanding these measures and reforms we arraign the Radical party for its disregard of right and the unparalleled oppression and tyranny which have marked its career.

After the most solemn and unanimous pledge of both Houses of Congress to prosecute the war exclusively for the maintenance of the Government and the preservation of the Union under the Constitution, it has repeatedly violated that most sacred pledge, under which alone was rallied that noble volunteer army which carried our flag to victory. (Cheers.) Instead of restoring the Union, it has, so far as in its power, dissolved it, and subjected ten States, in time of profound peace, to military despotism and negro supremacy. It has nullified there the right of trial by jury; it has abolished the *habeas corpus*, that most sacred writ of liberty; it has overthrown the freedom of speech and the press; it has substituted arbitrary seizures and arrests, and military trials and secret star-chamber inquisitions for the constitutional tribunals; it has disregarded in time of peace the right of the people to be free from searches and seizures; it has entered the post and telegraph offices, and even the private rooms of individuals, and seized their private papers and letters without any specific charge or notice of affidavit, as required by the organic law; it has converted the American Capitol into a bastile; it has established a system of spies and official espionage to which no constitutional monarchy of Europe would now dare to resort—(cheers)—it would abolish the right of appeal on important constitutional questions to the supreme judicial tribunal, and threatens to curtail or destroy its original jurisdiction, which is irrevocably vested by the Constitution, while the learned Chief-Justice—(loud cheering)—has been subjected to the most atrocious calumnies, merely because he would not prostitute his high office to the support of the false and partisan charges preferred against the President. Its corruption and extravagance have exceeded every thing known in history, and by its frauds and monopolies it has nearly doubled the burden of the debt created by the war. It has stripped the President of his constitutional power of appointment, even of his own Cabinet. Under its repeated assaults the pillars of the Government are rocking on their base, and should it succeed in November next and inaugurate its president, we will meet as a subjected and conquered people amid the ruins of liberty and the scattered fragment of the Constitution.

And we do declare and resolve that ever since the people of the United States threw off all subjection to the British crown the privilege and trust of suffrage have belonged to the several States, and have been granted, regulated, and controlled exclusively by the political power of each State respectively, and that any attempt by Congress, on any pretense whatever, to deprive any State of this right, or interfere with its exercise, is a flagrant usurpation of power which can find no warrant in the Constitution, and, if sanctioned by the people, will subvert our form of government, and can only end in a single centralized and consolidated Government in which the separate existence of the States will be entirely absorbed, and an unqualified despotism be established in place of a Federal Union of coequal States.

And that we regard the Reconstruction acts (so-called) of Congress, as such, as usurpations and unconstitutional, revolutionary and void.

That our soldiers and sailors who carried the flag of our country to victory against a most gallant and determined foe must ever be gratefully remembered, and all the guaranties given in their favor must be faithfully carried into execution. (Cheers.)

That the public lands should be distributed as widely as possible among the people, and should be disposed of either under the preemption of homestead lands, or sold in reasonable quantities, and to none but actual occupants, at the minimum price established by the Government. When grants of public land may be allowed, necessary for the encouragement of important public improvements, the proceeds of the sale of such lands, and not the lands themselves should be applied. (Cheers.)

That the President of the United States, Andrew Johnson—(applause)—in exercising the power of his high office in resisting the aggressions of Congress upon the constitutional rights of the States and the people, is entitled to the gratitude of the whole American people, and in behalf of the Democratic party we tender him our thanks for his patriotic efforts in that regard. (Great applause.)

Upon this Platform the Democratic party appeal to every patriot, including the conservative element and all who desire to support the Constitution and restore the Union, forgetting all past differences of opinion, to unite with us in the present great struggle for the liberties of the people—(cheers)—and that to all such, to whatever party they may have heretofore belonged, we extend the right hand of fellowship, and hail all such co-operating with us as friends and brethren. (Loud cheering.)

The platform was unanimously and most enthusiastically adopted.

BALLOTING FOR A PRESIDENTIAL CANDIDATE.

Next in order was the nomination of candidates for the presidency. The roll of States was called, and, as the various names were presented by the chairmen of the delegations they were greeted with hearty cheers. This over, it was proposed to ballot, but the hour being late the Convention adjourned.

On Tuesday six ballots were had without any candidate receiving even a majority of the votes cast; on Wednesday twelve more ballots were taken, and yet no nomination was made.

When the Convention met on Thursday, it was felt that a nomination would be made early in the day. Rumor had it that a letter from Mr. Pendleton, withdrawing his name, would be read, but as to whom his friends would transfer their votes was not known. During the previous evening a number of the leading supporters of Mr. Pendleton held a meeting and resolved to nominate Horatio Seymour and force the nomination upon him, but the plan coming to his knowledge he obtained a promise from them to relinquish it. Before taking the nineteenth ballot, Mr. Vallandigham, on behalf of the Ohio delegation, withdrew the name of George H. Pendleton as a candidate before the Convention, by virtue of the following letter:—

CINCINNATI, July 2, 1868.

WASHINGTON MCLEAN, *Fifth Avenue Hotel, New York:*—

MY DEAR SIR:—You know better than any one the feelings and principles which have guided my conduct since the suggestion of my name for the presidential nomination. You know that, while I covet the good opinion of my countrymen, and would feel an honest pride in so distinguished a mark of their confidence, I do not desire it at the expense of one electoral vote—(great applause)—or of the least disturbance of the harmony of our party. I consider the success of the Democratic party in the next election of far greater importance than the gratification of any personal ambition, however pure and lofty it might be. (Loud cheers.) If, therefore, at any time a man shall be suggested which, in the opinion of yourself and those friends who have shared our confidence, shall be stronger before the country, or which can more thoroughly unite our own party, I beg that you will instantly withdraw my name, and pledge to the Convention my hearty and zealous and active support for its nominee

Yours, very truly,
GEORGE H. PENDLETON.

Three ballots were then taken, and still the Convention appeared to be no nearer making a nomination than it did two days before. The roll was called for the twenty-second ballot. As the vote of each State was announced it was evident that Mr. Hendricks was gaining; Massachusetts cast four votes for Salmon P. Chase, which created some excitement; but the great event was yet to come. When Ohio was called, Gen. McCook startled the vast assemblage by saying:—

Mr. CHAIRMAN:—I arise at the unanimous request and the demand of the delegation from Ohio, and with the consent and approval of every public man in the State, including the Hon. George H. Pendleton, to again place in nomination, against his inclination, but no longer against his honor, the name of Horatio Seymour, of New York. (Rousing cheers and long-continued applause.) Let us vote, Mr. Chairman, and gentlemen of the Convention, for a man whom the presidency has sought, but who has not sought the presidency. (Applause.) I believe in my heart that it is the solution of the problem which has been engaging the minds of the Democrats and Conservative men of this nation for the last six months. ("Good," "good.") I believe it will have a solution which will drive from power the vandals who now possess the Capitol of the nation. (Applause.) I believe it will receive the unanimous assent and approval of the great bolt of States from the Atlantic—New York, New Jersey, Pennsylvania, Ohio, Indiana, Michigan, Illinois, and Missouri, and away West for quantity—to the Pacific Ocean. (Applause.) I say that he has not sought the presidency, and I ask—

not demand—I ask that this Convention shall demand of him that, sinking his own inclination and the well-known desires on his part, he shall yield to what we believe to be the almost unanimous wish and desire of the delegates to this Convention. (Great applause, and three cheers.) In my earnestness and enthusiasm, I had almost forgotten to cast the twenty-one votes of Ohio for Horatio Seymour. (Tremendous excitement, and nine cheers for Horatio Seymour.)

It was several minutes before Governor Seymour could obtain a hearing, so prolonged were the demonstrations in his honor. At last, silence being restored, he said:—

GENTLEMEN OF THE CONVENTION: (Cheers)—The motion just made by the gentleman from Ohio excites in my mind the most mingled emotions. (Applause.) I have no terms in which to express my gratitude—(cheers)—for the magnanimity of his State and for the generosity of this Convention. (Cheers.) I have no terms in which to tell of my regret that my name has been brought before this Convention. God knows that my life and all that I value most in life I would give for the good of my country, which I believe to be identified with our own party. (Applause, and cries of "Take the nomination, then.") I do not stand here as a man proud of his opinions, or obstinate in his purposes, but upon a question of duty and of honor I must stand upon my own convictions against the world. (Applause, and a voice, "God bless you, Horatio Seymour.") Gentlemen, when I said here at an early day, that honor forbade my accepting a nomination by this Convention, I *meant* it. When, in the course of my intercourse with those of my own delegation and my friends, I said to them that I could not be a candidate, I *meant* it. And now permit me here to say that I know, after all that has taken place, I could not receive the nomination without placing, not only myself, but the great Democratic party in a false position. But, gentlemen of the Convention, more than that, we have had to-day an exhibition from the distinguished citizen of Ohio, that has touched my heart as it has touched yours. (Cheers.) I thank God, and I congratulate this country, that there is in the great State of Ohio, whose magnificent position gives it so great a control over the action of our country, a young man, rising fast into fame, whose future is all glorious, who has told the world he could tread beneath his feet every other consideration than that of duty, and when he expressed to his delegation, and expressed in more direct terms, that he was willing that I should be nominated, who stood in such a position of marked opposition to his own nomination, I should feel a dishonored man if I could not tread in the far distance, and in a feeble way, the same honorable pathway which he has marked out. (Great applause.) Gentlemen, I thank you, and may God bless you for your kindness to me; but your candidate I can not be. (Three cheers for Horatio Seymour.)

Cries of "No," "No, No," came from every part part of the house when Mr. Vallandigham declared for the Ohio delegation, that under no circumstances would they recede from their position. The call of the States was then resumed without any noticeable change in the votes, until Wisconsin was called; the chairman of its delegation announced that he was instructed to second the motion of Ohio, and cast the eight electoral votes of his State for Horatio Seymour. At once the chairman of each delegation was on his feet, struggling for recognition of the President, in order to transfer the vote of his State to Horatio Seymour. The scene at this point was most exciting, and lest our own description of it might be suspected of partiality, we transcribe the following account from the New York *Times* of Friday, July 10:—

"The end had come. Instantly all over the hall the delegations sprang to their feet, every chairman demanding recognition by voice and gesture. The lobbies broke out into tumultuous continuous cheers. Hats, fans, handkerchiefs were waved aloft, delegates seized the silken pennons of their States, and brandished them over the heads of the yelling crowd. The tumult swelled until it became confusion worse confounded. No single word could be heard; no individual voice recognized. The vigorous rapping of the President's gavel was unheard. Out of the uproar came in some instants of intervention, the announcement of some State wheeling into line for

Seymour. Maryland, Illinois, Texas, Delaware, Virginia, Vermont, Georgia and Louisiana were heard above the din, and such announcement added fuel to the roaring flame. Sovereign States scrambled forward with unseemly haste, and rudely jostled each other in their rush to be first in changing to Seymour. The end was seen, and the order issued for the battery in Union square, which had been waiting, for two days to belch forth the nominations from the cannon's mouth, to begin. With the roar of the first gun the crowd within the hall was invigorated, and began again to cheer continuously, lustily. There seemed no limit to their capacity for uproar, nor their endurance in maintaining it. All business and order was swept before the storm, and the officers strove in vain to restore some semblance of order. Accidentally or instinctively the Democracy had found a way out of the dead-lock of balloting, and borne along by the current, States were swept like straws in a rapid river. When at last the tumult partially subsided, through sheer exhaustion of the audience and delegates, the change of States was obtained and recorded."

The nomination of Horatio Seymour as the Democratic candidate for the Presidency was declared unanimous amid wild cheering within, and the booming of cannon without the hall. And here we subjoin a table of all the ballots for convenience of reference by the reader :—

TABLE OF ALL THE BALLOTS.

CANDIDATES.	1.	2.	3.	4.	5.	6.	7.	8.	9.	10.	11.	12.	13.	14.	15.	16.	17.	18.	19.	20.	21.	22.
Pendleton	105	104	119½	118½	122	122½	137½	156½	144	147½	141½	145½	134½	130	129½	07½	70½	56½	—	—	—	—
Andrew Johnson	65	52	34½	32	24	21	12½	6	5½	6½	5½	4½	4½	—	5½	5½	6	10	—	—	5	—
Hancock	33½	40½	45½	43½	46	47	42½	28	34½	34	32½	30	48½	56	79½	113½	137½	144½	135½	142½	135½	—
Church	33	33	33	33	33	33	33	—	—	—	—	—	—	—	—	—	—	—	—	—	—	—
Packer	26	26	26	26	27	27	26	26	26½	27	26	26	26	26	—	—	—	—	22	—	—	—
Joel Parker	13	15½	13	13	13	13	7	7	7	7		7	7	7	7	7	7½	3½	—	—	—	—
English	16	12½	7½	7½	7	6	6	6	6	—	—	—	—	—	—	—	—	—	6	16	19	—
Doolittle	13	12½	12	12	15	12	17	12	—	12	12½	12½	13	13	12	13	12	12	12	12	12	—
Reverdy Johnson	8½	8	11	8	—	—	—	—	12	—	—	—	—	—	—	—	—	—	—	—	—	—
Hendricks	2½	2	9½	11½	19½	30	34½	75	80½	82½	88	89	81	84½	82½	70½	80	87	107½	121	132	—
F. P. Blair, Jr.	½	10½	4½	2	9½	5	½	½	½	—	—	½		—	—	—	—	—	13½	13	—	—
Ewing	—	½	1	1	—	—	—	—	—	—	—	—	—	—	—	—	—	—	—	—	—	—
Horatio Seymour	—	—	—	9	—	—	—	—	—	—	—	—	—	—	—	—	—	—	—	—	—	317
J. Q. Adams	—	—	—	—	—	—	—	—	—	—	—	—	—	—	—	—	—	—	—	—	—	—
McClellan	—	—	—	—	—	—	—	—	—	—	—	1	—	—	—	—	—	—	—	—	½	—
Chase	—	—	—	—	—	—	—	—	—	—	—	½	½	—	—	—	½	½	½	—	4	—
Franklin Pierce	—	—	—	—	—	—	—	—	—	—	—	—	1	—	—	—	—	—	—	—	—	—
John T. Hoffman	—	—	—	—	—	—	—	—	—	—	—	—	—	—	—	—	3	3	—	2	½	—

THE NOMINATION FOR VICE-PRESIDENT.

The Convention proceeded at once to nominate a candidate for Vice-President. Illinois presented the name of Gen. John A. McClernand, who promptly insisted upon its withdrawal. Iowa proposed the name of the Hon. Aug. C. Dodge, and Kansas that of Gen. Thomas Ewing, Jr. Kentucky then presented, amid great cheering, the name of Francis P. Blair, Jr., of Missouri; Louisiana, in the person of Gen. Jas. B. Steedman, hastened to second the nomination; Gen. Wade Hampton, speaking for South Carolina, warmly indorsed it, and one by one each State, on the first ballot, recorded its entire vote for Gen. Blair, thus making his nomination unanimous. The result, as announced by the President, was received with intense enthusiasm.

The Convention had done its work and done it well. Resolutions of compliment to the officers of the body, to the Tammany Society, to the citizens of New York, and to the Press were adopted, and after giving a hearty round of cheers for Seymour and Blair, the Convention adjourned *sine die.*

CHAPTER XXV.

THE DEMOCRATIC PARTY AND HORATIO SEYMOUR.

Since the commencement of our Government, there have been substantially but two parties in the country. No matter what name the opposition to the Democratic party has assumed, the tendencies it has exhibited have always been in one direction, which was their desire for a centralized government, and a distrust, latent or recognized, of the unchecked will of the people. Hamilton advocated effective institutions, and rather doubted the ability of the people, without checks and balances, to govern themselves. And so did all the parties which succeeded the Federal in our history; whatever name they have assumed, they always favored a strong central Government, and the necessary crippling of local freedom.

The party of Jefferson, on the other hand, have ever held that the people should be trusted; that that government was best which governed least; that there was a soul of good in all popular movements; that the true political theory was not to attempt to train human nature in certain fixed ways —to put bandages round the growing limbs of the nation—but to recognize the essential good that exists in humanity, and which, if given free course, would justify the work of its Maker. In short, on this continent we have had the old strife between authority and liberty. Hence, whenever by any accident the authority party have got into power, we have fallen upon an era of high tariffs, lavish expenditures, violations more or less open of the traditions and of the organic law of the country, limiting the central authority. Its alien and sedition laws; its national banks; its encroachments upon the liberty of the individual; its impatience of all those wise provisions of our Constitution, which limit the powers of the General Government;—all these characteristics mark the Republican party, as they did the old Federal party.

Much astonishment has been expressed that after the war the Democratic party did not go to pieces. The vitality of that party lies in the fact that notwithstanding its mistakes, and occasional fits of forgetfulness of its own high mission, it has, after all, been true to the conception of its founder, Thomas Jefferson, and his faith in the doctrine of local self-government and individual rights. In the excitement and tempest of the war, the American people put every available weapon into the hands of the central Government, to put down the rebellion; and the Democratic party, true to its mission, true to the idea which gave it vitality, boldly braved the full fury of the popular tempest, in order to preserve inviolate the liberties of the people. No man, or set of men, should be trusted with unlimited power. The history of all nations shows that unchecked power is always abused; and hence, when Mr. Lincoln and his cabinet were given absolute control, instead of using it wholly against the enemies of their country, it was employed to put a stop to free thought, to check discussion, and to silence all opposition. Our greatest peril during the war lay not in the injuries that might be inflicted by the armies of the enemy, but in the danger that the American people might forget those principles of freedom and self-government which had been handed down to them from their fathers. It is to the lasting honor of the democratic party, that at the risk of being called disloyal, it dared to brave the tremendous power which had been created at Washington, and to insist that the powers of the Government should not be used to take away the liberties of the people of the North; and it was this attitude which laid them open to the suspicion of sympathizing with the enemies of their country. But the history of all free governments proves that if ever there is a time when a wise, prudent, and patriotic opposition is useful to the nation, it is during a war, especially a civil war. The danger is then imminent that in the desire to preserve the national existence, the people will be willing to give up individual liberty.

When the real history of this war comes to be written, our future Macaulays will distinguish among all the men of this country who deserve honor and credit, Horatio Seymour of New York. His protest against the banishment of Mr. Vallandigham, his earnest appeals to the people not to sustain the central Government in the assaults they were making upon State rights and individual liberty, will always redound to his credit. No civilian could have done more than he did to help forward all the efforts which the Government was making to put down the Rebellion. He spared neither money nor work, nor his own personal influence, to urge on volunteering, and to forward troops to the front. His record in this respect is unimpeachable. He did not believe the war was a necessary war. He was convinced that wise statesmanship might have settled the dispute without the dread resort to arms; and hence he was compelled by his position to arraign the party in power for helping to bring upon us all the miseries and horrors of an unnecessary civil war. He also early saw the danger which would result from giving unchecked power to the party in power. For the first year after the war opened, Mr. Lincoln's administration was absolutely supreme. There were no political parties in the country. Even the democratic city of New York sustained the administration in the first year after the war opened, by a very large majority. After this, unchecked power soon showed itself to be an element of weakness. Our first two years of war were years of disappointment and disaster. Without any opposition, without any great party or body of statesmen to criticise and condemn when necessary, the Lincoln administration went on from blunder to blunder, wasted lives, and squandered treasure without accomplishing any of the objects of the war. At the same time it developed a spirit of impatience at criticism, and having the passions of the nation on its side, did not hesitate to use its great power in putting down the home opposition which its own blunders had aroused. The tide turned in favor of the North only when the great democratic party, true to the instincts for popular liberty, in opposition to the concentration of too much power in the central Government, rose up all over the country, and called attention to and denounced the shortcomings and blunders of the then existing Administration. The elections of 1862, in which the democratic party swept like a wave over the great central States of the Union, New York, Pennsylvania, Ohio, and Indiana was the true turning point of the war. An opposition party was called into existence, and though the General Government did not give up the extraordinary power it had assumed, and though it had (and has even to this day) a body of extreme partisans, which has always sustained its most offensive measures, yet something was done to check its pretensions, and to turn its attention to the enemy by whom it had been beaten in the field, rather than to the patriotic opposition which was endeavoring to correct its irregularities, and to point out its short-comings to the people. Once this lesson given, and the efforts of the General Government to crush the Rebellion successful, the American people, always grateful and loyal, rallied around the Lincoln administration, and helped it to close the war successfully.

It is usual in every government for parties which oppose a war to lose the confidence of the people. It was so in the war of 1812, and in the Mexican war. It was not so in the late civil war for the reason that the Democratic party acted a patriotic part. No State of the North, no matter how strongly it had been attached to the faith of the Democratic party, failed to do its duty when the call to arms came. New Jersey, always a reliable democratic State, sent an excess of soldiers to the field, and New York City, with its enormous democratic majorities, not only furnished its own quotas, but was a general recruiting ground for the whole Union. I have no disposition to make unfavorable comparisons, but the only States which made any systematic efforts to fill their quotas outside of their own boundaries were the New England States, and notably Massachusetts.

The position of Governor Seymour during the war was one of great delicacy, and his success in retaining the confidence of his party, and of the most honorable and candid of his opponents, was due to his rare tact and high statesmanlike qualities. He was opposed to the political organization whose advent to power precipitated us into war. He believed honestly that the Republican party, however worthy its aims might have been,—for no great party can exist in a free community without some worthy aims —was the cause of the war. There is no doubt at all that the cardinal doctrine at the root of the Republican party, its opposition to the extension of slavery, is one which will redound to its credit in all future time. But a distinction should be made between worthy aims and most unworthy and reprehensible methods of accomplishing those aims. The temper, the policy, the bearing of that party was offensive in the extreme. It was the first party that divided the country sectionally in a Presidential contest. It put forth a sectional ticket, appealed wholly to Northern voters, and was put into power entirely by Northern ballots. Its temper was aggressive and uncompromising, and, being met with equal temper and with equal violence, a collision was precipitated.

A few good, wise and sagacious statesmen at the South and a few at the North did what they could to allay the storm of passion, and naturally enough, Governor Seymour, living at the North, and being brought into personal contact with the leaders of the Republican party, blamed them for the temper they brought into the discussion of great public questions.

That party once in power, a wise forbearance, statesmanlike caution, some little of that prescience without which successful government is impossible, would have enabled them to avoid the necessity of a civil war, and would have postponed if not forever prevented any possibility of war on the subject of slavery. A charge has been made against Governor Seymour that he did not denounce the Southern statesmen in his speeches pending the outbreak of hostilities. It must be remembered, however, that he was a recognized party chief, whose duty it was to point out the short-comings of the section to which he belonged, and the people to whom he spoke. His criticisms upon the men and the policy of the republican party pending the quarrel, were necessarily from a home point of view, and were attended with immediate results in the Northern States. But once the civil war was fairly under way, Governor Seymour did not hesitate. The flag of his country had been insulted; men were in arms all over the South to rend the Union asunder. He never held any divided allegiance. Before the war, during the war, and since the war, his motto has been, "The Union and the Constitution." Never has he faltered, never wavered, from maintaining the Federal Union against all its opponents North and South. While he would have tried to prevent the war, he saw no way to get out of it but to fight it out when once war was commenced, though in spite of his warning and against his protests.

Knowing the temper of the leaders of the republican party, and seeing the power which had been conferred upon them by the thoughtless generosity of the American people, he saw with dismay, but without much surprise, that they were using the forces of the Government not for the purpose of putting down the rebellion, but for consolidating and increasing their own power, and removing impediments to unchecked authority, all of which was to have been expected from their antecedents and the theory of government at the bottom of every organization which has opposed the democratic party since the War for Independence.

Mr. Seymour possesses moral courage in a very high degree. He is always willing to sacrifice himself and the temporary good opinion, if need be, of those with whom he is associated if a great public good is to be gained thereby. Hence, in spite of the calumny which he knew would be heaped upon him; in spite of the false attitude in which he would be placed, toward those who honestly but unthinkingly sustained the war, he did not hesitate a moment to brave the Government, to brave popular clamor and feeling when he saw that by so doing he might protect popular rights and local independence. A State-Rights Democrat, he could not but view with alarm the encroachments of the Federal Government upon the authority of the States. By all his instincts and education strongly prepossessed in favor of the democratic ideal of a government in which the individual should have the right to the full play of his faculties, the only check being the right of his neighbors to protection, he could not sympathize with that unthinking and passionate loyalty which insisted upon striking down all opposition during the continuance of the civil war. His protest against the sentence and banishment of Mr. Vallandigham showed rare and knightly courage. He knew he would be misunderstood, knew he would be denounced as a sympathizer with traitors: but he loved his country; he loved too well the principles of democratic liberty in which he had been reared to consider what would be the effect upon his personal fortunes of a bold and brave protest against what he believed to be an act of wanton power in order to check and limit free discussion. His course during the famous riots of New York, in the year 1863, also have exposed him to the most cruel misrepresentations; but now, read in the light of all the evidence, it will be seen that Governor Seymour, in that as well as in any other emergency acted with courage as well as with rare discretion. The testimony of all the officials with whom he acted—Mayor

Opdyke and the military officers—proves him to be a man eminently fit to deal with the gravest emergencies which arise in a State or nation.

There is an impression abroad that there is great dissimilarity of character between Horatio Seymour and General Frank P. Blair, but really they have much in common. The pluck and positiveness of General Blair's character, which every one recognizes, are quite as marked in Governor Seymour's personal deportment, except that it is veiled by a more cautious form of statement and by that culture which obtains in the older communities. Gen. Blair, upon his advent as a Free-Soiler in Missouri showed very great physical and moral courage; but the refinements of deportment, of style, and of sentiment which would have been effective in an old State like New York, would have been out of place in the political agitator about entering upon public life in so turbulent a community as that of Missouri in those days. Governor Seymour's frank opposition to the administration when it was in the plenitude of its power, and when the people unthinkingly stood by it, regarding its cause as the cause of the nation; his protest against the banishment of Mr. Vallandingham and his speech at the City Hall during the riot week, all show him to be a man of rare courage, high temper, and unflinching bravery. But his education, habits of life, the community in which he had always lived, his disposition to conciliate, and the kindly temper of the man, all tended to make the general public blind to those bolder, nobler, and higher traits of his character which only a great public emergency could call out. Passion and force and courage in the one case were more open, avowed, pronounced; in the other they were tempered by circumstance, by education, and the necessity of winning rather than driving people to indorse his views.

It is charged by the Republican journals that Gov. Seymour wished to be nominated at New York, although he repeatedly urged that body not to bring forward his name. They impute to him a burning ambition to be made President of the United States. If this charge be true, how did it happen that President Lincoln was unable to swerve him from what he deemed to be his line of duty, by a proposal that he should be made his successor if he would only give up his own ideas of right and conform to the policy marked out by Mr. Lincoln? The world knows how many were bribed to leave the Democratic ranks by less tempting offers than this. Mr. Thurlow Weed, a political enemy of Mr. Seymour, states this fact in the following words:—

"Soon after the election of 1862, Mr. Lincoln remarked to me that, as the Governor of the Empire State and the Representative Man of the Democratic party, Gov. Seymour had the power to render great public service, and that if he exerted that power against the rebellion and for his country, he would be our next President."

This fact was also known to others, and it is true that Mr. Lincoln did write a letter to Mr. Seymour proposing to open a correspondence with regard to public affairs. This letter was followed by messengers from Washington, authorized to use language more explicit than the expressions used in his own written communication.

It appears, then, that the republican party have not found Mr. Seymour so ambitious that they could tempt him, as they have tempted others, by any offers of any position. It should be borne in mind, that when this offer was made the democratic party seemed to be in a hopeless minority, while the Republican organization was at the height of power and in the enjoyment of the enormous patronage growing out of the war, with the control of an army of nearly one million men.

CHAPTER XXVI.

HORATIO SEYMOUR AS A MAN, AN ORATOR, AND A STATESMAN.

Governor Seymour's bitterest enemy has never dared to impugn his private character. In that respect he is unassailable. He never wronged a human being in person or purse. With ample private means and simple tastes, he has had none of the ordinary temptations to increase his possessions by questionable means. Among his neighbors, his word has always been as good as his bond. During his legislative and executive career, he was never charged with giving a corrupt vote in helping any measure which would inure to his own private advantage.

His habits also are above reproach. He rarely takes wine and seldom smokes; when he does, it is generally out of compliment to his host or guests or because he does not wish to appear singular in the circle in which he moves. Nor does he use profane language. A cultured Christian gentleman, he is ever conscious of the impropriety (to use no stronger term) of those irreverent expletives, which form so large a part of the ordinary language of American men, when away from the presence of the other sex.

Yet there is nothing puritanical about Horatio Seymour. He is tolerant, kindly and genial in his deportment toward all with whom he is associated. Strict in his judgment of his own habits and language, he does not permit himself to criticise or condemn his fellow-men. Accustomed in his long political career to mix with all kinds of people, he has found a large charity in this regard to be as convenient as it is necessary and wise.

As a popular speaker, Governor Seymour has long been without a superior in his own State. Graceful, fluent, profound, powerful, yet always conciliatory, concise, instructive, and just, he never fails to interest and impress an audience. In this respect an English traveler of uncommon intelligence, years ago, said of him that he approached the type of the best class of English statesmen more nearly than did any other man he met in America. Professor Wilson, of Hobart College, himself a Republican, in a recent address before the upper class-men of his college, referred to Governor Seymour as the best living example of a popular orator, partaking in his style of the logic of Webster, the analysis of Calhoun, the grace of Clay, and the fluency of Choate.

He is peculiarly an extemporaneous speaker. In oratory more than in any other thing, has nature endowed him royally. He is the happiest when called out unexpectedly. He often writes or dictates his speeches but never memorizes them, and rarely follows his manuscript closely. The thought and the course of argument are retained, but it is noticeable that his language is better, if possible, in his impromptu speech than in the written draft of it. The inspiration of the audience and the scene make his words more graceful and effective, more fluent and energetic. The electrical bursts of eloquence which have given him fame, have been those which were evoked by the inspiration of the moment. The presence of an audience, the inspiriting effect of the scene and the occasion, rouse all his faculties and exhibit his most admirable and commanding capacities.

Take him "for all in all," he is one of the few men in the country fitted by deportment and training to be President of the United States. Trained to public life, thoroughly conversant with all public questions, wise in council, willing to take responsibility, discreet in action, ready of speech, affable, of kindly temper, he would dignify and adorn the highest office in the gift of the people.

CHAPTER XXVII.

LOOKING AHEAD—RESULT OF THE ELECTION.

The nomination of Horatio Seymour for President, and of Francis P. Blair, Jr., for Vice-President, necessitates a change in the calculations of those who, previous to these nominations, were rash enough to count as sure the election of Grant and Colfax. If popular enthusiasm form an element in the forecasting of the result of an election—and who will affirm that it does not?—the problem before us is easy of solution. High as General Grant had stood in public esteem, his nomination as the candidate of the republican party for the Presidency met with no popular response. On the contrary, so soon as it was known that the democratic party had nominated Horatio Seymour as its standard-bearer in the present campaign, the whole party heartily approved its action, and its adherents were unusually demonstrative.

But expressions of popular enthusiasm may be deceptive. What is needed is not cheers but votes. The main question, then, is whether the requisite number of votes can be obtained to elect Horatio Seymour, President, and Francis P. Blair, Jr., Vice-President, of the United States? To answer this question intelligently, it is necessary to examine certain political statistics. It is proposed first to review the vote cast by each State for Mr. Lincoln, in 1864; the vote of each State at its last general election; and then to compare the two, from which comparison alone, it is possible to forecast intelligently the result of the Presidential campaign of the present year. It will also be necessary to examine the votes of the Southern States since the close of the war, though an examination of this character must, perforce, be far less satisfactory than one could desire. That each step may be clear as the reader proceeds, it is proposed to consider each State by itself, and then recapitulate in tabular form, all that has been ascertained in the investigation; by each State, in this connection, is meant each State that took part in the Presidential election of 1864.

Naturally, we begin with Maine, and in all these observations upon particular States our aim will be to be as brief as possible, lest the reader be taxed with wearisome details. "As goes Maine, so goes the Union," ran the proverb in the days when it was a democratic State, simply because at that time it was the first of all the States, in which the issue was doubtful, to hold its election for State officers prior to the Presidential election. It gave a majority of 21,122 for Mr. Lincoln, in 1864, but in 1867 elected the republican candidate for Governor by a majority of only 11,818.

New Hampshire's majority for Mr. Lincoln, in 1864, was 3,529, but last spring it re-elected its republican Governor by a bare majority of 2,493.

Vermont, Massachusetts, and Rhode Island, of

course, are sure to be carried by the Republicans, though, in Massachusetts, the republican majority of 78,727, in 1864, was, in 1867, reduced to 27,946.

Connecticut may be counted upon for the Democrats, since its republican majority of 2,406, in 1864, was, in 1867, changed to a democratic majority of 1,772.

The same is true of New York. It gave Mr. Lincoln a majority of 6,749, but in November, 1867, elected a democratic Secretary of State by a majority of 47,930.

Counting New Jersey and Maryland as democratic—which no one will gainsay—Pennsylvania is the next State in the list which has showed a change in political sentiment since 1864. In that year it returned for Mr. Lincoln a majority of 20,075, but in 1867 it returned a democratic majority of 927.

In the Western States, no important political changes were noticeable, save in Ohio, Kansas, Minnesota and Michigan. In 1867, the question of negro suffrage was presented to the electors of Ohio, and it was decided in the negative by 50,253 majority; at the same election, the Democrats obtained a majority in the Legislature, resulting in the election of Allen G. Thurman (Democrat), United States Senator, to succeed Benjamin F. Wade, whose term expires March 4, 1869. The republican candidate for Governor, however, was elected by the meager majority of 2,983. In 1864, Ohio gave Mr. Lincoln a majority of 59,586.

In Kansas, the question of negro suffrage was submitted to the people in 1867, and rejected by a majority of 8,938, though Mr. Lincoln's majority in this State in 1864, was just 12,000, including the soldiers' votes, and without them, 10,400.

A similar question was presented to Minnesota in 1867, and a similar decision was rendered, the majority against negro suffrage being 1,288; at the same election a republican Governor was chosen by 5,314 majority. In 1864, Mr. Lincoln's majority was 7,615.

In Michigan a new constitution, involving negro suffrage, was submitted to the people in the spring of 1868, and it was rejected by 38,849 majority. It should be added that in each of the last three States just mentioned, the sole advocates of negro suffrage were Republicans, and its chief opponents were Democrats.

With these preliminary observations, we may advance to a more detailed examination of the probabilities of the issue of the present campaign; and in order to facilitate such an examination, the reader's attention is asked to the following table. The first two columns show the popular vote of each State for the Presidency in 1864; the last two, the vote of the same States at their last election for State officers. Some of these States, such as Indiana, have not held a general election since 1866; others, like New York, chose certain State officers in 1867; while still others, such as Connecticut, have held a general election in the present year. But in every instance is given the last vote of each State upon an issue in which party politics were clearly presented. For this reason the figures accredited to Ohio are those of the vote for Governor in 1867, though the main issue of that election was negro suffrage (which was defeated by over 50,000 majority), and the Democrats secured a majority in the State Legislature. And here, it may be observed, that in every case of doubt the benefit of the doubt has been given to the Republicans. Subjoined is the table already mentioned:—

STATES.	1864.		1866-7-8.	
	DEM.	REP.	DEM.	REP.
California, . . .	43,841	62,134	49,905	40,359
Connecticut, . .	42,285	44,691	50,551	48,779
Delaware, . . .	8,767	8,155	9,810	8,598
Illinois, ...	158,370	189,496	147,058	203,045
Indiana, ...	130,233	150,422	155,102	169,618
Iowa, ...	49,596	89,075	58,880	90,789
Kansas, ...	3,691	16,441	19,421	10,483
Kentucky, . . .	64,301	27,786	90,225	33,939
Maine, ...	46,992	68,114	45,644	57,462
Maryland, . . .	32,739	40,153	63,739	22,110
Massachusetts, .	48,745	126,742	70,360	98,306
Michigan, . . .	74,604	91,521	55,865	80,819
Minnesota, . . .	17,375	25,060	29,543	34,887
Missouri, . . .	31,678	72,750	40,958	62,187
Nevada, ...	6,594	9,826	4,065	5,208
New Hampshire, .	32,871	36,400	37,262	39,785
New Jersey, . .	68,024	60,723	67,468	51,114
New York, . . .	361,986	368,735	373,029	325,099
Ohio, ...	205,568	265,154	240,622	243,605
Oregon, ...	8,457	9,888	11,789	10,580
Pennsylvania, . .	276,316	296,391	267,751	266,824
Rhode Island, . .	8,718	14,319	5,658	9,767
Vermont, . . .	13,321	42,419	11,510	31,694
West Virginia, .	10,438	23,152	13,393	14,674
Wisconsin, . . .	65,884	83,458	65,683	72,470
TOTAL, . . .	1,811,754	2,223,035	1,985,291	2,032,201

A few very obvious deductions are to be made from this table, which the reader will not allow to escape him. They are:—

1. That, whereas Mr. Lincoln's majority on the popular vote in 1864 was 411,281, the republican majority in these same States at the last general election in each, was only 46,910.

2. That, whereas it would have required a change of 205,641 votes (on the popular, not electoral vote) in 1864, from the republican to the democratic side, to have elected General McClellan instead of Mr. Lincoln, a like change of only 23,456 votes is all that is needful now to elect Horatio Seymour over General Grant in these States, supposing that in no State has there been any change in political sentiment since the holding of its last general election.

3. That, whereas the Republicans, with Mr. Lincoln as their standard-bearer, obtained a popular majority in twenty-two of the twenty-five States which voted in 1864, of these same States at their last general elections, they carried but fifteen, while the Democrats carried ten. It must be borne in mind that the remarkable change in political sentiment in this country since 1864 did not manifest itself to any great extent until the spring of 1867, since which time neither Illinois nor Indiana have held a general election, whence might be decided the political preference of their electors.

Attention is first asked to the following table, embracing a list of the Northern States, in which are included all but the ten Southern States (until recently denied representation in Congress) with the electoral vote to which each is entitled, and classified politically, in accordance with the preceding table.

DEMOCRATIC		REPUBLICAN.	
STATES.	VOTES.	STATES.	VOTES.
California,	5	Illinois,	16
Connecticut,	6	Indiana,	13
Delaware,	3	Iowa,	8
Kansas,	3	Maine,	7
Kentucky,	11	Massachusetts,	12
Maryland,	7	Michigan,	8
New Jersey,	7	Minnesota,	4
New York,	33	Missouri,	11
Oregon,	3	Nebraska,*	3
Pennsylvania,	26	Nevada,	3
		New Hampshire,	5
	104	Ohio,	21
		Rhode Island,	4
		Tennessee,*	10
		Vermont,	5
		West Virginia,	5
		Wisconsin,	8
			143

[* NOTE.—The above table includes the States of Tennessee and Nebraska, which were not represented in the electoral college of 1864.]

It is clear, from the above, that were no changes to be made next fall in the votes as recorded in the first table, and were Tennessee and Nebraska to continue republican, Horatio Seymour would be defeated in these States by twenty electoral votes, a majority of their electoral votes being 124. And here comes an important element in the calculation which as yet has not been mentioned. The drift of public sentiment for the last year and a half or two years has been against the republican party and in favor of the democratic party. In the spring of 1867 the republican majority in New Hampshire was materially reduced, and less than a month later the Democrats carried Connecticut; in August they carried California; in October they elected their candidates in Pennsylvania and Ohio, and reduced the republican majority in Iowa; in November they carried New York, New Jersey, and Kansas, and reduced the republican majorities in several other States. In the spring of 1868 they still further reduced the republican majority in New Hampshire, and nearly doubled their own majority in Connecticut. If these facts indicate any thing, it is that for eighteen months past a revulsion in political sentiment has been working in favor of the Democrats, whence it seems not unreasonable to infer that certain of the States credited to the Republicans in the table last given, may cast their vote for Seymour and Blair next November. These States, with the electoral vote to which they are entitled, are:

```
Illinois,..................................... 16
Indiana,...................................... 13
New Hampshire,................................  5
Ohio,......................................... 21
    Total,.................................... 55
```

Such a change as this—and it is not improbable—would make the next electoral vote of the Northern States stand as follows:—

For Seymour.	Vote.	For Grant.	Vote.
California...........	5	Iowa..............	8
Connecticut.........	6	Maine.............	7
Delaware............	3	Massachusetts.....	12
Illinois............	16	Michigan..........	8
Indiana.............	13	Minnesota.........	4
Kansas..............	3	Missouri..........	11
Kentucky............	11	Nebraska..........	3
Maryland............	7	Nevada............	3
New Hampshire.......	5	Rhode Island......	4
New Jersey..........	7	Tennessee.........	10
New York............	33	Vermont...........	5
Ohio................	21	West Virginia.....	5
Oregon..............	3	Wisconsin.........	8
Pennsylvania........	26		
Total...............	159		88

Should the Democrats carry the States accredited to them in the above table they would elect Horatio Seymour, even though all the Southern States, with their seventy electoral votes, should be carried for Grant. And now the question is, Will General Grant obtain a majority in each of the Southern States? At first thought, one would answer, Yes; upon reflection, one would be less positive. At best, it is impossible to render a definite decision. Figures in this instance afford no light. Yet, as a matter of record, we append the latest returns of elections in these States, premising that those marked with a star (*) are returns of the vote for and against a State Convention, the rest being the votes for or against the new State constitutions. The Democrats voted against both and the Republicans for them.

State.	Dem.	Rep.
Virginia*	61,887	107,342
North Carolina	71,820	92,590
South Carolina	27,288	70,758
Georgia	71,309	86,007
Alabama	1,005	69,807
Florida	9,491	14,520
Louisiana	48,739	66,152
Texas*	11,440	44,689
Mississippi*	6,277	69,739
Arkansas	26,597	27,913

Notwithstanding these figures, there is good reason for believing that upon a fair election a conservative majority can be obtained in Virginia, Georgia, Alabama, Texas, Mississippi, and Kansas; in fact, the Conservatives have just carried Mississippi by a large majority. Of the ten Southern States, the following have, by recent acts of Congress, been admitted to representation in Congress, and, hence, will be entitled to representation in the electoral college: Alabama, Arkansas, Florida, Georgia, Louisiana, North Carolina, and South Carolina. It is probable that the remaining States of Virginia, Texas, and Mississippi also will be admitted by Congress, thus entitling all to participate in the Presidential election. Upon a fair vote, the result would probably stand thus:—

For Seymour.	Vote.	For Grant.	Vote.
Virginia	10	North Carolina	9
Georgia	9	South Carolina	6
Alabama	8	Florida	3
Texas	6	Louisiana	7
Mississippi	7		
Arkansas	5		25
	45		

These votes, together with those credited to the Northern States in a previous table, foot up as follows:—

For Horatio Seymour	204
For Ulysses S. Grant	113
Majority for Seymour	91
Necessary for election	159

But all such calculations pertaining to the Southern States are idle in view of the fact that the Republicans in those States hold all the offices, have it in their power, by provision of the latest reconstruction acts and their new State constitutions, to order a new registration of votes prior to the Presidential election, from which registry they can exclude whom they choose, and from their decision there can be no appeal. It is possible that Seymour and Blair may carry some of these States, but more than probable that all of them will be carried for Grant and Colfax. The battle, then, is to be fought in the Northern States, and the main battle-ground will be the States of New Hampshire, Pennsylvania, Ohio, Indiana, and Illinois. These—all these—the Democrats must carry or General Grant will be the next President; if they do carry them Horatio Seymour will be elected.

We need go no further. Ingenuity may so combine the figures which have been given as to elect Seymour or elect Grant, according to the political preference of the calculator. Such is not our purpose. On the contrary, the aim has been to present in a clear light the chances which each party has for success, and leave each reader to determine for himself, after careful examination, his own opinion of the result of the Presidential election.

LIFE OF
GENERAL FRANCIS P. BLAIR, JR.

CHAPTER I.

HIS BIRTH, BOYHOOD, AND EARLY HISTORY.

In this country we have not permitted the growth of any families with special privileges apart from the rest of the community; yet it is notable that by mere force of character, or special aptitude for some department of public life, there have been several families all the members of which have become eminent.

The most noted of these is the Adams family, of which we now have the example of four generations of public men, all of whom have evinced a decided genius for diplomatic and legislative careers. There is no doubt that the younger scions of this house are well able to maintain the reputation so justly accorded to the elder branches. Then we have the example of the brothers Washburne, all of them active politicians and filling offices of public trust and honor, though none of them quite reach the rank of first-class statesmen. In our own day the Lelands, Stetsons, and Colemans are noted for their success in hotel keeping,—some ten members, I believe, of the Leland family being proprietors of leading hotels in different cities of the country.

The Blair family are also among the most marked of these members of what Dr. Holmes has called the "Brahmin class." Francis P. Blair is always known as a politician and editor, was never suspected of any act inconsistent with personal honor. He was an able journalist, a shrewd adviser, and a sagacious observer of the tendencies of his times. His son, Montgomery Blair, is a statesman of no mean repute. He has wide political experience, great personal address, and is noted for his earnestness and vigor of character. He is suggestive, keenly sensitive to the tendencies of the times, and whatever criticism there has been on his conduct is due to the irritating effect which a man of great genius and high susceptibility, and keenly conscious of the influence of passing events, has upon his more sluggish and unimpressible associates. General Frank P. Blair, Jr., however, is a person of still more marked peculiarities. His most salient quality is his positive type of character. He is a man of rare courage, moral and physical.

It is the misfortune of our institutions that men of pluck and pronounced views are apt to be set aside in our political contests for an accommodating, compromising, calculating, and conciliating race of politicians. In our close contests, national and local, it is too often deemed prudent to select as candidates for office merely negative men, politicians without salient features of character, against whom nothing can be said, who have the tact to conceal views which may be objectionable to their own party, or to that undecided portion of the other party which it is possible to win over. We have had only one Jackson among all our Presidents, and such of our leading statesmen as have had pronounced views of their own have invariably been set aside when high offices were at stake, for men of much less force and genius, but who were more available. General Blair belongs to a type of statesmen whom it is desirable to retain in our public councils. With distinct views of public policy, never wavering in any set of opinions which have once been formed—for he stands to-day upon the same ground precisely on which he stood when he commenced his free-soil campaign in Missouri—General Blair is yet statesman enough to adapt himself to the varying phases of public opinion. One of the most curious results of the late civil war, was the damage it inflicted upon the lawyers and politicians who took a leading part in the conflict. Nearly all the Southern statesmen to whom were given independent commands, failed utterly in the field. The same is true of the Northern politicians who entered the ranks hoping to gain military glory for use in future political contests. It is needless to recite here the careers of Sickles, Banks, Butler, and the host of other politicians. General Frank P. Blair, Jr., alone, of the men who had been noted previous to the rebellion, came out of the war not only with his name untarnished, but with a great and honest addition to his deserved reputation. The conciliating, procrastinating, and compromising temper which is begotten in our political contests, gave our public men a habit of mind which entirely unfitted them for the ruder conflicts of war. The success of General Blair shows him to be of an entirely different type from the usual run of politicians. His boldness, his directness, his force of character, his promptness in emergencies, his knowledge of the salient points of the opposing force, are precisely the qualities which make good generals, and hence he succeeded when nearly all the others had failed. But this boldness of character, positiveness of view has been tempered by family influences and by his education in public life, so that even if he were elected to the highest office in the gift of the people, there would be no fear that this shrewd, brave soldier and statesman would do any thing to compromise his reputation or imperil the liberties of his country.

Francis Preston Blair, Jr., was born in the town of Lexington, Kentucky, on the 19th of February, in the year 1821, and is consequently now in his forty-eighth year. To these years, full of significant events, in which his force has always made him a leader, it is our purpose to direct attention. Unlike the Republican commander and candidate for the Presidency, General Blair has a name long known in those who bore it before him, and the subject of no conjecture now. Descended from the Blairs of Maryland on one side, and from the Prestons of Virginia on the other side, his father, Francis P. Blair, Sr., moved to the State of Kentucky only a few years before the birth of his son and namesake, and was even then a man of marked ability as a debater and lawyer. With a devotion to the Democratic party which has never faltered, and with a peculiar family preference for asserting its principles in its career of some commanding leader who would embody them in Government, the elder Blair, in Kentucky, became the warmest and ablest champion Andrew Jackson had in that then stronghold of the Whig power, where the name and the fame of Henry Clay were a subject of veritable idolatry.

The first seven years of young Francis' life were passed in Lexington, and while he was just emerging from infancy into mere boyhood, we may be sure that the exciting tides of political debate in the triangular Crawford-Jackson-Adams campaign, running with a violence to which the present furnishes no parallel, did not pass unnoticed by him. Controversy and courage in him bred in the bone, and bounding in the blood, were stimulated by the unconscious influences of partisanism that raged all across "the dark and bloody ground." Before he could realize their meaning, his home became the center of the astutest combinations, and the resort of the ablest men of the period. All the tendency which extraordinary events and the association of extraordinary men have to impress, was impressed on Frank P. Blair, Jr., from his earliest youth. In this fact we can see the reason for the depth of his convictions, for his intuitive aptitude and fondness for public life, and for the easy rapidity with which he stepped out among statesmen from his very first entrance into politics.

Absorbed as his father was as a man of affairs, he yet found or made time to superintend the education of his son. In the acquisition of the fundamental branches of learning, the boy displayed a precocity and an application which were thought remarkable even in a remarkable family. History, language, and mathematics were his favorite studies. Blessed with a constitution and a body that kept even pace with the development of his mind, prolonged mental labor did him no bodily harm. In this he was encouraged by the counsel and example of his father, who was careful to impress on him the necessity of curbing a facility which a very retentive memory gave him to learn by rote those studies requisite to be mastered in their relations and in their reasons. To show the tendency of Frank " to strike out for himself," it is related that when only a boy of nine, he employed a midsummer vacation in thoroughly absorbing a Latin grammar, and in characteristically launching into Horace before he had begun the primary period of Cæsar.

In common with all Kentuckians, he became a proficient in riding and shooting before he was much more than the height of a rifle. Both accomplishments indicated the practical daring form of his tastes. Both have stood him well in the subsequent career, whose opulent opportunities could then not even be guessed.

Events were preparing for his translation to a larger theater of life. Upon the accession of General

Andrew Jackson to the Presidency, he gathered at the capital a community of his most eminent adherents, to sustain the labors, if not to share the rewards of his illustrious administration. Among them was Hon. F. P. Blair, Sr., who became the confidential adviser of the warrior-statesman, and to whom the vindication and annunciation of the policy of the Executive were committed in the responsible conduct of the *Globe* newspaper, the organ of the party in power.

With the father came the son. Not yet in his teens, this keen observer was now at the capital of the country, at a time when his perceptive and receptive powers were putting forth their first exercises. Of this perilous period it were interesting to write, yet we **must** skip it in a paragraph. Blair, the boy, must yield to the consideration of Blair, the man. Only this we can state; young Frank certainly became the favorite of Andrew Jackson, who rarely unbent to children. That stanch patriot and game fighter fought his battles over again to the boy on his knee, and was known to keep even embassadors in waiting till he had finished a narration to the listening son of his trusted friend.

Five busy years passed pleasantly in Washington, with study of books the rule, and study of great men all around him, the not infrequent exception; at fifteen, young Blair was ready for college. He was sent to Princeton, New Jersey, and when just beyond nineteen, graduated with very high honors in his class. The venerable and recently retired President, John MacLean, at that time Vice-President of

Nassau Hall, bears testimony to this day, to the assiduity, courtesy, and temperance of the student, and is fond of asserting that at the time of his graduation in 1840, he was quick to predicate a distinguished career for young Blair. Nothing worthy of remark occurred during his collegiate course, except a noticeable fondness for oratory, and an unusual popularity with his classmates.

CHAPTER II.

HIS PROFESSIONAL AND EARLY POLITICAL CAREER—HE LEADS THE FREE SOIL MOVEMENT.

AFTER graduation, two years were consumed in the study of the law, under the direction of his father, in Montgomery County, Maryland, near the capital of the United States, and seeking Kentucky for that purpose, he was, in 1843, admitted to the bar of the Supreme Court of that State, in Lexington, his native town. At that time it was for some months an open question with him, whether to become a Washington lawyer, whose life is prolific of quiet fees, but barren of adventure and of the romance of the profession, or to settle down in some larger Eastern or Southern city, and pursue the plodding path of an attorney. Neither course was resolved upon. Washington was the field, as now, of gentlemen of the long robe. It brought from all States the ablest advocates, but could show few very able resident pleaders and counselors. The tendency of the talented and the young was toward the West. Thither the most ambitious and enterprising took their course. To St. Louis went Frank P. Blair, Jr., and set up as "Attorney and Counselor-at-Law." But it was not in the nature of the man to keep his light under a bushel, nor napkin his talent under ground. He became known at once, in that growing city, as a "man of mark." The first year or two cases were few, but of those he had, Mr. Blair made so much by appeal and constant, characteristic combat, as to command in months a reputation usually acquired by years of hard labor. His directness, his penchant for the substantial justice of equity, rather than its tortuous tides of ancient law, were abundantly satisfied by the admirable retention Missouri made of that fine feature of Gallic government, the Code Napoleon. This system allows of no red tape knots, and dispenses with all circumstantial delays, while it preserves all the wholesome axioms and wise prescriptions of the common law. The kind of practice it enforces was admirably adapted to the taste and temperament of our subject, and he soon became known as a pleader of no common power.

Yet in a sense the incidents of professional life in St. Louis were insufficient for the ambition, and a restraint upon the felt powers of Mr. Blair, young as he was. A frontier city was prolific of many phases of life, and photographed many kinds of character, yet the scope of these contests and their consequent reputation were quite local. We can credit the assertion, then, that as an attorney, young Blair chafed at the narrow limits of his legal life. He longed for more stirring scenes. Yet with a patience equal to his pluck afterward, he waited his time and did what he had to do conscientiously and well. The few leading lawyers between the Wabash and the Mississippi at that time could be counted on one's fingers. In Indiana, Thomas A. Hendricks; in Illinois, Browning, Douglas, and Abraham Lincoln, and in Missouri, Edward Bates, were all in that region of pronounced ability, and some of these owed quite as much to eccentricity as they did to excellence. These, while young Blair did not essay to rival he certainly did not fear, and they regarded him as a man, who by a few years of energy, had almost reached a plane to which they had struggled through half a lifetime. Mr. Bates, the most eminent professional of all named was kindness itself to our subject, and was not more gratified at his own success than in predicating it of his young friend.

It was plain, however, that Frank P. Blair, Jr., had not reached his proper place. Law with him, as it has been with many other of our public leaders, was calculated to prove an excellent preparatory step to a larger sphere of events. Born to be a leader of men, fitted to be a man of affairs, it is not unnatural that he was restive of the restraint of courts. His time was coming. The war with Mexico was the magnet that drew him out. Of the origin and cause of that dispute it is not necessary to write now. It only needs to say that we of the remoter East can not understand how popular that contest was, in the South and West. The call for volunteers was promptly responded to by Frank Blair, who closed up his office, transferred or settled his cases, and enlisting under the standard of Sterling Price, who won in that war the reputation as a leader, which he more than vindicated in larger and later conflict, was appointed a lieutenant in the infantry rifles; less than two months of 1846 had elapsed before he was one of the army of Zachary Taylor, and prominent in all the battles from Palo Alto to Benna Vista. Of his specific efforts in the Mexican war, the term of service was too brief, the succession of contests too rapid, and the subsequent campaign of Scott from the Gulf coast, inward, too furious in its fortunes and distracting in its details, to demand a lengthened reproduction here. As an officer of the army of the frontier, however, it is on record that Frank Blair was criticised for too much impetuosity, and that not even the swiftness of those bloody battles was enough for his spirit. He commanded the confidence of his superiors, and was twice exceptionally commended to General Taylor by General Price, " for gallantry and soldierly conduct," respectively, after the struggles at Monterey and Resaca de la Palma.

When the star of Scott rose above the horizon, many of the "year troops," under that old chief, preferred the activities of home to the monotonous prospect of mere guard duty, should they re-enlist, and home they came. Among them was Lieutenant Frank P. Blair. He reached St. Louis, after a short and brilliant service, in the first part of 1848. His reputation as a thorough officer and a furious fighter had reached the city of his residence, in advance of his return. A brilliant future lay ahead. The avenue of law opened wider and more invitingly than ever. But more offered. He who had helped the country deserved well of the State. Public life allured him. At this time Blair did an act which showed the independence of his mind, and his devotion to political conviction in the face of all adverse tendency of men and of the times. This act was the positive identification of himself with the Van Buren Free-Soil party of 1848. It mattered not to him that he was born in one slave State and domiciled in another. Convinced that slavery was economically, socially, and morally an evil, opposed to the spirit of the age and to the best interests of white and black alike, he pronounced against its further extension into free territory, and held, with that other great Missourian, Thomas Hart Benton, that it was purely a creature of local law. He foresaw with the prescience of a statesman that if not done away with by voluntary legislation, the system would plunge the whole nation into fratricidal strife. His remedy was, first, to stop its extension into free territory; second, to extinguish it in each State by the voluntary gradual abolition of it, with compensation to owners, by the government of each State. There he stood, and on that issue he fought, in the face of opposition, proscription, and even of violence. Mr. Van Buren was defeated, and under Mr. Fillmore, who succeeded General Taylor, was passed the fugitive-slave bill, which, with coincident legislation, marked the induction of the era which viewed slavery as national in its rights of recognition and migration. Through all those three years, Mr. Blair was the leader of the Free-Soil party in Missouri. What with the increasing numbers and the yielding sentiment of the city of St. Louis, a large portion of it became confirmed in the then anomalous faith.

Upon the opening of the Pierce-Scott campaign of

1851-52, Mr. Blair was chosen to the State Assembly of Missouri, and at that time his official political life may be said to have begun. In the Legislature of his adopted State he served two full terms, from 1852 to 1856, and fearlessly asserted the distinctive principles of the minority he represented. He was by all admitted to be leader of the opposition, yet his strict attention to the local interests of his city and county won him the esteem, as his manliness did the respect, of every voter. During this exciting time he steadily threw his influence and voice against the repeal of the Missouri Compromise and against the Lecompton Constitution of Kansas.

In 1856, closing his legislative services, Mr. Blair was advanced higher. From that date till the end of 1862, through three successive terms, he represented the St. Louis district in the House of Representatives, each time by decided and increasing majorities. His career in the National Legislature is familiar to the country. He was the leader of the Republican party in the House from the Northwest. As a debater he was the peer of any. As a worker, few were his equals. As a practical man he was prominent, and as an incorruptible representative was known as much by his associates as he was by his constituents. His identification with the leading articles of legislation of the Republican party, so long as it confined itself to the opposition to the extension of human slavery, and to non-interference with it in the States, is a matter of history. One project especially of Mr. Blair's, startled the country at the time, but commanded the assent of the leading thinkers of the period. It was this: In 1858 General Blair delivered, from his seat in the House, a very elaborate and able speech, practically proposing to end the slavery agitation by speedily and equitably ending the institution itself. His plan was to concentrate and colonize the black population then in servitude, in some suitable southern point, as the preventive of threatened mischief. His measure, and the argument he used to support it, commanded the assent at that time of the leading statesmen of the abolition party, North and West. Gerritt Smith, Theodore Parker, and others hailed it with cordial letters of thanks, as a happy harbinger of deliverance. Judge Trumbull, Judge Wade, Abraham Lincoln, in fact the whole Republican party, embraced the proposition.

The South was not then in a mood to accept this plan as a cure for the terrible malady which the sword was finally invoked to eradicate.

CHAPTER III.

HIS WAR RECORD.

LINCOLN tried, in the midst of war, the same experiment which General Blair had advocated in peace, but his own party would not support him. The beginning of the rebellion reveals to us the most distinguished, varied, and brilliant services General Blair has ever, in his career, rendered to the country. We are apt to think that the late contest, which rose to its highest tide-mark at Gettysburg, and finally was lost at Appomattox Court-House, was first foreseen and first opposed in the East. The red lane hewn through Baltimore, April 19th, was indeed the first blood shed after Sumter opened the ball. But to Frank P. Blair is due the credit of having been the very earliest to enroll in the defense of the Union. At once, following the election and preceding the inauguration of President Lincoln, Mr. Blair perceived, in advance of his party, that the South meant war, and that the western objective point would be the State of Missouri, the last of the slave, and the farthest of the border, States. The Administration of the State was committed to officials of secession sentiments. Though a majority of the people, counting in all classes, were in favor of the

Union, the wealth and property of the commonwealth leaned the other way, and the party that struck the first blow would carry the day. Frank Blair resolved to strike that first blow when the time was ripe, and save the State to the Union. Early in February, 1861, he secretly enrolled a full regiment of Federal volunteers, drilled them himself, and armed and uniformed them with his credit. They were 1,000 strong, were duly and fully officered, and were in the highest state of efficiency. How trustworthy the men were, can be told from the fact that ten hundred disciplined soldiers succeeded in keeping their organization a profound secret, and in meeting regularly and unnoticed in the heart of a hostile population, though environed by spies from the enemy, who were more openly organizing. A capacity for organization, a knowledge of men, a practical prescience such as this indicated, are attributes that mark the born soldier, and attributes such as General Blair demonstrated at the very beginning of the rebellion, and magnified to its close. This force was the very first organization armed against the rebellion as such. Its first enlisted man was Frank P. Blair, who wrote himself down private, and who was afterward regularly elected colonel.

When Washington was threatened, and when Baltimore had been bloodily traversed, before the Federals had established communication between the North and the Capital, and while the flushed Southern armies looked upon it as a fruit ripe to fall in their lap, the friends of the Confederacy were not less active or less daring in Missouri.

Claiborne Jackson was Governor; a wily, able, energetic man. Sterling Price was chief commander of the State Guard, a man of consummate ability, and veritably idolized by the young blood and the old culture of the State. Passive Unionists there were many. Active Unionists were confined to Frank Blair's Congressional corner in St. Louis.

Within seven days after the President's first call for troops, Col. Blair's already formed body of men were in the field and accepted as the First Missouri Regiment, while four others were in rapid formation. On the day succeeding the proclamation, April 20, the Western State Arsenal, at Liberty, Clay County, Missouri, was seized and sacked by the Confederate agents, who led on a small but sufficient force for that purpose. Arrangements were projected to seize the Federal arsenal at St. Louis. To this end, a force of the State Guard rendezvoused at Camp Jackson, near the city, under the command of Brigadier-General D. M. Frost. They affected peace. Time, location, every thing, however, showed they meant business. The arsenal was filled with valuable ordnance, arms, and ammunition, and was guarded by but a few hundred regulars, under Captain Lyon. On the night of the 25th of April, most of the arms were secretly conveyed to Alton, and thence to Springfield, Illinois, and on May 10th, Col. Blair and Captain Lyon surrounded Camp Jackson and secured the surrender of the place with its munitions. The captures comprised 20 cannon, 1,200 new rifles, several cases of muskets, and large quantities of ammunition, together with the whole force, near 3,000 militia, there gathered. The movement was planned by Colonel Blair, who contributed to its execution the whole force under his command, and who accompanied it to the field, and put himself in conjunction with the more experienced regulars of Captain Lyon. The result was bloodless, but of very great importance. The cause of the Confederacy was from that moment on the wane in Missouri. The State was welded by force to the Union. In less than forty days thereafter, the battle of Booneville, in which General Blair's troops, but not himself—he being in Washington—took principal part, left the secession Governor a fugitive, and his incoherent, half-armed forces demoralized. Only such a prompt putting the foot down would have secured Federal ends in that State. For this thoroughness and expedition, the country has to thank General Blair. The country did thank him. It rang with his praise. The President and Secretary of War testified their warmest indebtedness to him. He was constituted a Brigadier-General at once, and responded with his brigade with unequaled promptitude, and in full numbers. The troops accepted with eagerness, were merged into General Lyon's army, and did well at the gallant but unsuccessful battle of Wilson Creek, where their commander lost his life. At this time General Blair was unable to take the field, because his presence was needed in Congress as Chairman of the Military Committee of the House. The energy he infused into the campaigns of 1861 and 1862 can never be forgotten. He it was who drafted the bills calling for the supplies of the 500,000 men proclaimed for, soon after the disaster at Bull Run. As the Chairman of the most important Committee of the House, at the most perilous period of our recent history, his labors were herculean. On him devolved the military appropriation bills. He was in constant intercourse with the Generals, the President, the Secretary of War, and the thousand and one persons, by office or officiousness interested in the equipment of our field forces. Mr. Blair allowed himself no time for oratory. He wished to expedite the military business of the House, in order to hasten his return to the field. Only one notable occasion called him out. It was to refute the idea that President Lincoln had "hurricaned" General Scott into the battle of Bull Run before the latter was ready. In the same connection General Blair predicted, at that early day, with prophetic accuracy, what would be the plan of the Confederates during the ensuing rebellion. How truly events bore out this statement: "They desire to make the whole of this war within the Border States, so as to let the Cotton States escape scot-free —not only free from Scott, but from all other generals. They wish to enjoy their quietude so that they may raise their cotton; that they may hold it out as a bribe to foreign nations to break our blockade." Remember, these words were uttered just after the battle of Bull Run, when the purposes of the Confederate chief were all conjecture, and when Mr. Blair's theory was offset in many minds by a belief that the Southerners would pursue a Fabian policy, and woo our armies far South to their own destruction. That Mr. Blair divined the purposes of the rebellion while it was yet inchoate, will exhibit his forecast in no inconsiderable degree.

Congress sat very late that year, and Congressman Blair's labors were unremitting. On November 29, 1862, President Lincoln promoted him to be Major-General of Volunteers, and he at once set out for the army of the West, under Grant. That officer assigned General Blair to a command of a brigade in the division of General Frederick Steele, then stationed at Helena, Arkansas. To stay in camp during the winter months was disappointing to expectation, and after the reverses in the East, was not encouraging. But a better prospect was in store; at least a more animated one was at hand. General Steele's division was spoiling for a fight, and of the division none were more eager than the brigade of General Blair. The work before them was none other than the attempted reduction of Vicksburg by assault. On the 20th of September, 1862, General Sherman embarked from Memphis with the right wing of the Thirteenth Corps, for the mouth of the Yazoo River, to begin the contemplated movement. The division of General Steele, comprising the brigades of Generals F. P. Blair, Jr., C. E. Hovey, John M. Thayer, and C. W. Dayman, was taken on at Helena, and the whole force rendezvoused at Friar's Point, on the Mississippi, just below Helena.

In considering the important part borne by General Blair in this unsuccessful yet well-sustained assault, it will be necessary to view correlatively the situation at that place. Sherman embarked to take

Vicksburg, but he hoped to be joined by Grant and the army from the banks of the Tennessee, and by Banks from Louisiana. Neither came to hand. The sudden capture of his depot of supplies at Holly Springs detained Grant. Banks was too busy attending receptions at Baton Rouge; Sherman resolved to go alone with 42,000 and odd men. Not to sketch the other dispositions, it is sufficient to say that General Morgan's division led the assault on Vicksburg from the river front, and that General Blair's brigade, detached from Steele, was in the van, was in fact, what in Napoleonic days were called "The Forlorn Hope." Four days had been spent in manœuvering, and on the 29th, the assault was made. A more spirited attack was never executed. It was a literal storming, under a direct and an enfilading fire. Behind the breastworks, however, were found the whole of Pemberton's army, from the Blackwater which Grant had not succeeded in keeping at bay, and our troops had only expected a minimum of Confederate defenders. If not outnumbered, the Federal forces were equaled by the enemy, besides the breastworks, which afterward stood such a protracted investiture, and succumbed to hunger, but never to assault. In the successive charges made, Blair's was the only brigade which reached the enemy's parapet, and alone of all the army planted its colors, and defended them, within the enemy's fortifications, till ordered, not forced, to retire. The superb conduct of General Blair and his special troops was the theme and the envy of the whole army of the Mississippi. It was the general's magnificent bravery and sudden exhibition of tactical skill in retiring from a position which he alone had been impetuous enough to reach, that forced General Grant, sufficiently out of his taciturnity to declare him "the ablest volunteer officer in the service."

Withdrawing his troops from Vicksburg, General Blair's brigade, still of General Steele's division, was attached to General McClernand's highly successful expedition against Arkansas Post, on the White River. This opened the way to Little Rock, and into the interior of the State whereof that town was the capital. In this engagement General Blair played a quiet but important part. The division in which his troops were, was stationed between the rear of the fort and the bayou that skirted it, and when Admiral Porter and General Sherman had successively shelled and assaulted General Churchill's six thousand men out of the intrenchments, General Blair's position in their rear compelled their surrender to the attacking force, by cutting off all escape.

Operations now immediately began against Vicksburg, under the direct command of General Grant. General Sherman was promoted to the command of the Fifteenth Corps, and General Blair, though the junior Major-General, in the force, succeeded Sherman in the charge of the grand second division of that corps. Within the limits of this biography it is impossible to trace minutely the responsible and brilliant services of General Blair, during the 109 days of that remarkable siege. He was the right-hand man of Sherman, who was the most trusted assistant of the General-in-Chief; always on hand, sharing from principle the fatigues of his men, ever soliciting, following where he himself always did the leading, he became the idol of his force, and shared the entire confidence of his associates and superiors. Throughout the famous three days' march of Sherman's army in detour behind Vicksburg, it is remarkable that Blair's division always was in the advance. In the final assault on the rear works of Vicksburg, July 2d, 1863, General Blair led Mower's brigade of his own division in person, amid a most tremendous fire, and with great loss, yet he planted his colors on the enemy's works, and held them there till ordered to retire at night-fall. This was the conclusion of the whole matter. The next day negotiations began, and on the 4th of July Pemberton's's army unconditionally surrendered.

After receiving the published thanks of Generals Grant and Sherman, General Blair was allowed the leave of absence he had so well won, and he remained North recruiting his shattered health during the cessation of hostilities that obtained all along the lines. The 11th of October, 1863, however, found him again with Sherman, who appointed him his second in command as before. In the march from Vicksburg to Corinth and thence to Tuscumbia, General Blair led the advance. Before reaching the latter place, his division had a short, sharp, and decisive engagement with General Stephen D. Lee's cavalry, which he easily drove, entering the town on the 27th of October. Meantime, Bragg had invested Rosecrans tightly in Chattanooga, and Sherman and Blair set out to raise the siege of that place.

Sherman now assumed command of the army of the Tennessee, and Blair again followed in his footsteps, taking Sherman's late command of the Fifteenth Corps, at the latter's special request. The historical events of that march and of the succeeding "battle above the clouds," are too recent and too many to receive or require recapitulation here. General Blair's corps bore no secondary part, and shared the honors equally with all their comrades of that extraordinary campaign. The degree of desert the troops of General Blair acquired under his command may be inferred from the fact that no sooner had Bragg been forced to retreat than General Grant, of all his army, selected the tireless and trusted Fifteenth Corps to march to the immediate relief of Knoxville where Burnside was then hemmed in by Longstreet. Before Blair reached the place, Longstreet retired in precipitation, and the jaded soldiers, who had marched from Memphis to Chattanooga, fought the battles of Lookout Mountain and Missionary Ridge, and then without rest had marched to Knoxville and back, were permitted a breathing spell.

Soon after this, the armies went into winter quarters. On making up his official report, General Grant thus spoke of the corps of General Blair: "I can not speak of the Fifteenth Corps without seeming vanity, but as I am no longer its commander, I assert that there is no better body of soldiers in America than it, or who have done more or better service. I wish all to feel a pride in its real honors." At this point General Logan relieved General

Blair of the command of the Fifteenth Corps, in accordance with the following order of Major-General Sherman:—

HEAD-QUARTERS DEPARTMENT AND ARMY OF THE TENNESSEE,
MARYSVILLE, TENNESSEE, December 7, 1863.

GENERAL ORDER NO. 5.—Major-General John A. Logan having reported for duty as commander of the Fifteenth Army Corps, will assume command thereof and enter upon his duties. Major-General F. P. Blair, Jr., now commanding the corps, will, with his assistant adjutant-general and present staff, proceed to Chattanooga, and turn over to General Logan the records of the corps, when they will be relieved from duty with the corps, and report for orders to Major-General Grant, commanding the military district of the Mississippi.

The general commanding avails himself of this opportunity to thank General Blair for the zeal, intelligence, courage, and skill with which he has handled the corps during the eventful period he has commanded it.

By order of
W. T. SHERMAN, MAJOR-GENERAL.
R. M. SAWYER, Assistant Adjutant-General.

Now that the troops were resting in quarters, General Blair, at the request of President Lincoln, resumed his seat in the Congress of 1863, and materially assisted the administration by his extraordinary energy and trained good sense. The accomplished and always successful soldier again approved his own great gifts and the flexibility of our institutions, by quietly becoming the industrious legislator and the ready orator, in the interest of those principles for which he had battled in the field.

But the Republicans were even then beginning to scheme against the President of the United States.

His request to General Blair to resume his seat in Congress, and the agreement to allow his *pro forma* resignation of the generalship to remain in abeyance, so that General Blair could resume the command on the adjournment of Congress, became the subject of a quixotic and unpatriotic examination by an administration committee. They made a report against the President's action in the matter, glad of an opportunity to hit at Mr. Lincoln, and through him, at "the ablest volunteer general in the service." The President not caring to risk the retention of General Blair in the service by any mere technicality, nominated him anew to be major-general of the volunteers. He was finally confirmed by a bare majority of one or two, by the Senate of the Thirty-eighth Congress. Without waiting, however, for their confirmation, General Blair had already joined Sherman's grand army in their march to the sea, and was in command of the Seventeenth Corps, the advance as of old, of Sherman's right wing. His corps comprised three divisions, commanded respectively by Leggett, Mower, and Giles A. Smith. This was after the razing of Atlanta. Consequent upon Joe Johnston's discreet but not damaging Fabian policy, the "lost army" had little to do but to smash their way to the sea, and to bisect the Confederacy. How thoroughly they did both is a matter of record, as well as the deep and long unrelieved solicitude that followed them on their winding way. Of active work, except extraordinary marching, little was done. Of co-operative work, how much was done can be inferred from the consequent crackling of the exhausted shell which had been the Southern Confederacy, when their march finally terminated on the plains of North Carolina. On the approach to Savannah, General Blair had several very active skirmishes before the taking of Fort McAllister by General Hazen. But no battle of moment occurred, nor did any opportunities present themselves either through Georgia or the Carolinas for the display of any other qualities than the solid ones of persistence, promptness, patience, and admirable disciplinary traits.

On July 11th, the Seventeenth Corps, which had won laurels for itself and its commander, was disbanded at Louisville. General Blair took occasion to issue a farewell address to his force. With modest merit he "begged to thank them for the reputation which their gallantry had conferred on him." After recurring to and recounting the triumphs which the troops and their commander had won, he added: "The rebellion has been crushed, but the invasion of our sister republic of Mexico, has, in a measure, been successful. Can it be said that we have triumphed, and that our republic has been re-established on solid and immovable foundations, so long as the Hapsburgs, supported by the bayonets of France, maintain themselves in Mexico?" He closed by spiritedly annunciating his readiness to lead his old troops against the oppressors of Mexico so soon as the occasion should present. The deposition of Maximilian, and the re-establishment of the Republican system in Mexico, happily obviated the necessity of any Federal intervention in that country. The Monroe doctrine had been vindicated by itself.

CHAPTER IV.

HIS RECENT POLITICAL HISTORY.

At the close of the war, General Blair for a year attended to his private affairs. They had been disorganized by the war and needed his immediate rearrangement. On the 16th March, 1866, President Johnson appointed him to the position of Internal Revenue Collector at St. Louis, for the district which he had so long and so ably represented in Congress. The office was one of large responsibility, but not of extended emolument. It was in spirit, however, a partial recognition of a brave soldier's claims on his country, a soldier who had periled life and sacrificed fortune and health in her defense, and whose record was only a record of victory.

Unfortunately, however, for his official advancement, General Blair had unequivocally identified himself with the restoration policy of President Lincoln, inherited and adopted by President Johnson. The party in the Senate who banded during the war against his confirmation the second time as Major-General, was larger now, and on May 3, 1866, General Blair's nomination was rejected by a vote of 8 to 20. General Grant, who was then a pronounced conservative, declared his "indignation and surprise;" asserted that General Blair "had held Missouri in the Union by his own hand," and that "then and since he had always rendered most important service to the country." As Slocum, McClernand, Steadman, McClellan, Pratt, and other Union generals were successively rejected by the Republican Senate, the enormity of General Blair's case grew larger in public estimation by the additions it had in these other equally illustrious examples.

At the next election ensuing after the war, in St. Louis, General Blair was confronted with the offensive test oath, adopted by the proscriptionists in that State. He refused to take it, but offered to swear that he was and ever had been loyal to the Constitution of the United States, and of the State of Missouri. The oath required a specific denial of no less than eighty-six *ex post facto* provisions as not then being done or *having been done*, and disfranchisement followed as a refusal to swear to any of them or from "the information of any loyal man," impeaching the denial of any voter. This oath ingeniously effected the disfranchisement of nearly every Conservative in the State. General Blair, though conscientiously able to swear to any number of oaths consistently and courageously refused to take the unconstitutional obligation, and appealed to the courts. Partisan prejudgment affirmed it against him at first, but the case is still in appeal; though on other suits, at the instance of lawyers and attorneys, the United States Supreme Court have decided it to be unconstitutional.

Since the war, besides exerting himself professionally, General Blair has labored with fine effect as a speaker for the Conservative cause. His efforts have extended through several States, especially in Connecticut, where first set in the reaction which is now sweeping over the country.

Having always had a clear purpose in his fighting, he maintained it in its unity to the end, and in the prosecution of the plans of peace. That object was the suppression of the rebellion simply and solely. The extinguishment of States, the degradation of the white below the black race, the supremacy of military over civil power, have received no countenance from him. Resuming with ripened and expanded convictions his position as statesman, and adding to it the record second to none, of eminent military qualities, he has labored with voice and pen as strenuously as he did with the sword to realize in peace the benefits he felt forced to seek by war. So orderly has been his mind, that he has always known where to stop. Believing in the negro's right to be free, he helped give him his freedom. Nothing less would suffice; nothing more was required. Devoted to the Union, zeal and intolerance never tided him over into disunion in the name of Union. He has never prostituted the name of liberty into tyranny, the name of loyalty into proscription of the white race, the name of anti-slavery into the enormities of negro supremacy. The issues of the war unaccomplished, made him a radical. The issues of the war finally accomplished, left him a conservative.

To speak of his magnanimity, bravery, and popularity would only repeat the record of his soldierly career. Sherman kept him closer to him than his own shadow during all the war, and always had him for his second in command. His officers loved him: his men worshiped him. He was never defeated. Successive promotions in rank and power flowed in on him. He gave to each advanced responsibility a more brilliant discharge than the preceding one. No fraud taints his hands. No tyranny stamps his record.

In war, he was a relentless, sleepless, always victorious enemy: in peace he has proved a thorough, all-forgetting, wholly-trusting, magnanimous friend. His record is as consistent as it is patriotic. Those whom he regards as Northern rebels now, he opposes with as much fire and force as he did Southern rebels in the past.

His address is singularly popular and unaffected. He is accessible to the humblest, and serene among the highest. His personal power almost amounts to magnetism. He can mold men to the purpose he wishes. Not reticent, he is yet prudent. Emphatically, he possesses that equilibrium of all the faculties known as common sense.

His life has been almost a romance. Converting a State to freedom, and then saving it to the Union; the hero of two wars, and deservedly eminent in both; a business man of the highest integrity of mind and temperance of habit; an orator of great ability; a statesman of rare faculty and foresight; a man of indomitable will: his traits are all positive to the highest degree. In gameness, in clearness, in pureness, in combativeness, in statesmanship, he is a veritable Andrew Jackson. We have given his record. Further to reason from it would be supererogation. The country knows him, and, above all, his comrades in arms revere and love him.

As a stronger addition than any thing we can say in favor of General Blair, and to exhibit the warm estimation he is held in by his comrades in arms, we submit the following correspondence:—

[Copy.]
GENERAL BLAIR TO GENERAL SHERMAN.

St. Louis, June 22, 1866.

Major-General Sherman:—Dear General, a report was put in circulation soon after the battle before Atlanta, on the 22d of July, 1864, by some irresponsible letter-writer, to the effect that the death of Maj.-Gen. McPherson was the direct result of my mismanagement and improper disposition of the troops under my command. This report is received and reiterated by persons who are displeased with my political sentiments, whenever it promises to give them any advantage.

Every soldier and officer who served under your orders has a right to appeal to you against any injustice sought to be inflicted on him while under your command, and as I know that nothing will be more unjust and injurious than this accusation, I ask you to say whether there is any foundation, or even color of truth, in the statement to which I have referred. I have only to add that it is my intention to publish your reply to this note. Respectfully,

Your friend and obedient servant,
FRANK P. BLAIR, Jr.

[Copy.]
GENERAL SHERMAN TO GENERAL BLAIR.

Head-quarters Mil. Div. of the Mississippi, }
St. Louis, Mo., June 23, 1866. }

Gen. F. P. Blair, St. Louis, present:

Dear Gen.—I am this moment in receipt of your note of yesterday, in which you state that certain parties differing from you in political sentiments, have raised the story that the death of our mutual friend, Gen. McPherson, July 22, 1864, resulted from your mismanagement and faulty disposition of troops.

It seems impossible to fix a limit to the falsehoods that politicians will resort to to accomplish their ends; but this goes beyond all decency. The truth was, and is, that General McPherson in person placed in their position the two divisions which composed your corps, the Seventeenth, and instead of refusing the extreme left, he had in person extended it forward, and detached a party still more to the left and front to secure a position from which he proposed to batter the large rolling mill in Atlanta. Having about that time of the day, say 10 A. M., received from me a note telling him not to extend too far to his left, he left you and came to me, then near the center of the general line, and urged on me the importance of using Dodge's two divisions, then moving toward that flank, to extend still more your line. I had consented to modify my former orders in part, and he was returning to that flank when he was killed.

You were in no manner the cause, nor was it your business to alter the disposition of the troops, just as General McPherson had made them himself. You had no reason to apprehend danger to your left or rear, nor from the nature of the ground could you have seen the movement by which the enemy's skirmishers reached the wooded space in passing which General McPherson was shot.

Our military maps are now so perfect and public, and the official reports of the facts so full and clear, that I must say it augurs a very bad heart to lay this charge to you, from which, as your common commander, I exonerate you absolutely.

With great respect,
(Signed)   W. T. SHERMAN, MAJ.-GEN.

The unsolicited compliment from Major-General Howard below given, explains itself, as a spontaneous and chivalrous instance of the amenities of arms.

GENERAL HOWARD TO GENERAL BLAIR.

HEADQRS. ARMY OF THE TENNESSEE,
PETERSBURG, VA., May 7, 1865.

MAJOR-GENERAL F. P. BLAIR,
        Commanding Seventeenth Corps:

MY DEAR SIR.— Hearing that you intended soon to leave the service, I wish to thank you for the genuine kindness and uniform hearty support you have ever extended to me, from the time I took command, through all the varied and trying circumstances of hard campaigning up to the present time. I take great pleasure and pride in acknowledging your ability and success as a commanding officer, and if I can at any time be of service to yourself I trust you will not fail to call upon me as a friend. With high esteem, I subscribe myself,

Yours sincerely,
(Signed)   O. O. HOWARD, MAJ.-GEN.

This letter was sent to General Blair voluntarily by General Howard, and was quite unusual and out of the military way. It was doubtless prompted by the peculiar circumstances growing out of General Howard's assignment to command of the Army of the Tennessee, which met considerable opposition and jealousy, but in which he was warmly sustained by General Blair at a time he regarded as very trying.

FOLDO

DOUT

APPENDIX.

CONGRESSIONAL RECONSTRUCTION.

THE ORIGINAL RECONSTRUCTION ACT.

AN ACT to provide for the more efficient government of the rebel States.

WHEREAS no legal State governments or adequate protection for life or property now exists in the rebel States of Virginia, North Carolina, South Carolina, Georgia, Mississippi, Alabama, Louisiana, Florida, Texas, and Arkansas: and whereas it is necessary that peace and good order should be enforced in said States until loyal and republican State governments can be legally established: Therefore—

Be it enacted by the Senate and House of Representatives of the United States of America in Congress assembled, That said rebel States shall be divided into military districts and made subject to the military authority of the United States, as hereinafter prescribed, and for that purpose Virginia shall constitute the first district; North Carolina and South Carolina the second district; Georgia, Alabama, and Florida, the third district; Mississippi and Arkansas the fourth district; and Louisiana and Texas the fifth district.

SEC. 2. *And be it further enacted,* That it shall be the duty of the President to assign to the command of each of said districts an officer of the army, not below the rank of brigadier-general, and to detail a sufficient military force to enable such officer to perform his duties and enforce his authority within the district to which he is assigned.

SEC. 3. *And be it further enacted,* That it shall be the duty of each officer assigned as aforesaid to protect all persons in their rights of person and property, to suppress insurrection, disorder, and violence, and to punish, or cause to be punished, all disturbers of the public peace and criminals, and to this end he may allow local civil tribunals to take jurisdiction of and to try offenders, or, when in his judgment it may be necessary for the trial of offenders, he shall have power to organize military commissions or tribunals for that purpose; and all interference under color of State authority with the exercise of military authority under this act shall be null and void.

SEC. 4. *And be it further enacted,* That all persons put under military arrest by virtue of this act shall be tried without unnecessary delay, and no cruel or unusual punishment shall be inflicted; and no sentence of any military commission or tribunal hereby authorized, affecting the life or liberty of any person, shall be executed until it is approved by the officer in command of the district; and the laws and regulations for the government of the army shall not be affected by this act, except in so far as they conflict with its provisions: *Provided,* That no sentence of death under the provisions of this act shall be carried into effect without the approval of the President.

SEC. 5. *And be it further enacted,* That when the people of any one of said rebel States shall have formed a constitution of government in conformity with the Constitution of the United States in all respects, framed by a convention of delegates elected by the male citizens of said State twenty-one years old and upward, of whatever race, color, or previous condition, who have been resident in said State for one year previous to the day of such election, except such as may be disfranchised for participation in the rebellion or for felony at common law; and when such constitution shall provide that the elective franchise shall be enjoyed by all such persons as have the qualifications herein stated for electors of delegates, and when such constitution shall be ratified by a majority of the persons voting on the question of ratification who are qualified as electors for delegates, and when such constitutions shall have been submitted to Congress for examination and approval, and Congress shall have approved the same, and when said State, by a vote of its legislature elected under said constitution, shall have adopted the amendment to the Constitution of the United States, proposed by the thirty-ninth Congress, and known as article fourteen, and when said article shall have become a part of the Constitution of the United States, said State shall be declared entitled to representation in Congress, and Senators and Representatives shall be admitted therefrom on their taking the oath prescribed by law, and then and thereafter the preceding sections of this act shall be inoperative in said State: *Provided,* That no person excluded from the privilege of holding office by said proposed amendment to the Constitution of the United States shall be eligible to election as a member of the convention to frame a constitution for any of said rebel States, nor shall any such person vote for members of such convention.

SEC. 6. *And be it further enacted,* That until the people of said rebel States shall be by law admitted to representation in the Congress of the United States, any civil governments which may exist therein shall be deemed provisional only, and in all respects subject to the paramount authority of the United States at any time to abolish, modify, control, or supersede the same; and in all elections to any office under such provisional governments all persons shall be entitled to vote, and none others, who are entitled to vote under the provisions of the fifth section of this act; and no person shall be eligible to any office under any such provisional governments who would be disqualified from holding office under the provisions of the third article of said constitutional amendment.

Passed over the Veto, March 2, 1867.

THE FOURTEENTH AMENDMENT.

The following is the Amendment to the Constitution of the United States referred to in section five of the above act

ARTICLE XIV.

SECTION 1. All persons born or naturalized in the United States, and subject to the jurisdiction thereof, are citizens of the United States and of the State wherein they reside. No State shall make or enforce any law which shall abridge the privileges or immunities of citizens of the United States; nor shall any State deprive any person of life, liberty, or property, without due process of law, nor deny to any person within its jurisdiction the equal protection of the laws.

SEC. 2. Representatives shall be apportioned among the several States according to their respective numbers, counting the whole number of persons in each State, excluding Indians not taxed. But when the right to vote at any election for the choice of electors for President and Vice-President of the United States, representatives in Congress, the executive and judicial officers of a State, or the members of the legislature thereof, is denied to any of the male inhabitants of such State, being twenty-one years of age, and citizens of the United States, or in any way abridged, except for participation in rebellion or other crime, the basis of representation therein shall be reduced in the proportion which the number of such male citizens shall bear to the whole number of male citizens twenty-one years of age in such State.

SEC. 3. No person shall be a senator or representative in Congress or elector of President and Vice-President, or hold any office, civil or military, under the United States, or under any State, who having previously taken an oath as a member of Congress, or as an officer of the United States, or as a member of any State legislature, or as an executive or judicial officer of any State, to support the Constitution of the United States, shall have engaged in insurrection or rebellion against the same, or given aid or comfort to the enemies thereof. But Congress may, by a vote of two-thirds of each house, remove such disability.

Sec. 4. The validity of the public debt of the United States, authorized by law, including debts incurred for payment of pensions and bounties for services in suppressing insurrection or rebellion, shall not be questioned. But neither the United States nor any State shall assume or pay any debt or obligation incurred in aid of insurrection or rebellion against the United States, or any claim for the loss or emancipation of any slave; but all such debts, obligations, and claims shall be held illegal and void.

Sec. 5. That Congress shall have power to enforce, by appropriate legislation, the provisions of this article.

Resolution proposing passed June 13, 1866.

THE FIRST SUPPLEMENTARY RECONSTRUCTION ACT.

Passed over the Veto, March 23, 1867.

AN ACT supplementary to an act entitled "An act to provide for the more efficient government of the rebel States." passed March two, eighteen hundred and sixty-seven, and to facilitate restoration.

Be it enacted by the Senate and House of Representatives of the United States of America in Congress assembled, That before the first day of September, eighteen hundred and sixty-seven, the commanding general in each district, defined by an act entitled "An act to provide for the more efficient government of the rebel States," passed March second, eighteen hundred and sixty-seven, shall cause a registration to be made of the male citizens of the United States, twenty-one years of age and upward, resident in each county or parish in the State or States included in his district, which registration shall include only those persons who are qualified to vote for delegates by the act aforesaid, and who shall have taken and subscribed to the following oath or affirmation: "I, ——— ———, do solemnly swear (or affirm), in the presence of Almighty God, that I am a citizen of the State of ———; that I have resided in said State for ——— months next preceding this day, and now reside in the county of ———, or parish of ———, in said State (as the case may be); that I am twenty-one years old; that I have not been disfranchised for participation in any rebellion or civil war against the United States, nor for felony committed against the laws of any State or of the United States; that I have never been a member of any State legislature, nor held any executive or judicial office in any State, and afterward engaged in insurrection or rebellion against the United States or given aid or comfort to the enemies thereof; that I have never taken an oath as a member of Congress of the United States, or as an officer of the United States, or as a member of any State legislature, or as an executive or judicial officer of any State, to support the Constitution of the United States, and afterward engaged in insurrection or rebellion against the United States or given aid or comfort to the enemies thereof; that I will faithfully support the Constitution and obey the laws of the United States, and will, to the best of my ability, encourage others so to do, so help me God;" which oath or affirmation may be administered by any registering officer.

SEC. 2. *And be it further enacted*, That after the completion of the registration hereby provided for in any State, at such time and places therein as the commanding general shall appoint and direct, of which at least thirty days' public notice shall be given, an election shall be held of delegates to a convention for the purpose of establishing a constitution and civil government for such State loyal to the Union, said convention in each State, except Virginia, to consist of the same number of members as the most numerous branch of the State legislature of such State in the year eighteen hundred and sixty, to be apportioned among the several districts, counties, or parishes of such State by the commanding general, giving to each representation in the ratio of voters registered as aforesaid as nearly as may be. The convention in Virginia shall consist of the same number of members as represented the territory now constituting Virginia in the most numerous branch of the legislature of said State in the year eighteen hundred and sixty, to be apportioned as aforesaid.

SEC. 3. *And be it further enacted*, That at said election the registered voters of each State shall vote for or against a convention to form a constitution therefor under this act. Those voting in favor of such a convention shall have written or printed on the ballots by which they vote for delegates, as aforesaid, the words "For a convention," and those voting against such a convention shall have written or printed on such ballots the words "Against a convention." The persons appointed to superintend said election, and to make return of the votes given thereat, as herein provided, shall count and make return of the votes given for and against a convention; and the commanding general to whom the same shall have been returned shall ascertain and declare the total vote in each State for and against a convention. If a majority of the votes given on that question shall be for a convention, then such convention shall be held as hereinafter provided; but if a majority of said votes shall be against a convention, then no such convention shall be held under this act; *Provided*, That such convention shall not be held unless a majority of all such registered voters shall have voted on the question of holding such convention.

SEC. 4. *And be it further enacted*, That the commanding general of each district shall appoint as many boards of registration as may be necessary, consisting of three loyal officers or persons, to make and complete the registration, superintend the election, and make return to him of the votes, lists of voters, and of the persons elected as delegates by a plurality of the votes cast at said election; and upon receiving said returns he shall open the same, ascertain the persons elected as delegates according to the returns of the officers who conducted said election, and make proclamation thereof; and if a majority of the votes given on that question shall be for a convention, the commanding general, within sixty days from the date of election, shall notify the delegates to assemble in convention at a time and place to be mentioned in the notification, and said convention, when organized, shall proceed to frame a constitution and civil government according to the provisions of this act, and the act to which it is supplementary: and when the same shall have been so framed, said constitution shall be submitted by the convention for ratification to the persons registered under the provisions of this act at an election to be conducted by the officers or persons appointed or to be appointed by the commanding general, as hereinbefore provided, and to be held after the expiration of thirty days from the date of notice thereof, to be given by said convention; and the returns thereof shall be made to the commanding general of the district.

SEC. 5. *And be it further enacted,* That if, according to said returns, the constitution shall be ratified by a majority of the votes of registered electors qualified as herein specified, cast at said election (at least one-half of all the registered voters voting upon the question of such ratification), the president of the convention shall transmit a copy of the same, duly certified, to the President of the United States, who shall forthwith transmit the same to Congress, if then in session, and if not in session, then immediately upon its next assembling, and if it shall moreover appear to Congress that the election was one at which all the registered and qualified electors in the State had an opportunity to vote freely, and without restraint, fear, or the influence of fraud, and if Congress shall be satisfied that such constitution meets the approval of a majority of all the qualified electors in the State, and if the said constitution shall be declared by Congress to be in conformity with the provisions of the act to which this is supplementary, and the other provisions of said act shall have been complied with, and the said constitution shall be approved by Congress, the State shall be declared entitled to representation, and Senators and Representatives shall be admitted therefrom as therein provided.

SEC. 6. *And be it further enacted,* That all elections in the States mentioned in the said "Act to provide for the more efficient government of the rebel States," shall, during the operation of said act, be by ballot; and all officers making the said registration of voters and conducting said elections shall, before entering upon the discharge of their duties, take and subscribe to the oath prescribed by the act approved July 2, 1862, entitled "An act to prescribe an oath of office." *Provided,* That if any person shall knowingly and falsely take and subscribe any oath in this act prescribed, such person so offending and being thereof duly convicted, shall be subject to the pains, penalties, and disabilities which by law are provided for the punishment of the crime of wilful and corrupt perjury.

SEC. 7. *And be it further enacted,* That all expenses incurred by the several commanding generals, or by virtue of any orders issued, or appointments made, by them, under or by virtue of this act, shall be paid out of any moneys in the treasury not otherwise appropriated.

SEC. 8. *And be it further enacted,* That the convention for each State shall prescribe the fees, salary, and compensation to be paid to all delegates and other officers and agents herein authorized or necessary to carry into effect the purposes of this act not herein otherwise provided for, and shall provide for the levy and collection of such taxes on the property in such State as may be necessary to pay the same.

SEC. 9. *And be it further enacted,* That the word article, in the sixth section of the act to which this is supplementary, shall be construed to mean section.

Passed over the Veto March 23, 1867.

THE SECOND SUPPLEMENTARY RECONSTRUCTION ACT.

AN ACT supplementary to an act entitled "An act to provide for the more efficient government of the rebel States," passed on the second day of March, eighteen hundred and sixty-seven, and the act supplementary thereto, passed on the twenty-third day of March, eighteen hundred and sixty-seven.

Be it enacted by the Senate and House of Representatives of the United States of America in Congress assembled, That it is hereby declared to have been the true intent and meaning of the act of the second day of March, one thousand eight hundred and sixty-seven, entitled "An act to provide for the more efficient government of the rebel States," and of the act supplementary thereto, passed on the twenty-third day of March, in the year one thousand eight hundred and sixty-seven, that the governments then existing in the rebel States of Virginia, North Carolina, South Carolina, Georgia, Mississippi, Alabama, Louisiana, Florida, Texas, and Arkansas, were not legal State governments; and that thereafter said governments, if continued, were to be continued subject in all respects to the military commanders of the respective districts, and to the paramount authority of Congress.

SEC. 2. *And be it further enacted,* That the commander of any district named in said act shall have power, subject to the disapproval of the General of the army of the United States, and to have effect till disapproved, whenever in the opinion of such commander the proper administration of such act shall require it, to suspend or remove from office, or from the performance of official duties and the exercise of official powers, any officer or person holding or exercising, or professing to hold or exercise, any civil or military office or duty in such district under any power, election, appointment, or authority derived from, or granted by, or claimed under, any so-called State or the government thereof, or any municipal or other division thereof; and upon such suspension or removal, such commander, subject to the disapproval of the General as aforesaid, shall have power to provide from time to time for the performance of the said duties of such officer or person so suspended or removed, by the detail of some competent officer or soldier of the army, or by the appointment of some other person, to perform the same, and to fill vacancies occasioned by death, resignation, or otherwise.

SEC. 3. *And be it further enacted,* That the General of the army of the United States shall be invested with all the powers of suspension, removal, appointment, and detail granted in the preceding section to district commanders.

SEC. 4. *And be it further enacted,* That the acts of the officers of the army already done in removing in said districts persons exercising the functions of civil officers, and appointing others in their stead, are hereby confirmed: *Provided,* That any person heretofore or hereafter appointed by any district commander to exercise the functions of any civil office may be removed either by the military officer in command of the district, or by the General of the army. And it shall be the duty of such commander to remove from office, as aforesaid, all persons who are disloyal to the government of the United States, or who use their official influence in any manner to hinder, delay, prevent, or obstruct the due and proper administration of this act and the acts to which it is supplementary.

SEC. 5. *And be it further enacted,* That the boards of registration provided for in the act entitled " An act supplementary to an act entitled ' An act to provide for the more efficient government of the rebel States,' passed March two, eighteen hundred and sixty-seven, and to facilitate restoration," passed March twenty-three, eighteen hundred and sixty-seven, shall have power, and it shall be their duty before allowing the registration of any person, to ascertain, upon such facts or information as they can obtain, whether such person is entitled to be registered under said act, and the oath required by said act shall not be conclusive on such question, and no person shall be registered unless such board shall decide that he is entitled thereto; and such board shall also have power to examine under oath, to be administered by any member of such board, any one touching the qualification of any person claiming registration, but in every case of a refusal by the board to register an applicant, and in every case of striking his name from the list as hereinafter provided, the board shall make a note or memorandum, which shall be returned with the registration list to the Commanding General of the district, setting forth the grounds of such refusal, or such striking from the list. *Provided,* That no person shall be disqualified as a member of any board of registration by reason of race or color.

SEC. 6. *And be it further enacted,* That the true intent and meaning of the oath prescribed in said supplementary act is, among other things, that no person who has been a member of the Legislature of any State, or who has held any executive or judicial office in any State, whether he has taken an oath to support the Constitution of the United States or not, and whether he was holding such office at the commencement of the rebellion, or had held it before, and who was afterward engaged in insurrection or rebellion against the United States or giving aid or comfort to the enemies thereof, is entitled to be registered or to vote, and the words "executive or judicial office in any State" in said oath mentioned, shall be construed to include all civil offices created by law for the administration of any general law of a State or for the administration of justice.

SEC. 7. *And be it further enacted*, That the time for completing the original registration, provided for in said act may, in the discretion of the commander of any district, be extended to the 1st day of October, 1867, and the boards of registration shall have power, and it shall be their duty, commencing fourteen days prior to any election under said act, and upon reasonable public notice of the time and place thereof, to revise, for a period of five days, the registration list, and upon being satisfied that any person not entitled thereto has been registered, to strike the name of such person from the list, and such persons shall not be allowed to vote. And such board shall, also, during the same period add to such registry the names of all persons who at that time possess the qualifications required by said act, who have not been already registered, and no person shall at any time be entitled to be registered or to vote by reason of any executive pardon or amnesty for any act or thing which, without such pardon or amnesty, would disqualify him from registration or voting.

SEC. 8. *And be it further enacted*, That section four of said last-named act shall be construed to authorize the commanding general named therein, whenever he shall deem it needful, to remove any member of a board of registration and to appoint another in his stead, and to fill any vacancy in such board.

SEC. 9. *And be it further enacted*, That all members of said boards of registration, and all persons hereafter elected or appointed to office in said military districts under any so-called State or municipal authority, or by detail or appointment of the district commanders, shall be required to take and to subscribe the oath of office prescribed by law for officers of the United States.

SEC. 10. *And be it further enacted*, That no district commander or member of the board of registration, or any of the officers or appointees acting under them shall be bound in his action by any opinion of any civil officer of the United States.

SEC. 11. *And be it further enacted*, That all the provisions of this act and the acts to which this is supplementary, shall be construed liberally, to the end that all the intents thereof may be fully and perfectly carried out.

Passed over the Veto, July 19, 1867.

THE THIRD SUPPLEMENTARY RECONSTRUCTION ACT.

AN ACT to amend the act passed March twenty-third, eighteen hundred and sixty-seven, entitled "An act supplementary to 'An act to provide for the more efficient government of the rebel States,' passed March second, eighteen hundred and sixty-seven, and to facilitate their restoration."

Be it enacted by the Senate and House of Representatives of the United States of America in Congress assembled, That hereafter any election authorized by the act passed March twenty-three, eighteen hundred and sixty-seven, entitled "An act supplementary to 'An act to provide for the more efficient government of the rebel States,' passed March *two* [second], eighteen hundred and sixty-seven, and to facilitate their restoration," shall be decided by a majority of the votes actually cast; and at the election in which the question of the adoption or rejection of any constitution is submitted, any person duly registered in the State may vote in the election district where he offers to vote when he has resided therein for ten days next preceding such election, upon presentation of his certificate of registration, his affidavit, or other satisfactory evidence, under such regulations as the district commanders may prescribe.

SEC. 2. *And be it further enacted,* That the constitutional convention of any of the States mentioned in the acts to which this is amendatory, may provide that at the time of voting upon the ratification of the constitution the registered voters may vote also for members of the House of Representatives of the United States, and for all elective officers provided for by the said constitution; and the same election officers who shall make the return of the votes cast on the ratification or rejection of the constitution, shall enumerate and certify the votes cast for members of Congress.

Became an Act, March 10, 1868, *by expiration of constitutional ten days.*

THE ARKANSAS ACT.

AN ACT to admit the State of Arkansas to representation in Congress.

WHEREAS, The people of Arkansas, in pursuance of the provisions of an act entitled "An act for the more efficient government of the rebel States," passed March second, eighteen hundred and sixty-seven, and the acts supplementary thereto, have framed and adopted a constitution of State government which is republican in form, and the Legislature of said State has duly ratified the amendment to the Constitution of the United States, proposed by the XXXIXth Congress and known as Article 14: Therefore—

Be it enacted by the Senate and House of Representatives of the United States of America, in Congress assembled, That the State of Arkansas is entitled and admitted to representation in Congress as one of the States of the Union upon the following fundamental condition: That the constitution of Arkansas shall never be so amended or changed as to deprive any citizen or class of citizens in the United States of the right to vote who are entitled to vote by the constitution herein recognized, except as a punishment for such crimes as are now felonies at common law, whereof they have been duly convicted under laws equally applicable to all the inhabitants of said State; provided, that any alteration of said constitution, prospective in its effect, may be made in regard to time and place of residence of the voters.

Passed over the Veto, June, 1868.

"THE OMNIBUS BILL."

AN ACT to admit the States of North Carolina, South Carolina, Louisiana, Georgia, Alabama, and Florida to representation in Congress.

WHEREAS, The people of North Carolina, South Carolina, Louisiana, Georgia, Alabama, and Florida have, in pursuance of an Act entitled "An Act for the more efficient government of the rebel States," passed March second, eighteen hundred and sixty-seven, and the acts supplementary thereto, framed constitutions of State government which are republican, and have adopted said constituions by large majorities of the votes cast at the election held for the ratification or rejection of the same: Therefore—

SECTION 1. *Be it enacted by the Senate and House of Representatives of the United States of America, in Congress assembled,* That each of the States of North Carolina, South Carolina, Louisiana, Georgia, Alabama, and Florida, shall be entitled and admitted to representation in Congress as a State of the Union when the Legislature of such State shall have duly ratified the amendment to the Constitution of the United States, proposed by the Thirty-ninth Congress, and known as article fourteen, upon the following fundamental conditions: That the constitutions of neither of said States shall ever be so amended or changed as to deprive any citizen or class of citizens in the United States of the right to vote, who are entitled to vote in said State by the constitution thereof herein recognized, except as punishment for such crimes as are now felonies at common law, whereof they shall have been duly convicted under laws equally applicable to all the inhabitants of said States; provided that alterations of said constitutions, prospective in its effect, may be made in regard to time and place of residence of the voters; and the State of Georgia shall only be entitled and admitted to representation upon this further fundamental condition: that the first and third subdivisions of section seventeen of the fifth article of the constitution of said State, except the proviso to the first subdivision, shall be null and void, and that the General Assembly of said State by solemn public act shall declare the assent of the State to the foregoing fundamental condition.

SEC. 2. *And be it further enacted*, That if the day fixed for the meeting of the Legislature of either of said States by the constitution thereof shall have passed, or shall have so nearly arrived before the passage of this act that there shall not be time for the Legislature to assembl oat the time fixed by the convention of said State, such Legislature shall convene at the end of twenty days from the time this act takes effect, unless the Governor shall sooner convene the same.

SEC. 3. *And be it further enacted*, That the first section of this act shall take effect as to each State, except Georgia, when such State by its Legislature duly ratify article 14 of the amendment to the Constitution of the United States proposed by the Thirty-ninth Congress, and as to the State of Georgia, when it shall, in addition, give the assent of said State to the fundamental condition hereinbefore imposed upon the same; but no person prohibited from holding office under the United States or under any State by section three of the proposed amendment to the Constitution of the United States, known as article 14, shall be deemed eligible to any office in either of said States, unless relieved from disability as provided in said amendment. And it is hereby made the duty of the President, within ten days after receiving official information of the ratification of said amendment by the Legislature of either of the States, to issue a proclamation announcing that fact.

Passed over the Veto, June 25, 1868.

RECONSTRUCTION STATISTICS.

THE DISTRICT COMMANDANTS.

On the passage of the Reconstruction act of March 2, 1867, over his veto, the President appointed commandants for the several military districts, and these original appointments, with those afterward made from various causes, stand thus:

First Military District (State of Virginia), Bvt. Maj.-Gen. J. M. Schofield, assigned, March 11, 1867; assumed command, March 13, 1867; confirmed as Secretary of War, March 29, 1868; succeeded by Bvt. Maj.-Gen. Geo. Stoneman, assigned, June 1, 1868; assumed command, June 2, 1868. Head-quarters, Richmond, Va.

Second Military District (States of North Carolina and South Carolina), Maj.-Gen. D. E. Sickles, assigned, March 11, 1867; assumed command, March 21, 1867; relieved, Sept. 1, 1867, by Maj.-Gen. E. R. Canby, assigned by order dated August 26, 1867. Head-quarters, Charleston, S. C.

Third Military District (States of Georgia, Alabama, and Florida), Maj.-Gen. Geo. H. Thomas, assigned, March 11, 1867; relieved at own request, March 15, 1867, and succeeded by Bvt. Maj.-Gen. Jno. Pope, assigned same day; assumed command, April 1, 1867; relieved, Dec. 28, 1867; succeeded by Maj.-Gen. Geo. G. Meade, assigned same day; assumed command, Jan. 6, 1868. Head-quarters, Atlanta, Ga.

Fourth Military District (States of Mississippi and Arkansas), Bvt. Maj.-Gen. E. O. C. Ord, assigned, March 11, 1867; assumed command, March 26, 1867; relieved, Dec. 28, 1867, by Bvt. Maj.-Gen. A. C. Gillem, assigned to duty till arrival of Bvt. Maj.-Gen. Irwin McDowell, who assumed command, June, 1868; relieved at own request, July 1, 1868, and succeeded by Bvt. Maj.-Gen. A. C. Gillem same day.

Fifth Military District (States of Louisiana and Texas), Maj.-Gen. P. H. Sheridan, assigned, March 11, 1867; relieved, Sept. 1, 1867, by order of Aug. 17, 1867, which appointed Maj.-Gen. Geo. H. Thomas to succeed. That officer's health being certified to as not permitting him to go south, Maj.-Gen. W. S. Hancock was, by order dated August 26, 1867, appointed in his stead, the officer next in rank to Gen. Sheridan (Gen. Griffin) to command till his arrival. Gen. Griffin died, Sept. 16, 1867, and Bvt. Maj.-Gen. Mower assumed command same day, holding till Nov. 29, 1867, when Gen. Hancock assumed command; relieved, at own request, and succeeded by Bvt. Maj.-Gen. R. C. Buchanan, March, 1868. Head-quarters, New Orleans.

PERSONS REGISTERED AS VOTERS IN THE SOUTH UNDER THE RECONSTRUCTION ACTS.

STATE.	Whites.	Negroes.	Aggregate.	White Maj.	Negro Maj.
Alabama,	61,295	104,518	165,813		43,223
Arkansas,	43,470	23,361	66,831	20,109	
Florida,	11,914	16,089	28,003		4,175
Georgia,	96,333	95,168	191,501	1,165	
Louisiana,	45,218	84,436	129,654		39,218
Mississippi,	59,330	80,360	139,690		21,030
North Carolina,	106,721	72,932	179,653	33,789	
South Carolina,	46,882	80,550	127,432		33,668
Texas,	59,633	49,497	109,130	10,136	
Virginia,	120,101	105,832	225,933	14,269	
Total	650,897	712,743 / 650,897	1,363,640	79,468	141,314 / 79,468
Negro Majority,		61,846			61,846

VOTE ON THE QUESTION OF CONVENTION.

STATE.	For a Convention.	Against a Convention.	Not Voting.	Vote for a convention more or less than a majority of the total registered vote.	
				More.	Less.
Alabama	90,283	5,583	69,947	7,376	
Arkansas	27,576	13,558	25,697		5,840
Florida	14,300	203	13,500	298	
Georgia	102,283	4,127	85,091	6,532	
Louisiana	75,083	4,006	50,565	10,255	
Mississippi	69,739	6,277	63,674		107
North Carolina	93,006	32,961	53,686	3,179	
South Carolina	68,768	2,278	56,386	5,051	
Texas	44,689	11,440	53,001		9,877
Virginia	107,342	61,887	56,704		5,625
Total	693,069	142,320	528,251	32,691	21,449

NOTE.—The large number of those not voting arises from the fact that at the time of these convention elections the whites very generally kept away from the polls, the reconstruction acts at that time rendering this course equivalent to voting against a convention. Those voting for convention were almost entirely negroes, as may be better seen in the annexed table of the vote by race, in those seven of the ten Southern States where the vote was so kept.

THE CONVENTION VOTE BY RACE.

STATE.	For a Convention.		Against a Convention.	
	Whites.	Negroes.	Whites.	Negroes.
Alabama	18,553	71,730	61,249	None.
Florida	1,220	13,080	203	"
Georgia	32,000	70,283	4,000	127
North Carolina	31,284	61,722	32,961	None.
South Carolina	2,350	66,418	2,278	"
Texas	7,757	36,932	10,622	818
Virginia	14,835	92,507	61,249	638
Total	107,999	412,672	172,562	1,583
		107,999		1,583
Majority		304,673	170,979	

THE RECONSTRUCTION CONVENTIONS.

STATE	ELECTION.	MET.	Delegates. Whites. Native.	Delegates. Whites. Imported.	Delegates. Negroes. Native.	Delegates. Negroes. Imported.	Total.	PRESIDENTS.	Adjourned.	Days in Session.	Per Diem.
Alabama	Oct. 1, 2, 3, 1867	Montgomery, Nov. 5, 1867	24	60	12	4	100	E. W. Peck	Dec. 6, 1867	82	$10
Arkansas	Nov. 6-16, 1867	Little Rock, Jan. 7, 1868	25	42	6	2	76	Thos. M. Bowen	Feb. 14, 1868	89	8
Florida	Nov. 14-16, 1867	Tallahassee, Jan. 20, 1868	10	19	14	4	46	Horatio Jenkins*	Feb. 25, 1868	87	8
Georgia	Oct. 29-31, 1867	Atlanta, Dec. 9, 1867	58	75	20	16	169	J. R. Parrott	March 11, 1868	79†	8
Louisiana	Sept. 27, 28, 1867	New Orleans, Nov. 23, 1867	13	36	46	8	98	Jas. G. Taliaferro	March 9, 1868	108	10
Mississippi	Nov. 19-26, 1867	Jackson, Jan. 7, 1868	5	78	6	11	100	Beroth B. Eggleston	May 18, 1868	133	10
North Carolina	Nov. 19, 20, 1867	Raleigh, Jan. 14, 1868	54	33	11	2	120	Calvin J. Cowles	March 17, 1868	64	8
South Carolina	Nov. 19, 20, 1867	Charleston, Jan. 14, 1868	28	28	57	16	124	A. G. Mackey	March 17, 1868	64	11
Texas	Feb. 10-14, 1868	Austin, June 1, 1868	20	61	8	1	90	F. J. Davis			8
Virginia	Oct. 22-24, 1867	Richmond, Dec. 3, 1867	88	42	24	1	105	Jno. C. Underwood	April 17, 1868	137	10

* There were two reconstructing conventions in Florida and two constitutions framed, but the one presided over by H. Jenkins was the one recognized by the military.

† Took a recess from December 23, 1867, to January 8, 1868.

VOTE ON RATIFICATION OF THE RECONSTRUCTED CONSTITUTION.

STATE.	Election.	For.	Agst.	Over or under maj. registered vote.	
				Over.	Under.
Alabama.......	Feb. 4–8, 1868.	69,807	1,005	......	15,609
Arkansas.....	March 13, 1868.	27,913	26,597	......	8,970
Florida.......	May 4–6, 1868.	14,520	9,491	......	1,230
Georgia	April 20–23, 1868.	89,007	71,309	......	16,993
Louisiana.....	April 17–18, 1868.	66,152	48,739	1,324	21,445
Mississippi....	June 22– , 1868.	56,231	63,860	......	....
North Carolina	April 21–23, 1868.	92,590	71,820	......	5,847
South Carolina	April 14–16, 1868.	70,758	27,288	6,041	....

NOTE.—Texas has not as yet had any reconstructed constitution framed for her, and in Virginia no time has been set for election on the one there formed.

THE RECONSTRUCTED GOVERNORS.

State.   *Governor.*

Alabama.................... Wm. H. Smith, of Alabama.
Arkansas .... Powell Clayton, of Pennsylvania.
Florida..................... Harrison Reed, of Wisconsin.
Georgia..................... Rufus B. Bullock, of Connecticut.
Louisiana................... Henry C. Warmoth, of Illinois.
North Carolina.............. Wm. W. Holden, of North Carolina.
South Carolina.............. Robt. K. Scott, of Pennsylvania.

Of the above Smith was Chief of Registration in Alabama; Clayton had a command in the Kansas troops during the war; Reed is the special mail agent of the P. O. department for Alabama and Florida; Bullock has been an express agent for some years past in Georgia; Warmoth was an officer of Missouri troops and acted as Butler's provost-marshal in New Orleans; Holden was the provisional governor of North Carolina under the presidential policy of recoustruction; and Scott was a brigadier-general of Ohio troops and the commissioner of the Freedmen's Bureau for North Carolina. In Louisiana a negro is Lieutenant-Governor, and in South Carolina another negro is Secretary of State.

THE RECONSTRUCTED SENATORS.

ARKANSAS................... { Benj. F. Rice, of Minnesota.
 Alexander McDonald, of Kansas.

FLORIDA.................... { A. S. Welsh, of Michigan.
 T. W. Osborn, of New York.

LOUISIANA.................. { W. P. Kellogg, of Illinois.
 Jno. S. Harris, of Pennsylvania.

NORTH CAROLINA............ { J. D. Abbott, of New Hampshire.
 Jno. Pool, of North Carolina.

SOUTH CAROLINA............ { F. A. Sawyer, of Massachusetts.
 T. J. Robertson, of South Carolina.

There have been no other reconstructed Senators elected.

THE RECONSTRUCTED CONGRESSMEN.

State.	District.	Name.
ALABAMA	I.	F. W. Kellog, of Michigan.
	II.	Chas. W. Buckley, of Mass.
	III.	Benj. W. Norris, of Maine.
	IV.	Chas. W. Pierce, of Mass.
	V.	Joseph W. Burk, of Ala.
	VI.	Thomas Haughey, of Scotland.
ARKANSAS	I.	Logan H. Roots, of Illinois.
	II.	James Hinds, of Minnesota.
	III.	Thos. Bolles, of Arkansas.
FLORIDA	I.	Chas. M. Hamilton, of Wisconsin.
GEORGIA	I.	J. W. Clift, of Mass.
	II.	*Nelson Tift, of Georgia.
	III.	Wm. P. Edwards, of Georgia.
	IV.	Saml. F. Gove, of Mass.
	V.	Chas. H. Prince, of Maine.
	VI.	*Jno. H. Christy, of Georgia.
	VII.	*P. M. B. Young, of Georgia.
LOUISIANA	I.	J. H. Sypher, of Penn.
	II.	*Jas. Mann, of N. Y.
	III.	Jos. P. Newsham, of N. Y.
	IV.	Michael Vidal, of France.
	V.	W. J. Blackburn, of Tennessee.
NORTH CAROLINA	I.	Jno. R. French, of New Hampshire.
	II.	David Heaton, of Ohio.
	III.	Oliver H. Dockery, of North Carolina.
	IV.	Jno. I. Dervees, of Indiana.
	V.	Israel G. Losh, of North Carolina.
	VI.	*Israel Boyden, of Mass.
	VII.	Alex. H. Jones, of North Carolina.
SOUTH CAROLINA	I.	B. F. Whittemore, of Mass.
	II.	C. C. Bowen, of Rhode Island.
	III.	Simon Corley, of South Carolina.
	IV.	Jas. H. Goss, of South Carolina.

RECAPITULATION.—5 Democrats and 28 Radicals, total 33. Of these 17, or a majority, went South after the war.

THE RECONSTRUCTED CONSTITUTIONS.

The following synopsis will give an idea of the main provisions of the several constitutions framed for the Southern States under the reconstruction acts of Congress.

REGISTRATION.

By the reconstructed constitutions of Arkansas, Florida, Louisiana, Mississippi, and Virginia, it is made the duty of the Legislature at its first session thereunder to provide by law for the registration of all electors. The reconstructed constitutions of Alabama, Georgia, North Carolina, and South Carolina, prescribe that the same shall be done from time to time.

SUFFRAGE AND ELIGIBILITY TO OFFICE.

In Alabama, Arkansas, and Mississippi, no one is to be a voter unless he will swear to "accept the civil and political equality of all men." In Florida, North Carolina, and Virginia the voter's oath is to support the constitutions of those States respectively, each of which recognize in express terms the same doctrine of civil and political equality. The voter's oath in Georgia is, that he has neither given nor received any thing to affect his own or another's vote. In Louisiana those who held civil or military office for a year or more under the Confederate government, secession editors or preachers, signers of a secession ordinance, registered enemies, and leaders of guerrilla bands are disfranchised. In South Carolina all now or hereafter to be disfranchised by the U. S. Constitution are disfranchised. In all these States it is proper to say that the power given the legislatures to pass registration laws carries with it the power to prescribe an oath of acceptance of the civil and political equality of all men as an indispensable prerequisite to suffrage. No person is to be disfranchised for felony committed when a slave, which gives a negro homicide, house-burner, ravisher, or robber the franchise, when a white man convicted of like offenses loses it. In Alabama, Arkansas, Louisiana, Mississippi, and Virginia, no one is eligible to office who will not swear that he accepts the civil and political equality of all men.

SOCIAL EQUALITY.

In Alabama all citizens have "equal civil and political rights and public privileges." In Arkansas no citizen shall ever be deprived of any right, privilege, or immunity, nor exempted from any burden or duty on account of race, color, or previous condition. In Florida "there shall be no civil or political distinction." In Georgia "no laws shall be made or enforced which shall abridge the privileges or immunities of citizens of the United States," and "the social status of the citizen shall never be the subject of legislation." In Louisiana "all persons shall enjoy equal rights and privileges upon any conveyance of a public character; and all places of business, or of public resort, or for which a license is required by either state, parish, or municipal authority, shall be deemed places of a public character, and shall be opened to the accommodation and patronage of all persons, without distinction or discrimination on account of race or color." In Mississippi no distinction to be made on public conveyances. In South Carolina "all classes of citizens shall enjoy equally all common public, legal, and political privileges." In Virginia "all citizens are to have equal civil and political rights and public privileges."

EDUCATION.

All distinction of races in schools is expressly forbidden in all the reconstructed constitutions. In Arkansas, South Carolina, and North Carolina, education at the common schools is compulsory, unless private tuition is given. In the other States, boards of education with full legislative powers, ample to, in like manner, compel attendance, have charge of the entire subject, choice of books, selection of teachers, etc., and are empowered to levy taxes.

MILITIA.

In Alabama all able-bodied male inhabitants between 18 and 45 are subject to militia duty. In Arkansas no one is to be a militiaman who does not swear to accept the civil and political equality of all men. In Florida no religious scruples are to exempt unless the Legislature says so. In Georgia able-bodied males between 18 and 45, subject to the paramount authority of Congress. In Louisiana all militia officers must take the test oath. In Mississippi the militia must swear to accept the civil and political equality of all men, and the officers must take the test oath. In North Carolina able-bodied citizens 21 to 40. In South Carolina, same from 18 to 45. In Virginia all able-bodied male persons between the ages of 18 and 45.

VETO.

By the reconstructed constitution of North Carolina there is no veto. In Alabama and Arkansas a majority can override the veto: in all the others the usual two-thirds.

LEGISLATURES.

		In Senate.	In House.	Joint House.
Alabama,	members	33	100	133
Arkansas,	"	26	82	108
Florida,	"	24	53	77
Georgia,	"	44	175	219
Louisiana,	"	36	101	137
Mississippi,	"	33	107	140
North Carolina,	"	50	120	170
South Carolina,	"	32	124	176
Virginia,	"	43	138	181

AMENDMENTS.

In Alabama the reconstructed constitution can only be amended by a two-thirds vote of both houses of two successive Legislatures, necessarily occupying four years, and then by a majority vote of the people. In Arkansas one Legislature is to propose by a two-thirds vote, the amendment is then to be submitted to the people at the election for a second, and, if carried, this second Legislature is to submit it to the people the second time, " in such manner and at such time," as it may see fit. In Florida exactly the same procedure is to be had. In Georgia the constitution can only be carried by a two-thirds vote of two successive Legislatures, and by a submission to the voters for final ratification, no time for such submission being made imperative. In Louisiana one Legislature is to propose by a two-thirds vote, and at the election for the next the people are to ratify or reject. In Mississippi almost exactly the same provision, save that after the people have ratified, the second Legislature is to insert within its term. In North Carolina any amendment must receive a three-fifths vote in the Legislature proposing, then a popular vote, then a two-thirds vote in the second Legislature, and then " said general assembly shall prescribe a mode" of submission thereof to the people. In South Carolina there is to be no ratification save on a two-thirds vote of the Legislature proposing, then a popular vote, and then a two-thirds vote by a second Legislature. In Virginia there must be a majority vote in two successive Legislatures and then a final submission to the people, " in such manner and at such time as the general assembly shall prescribe." These provisions, as will be seen, render any amendment almost impossible.

STATES.	ADMITTED INTO THE UNION.	VOTE IN 1860.
Alabama	December 14, 1819	90,357
Arkansas	June 15, 1836	54,053
Florida	March 3, 1845	14,347
Georgia	One of the Old Thirteen	106,365
Louisiana	April 8, 1812	50,150
Mississippi	December 10, 1817	69,120
North Carolina	One of the Old Thirteen	96,230
South Carolina	" " "	43,000
Texas	December 29, 1845	62,986
Virginia	One of the Old Thirteen	167,223
Total		754,191

SOUTHERN FINANCES.

The subjoined table will be found to give the wealth of the ten reconstructed States in the year 1860 and the same item for six of the number in 1866.

	Real Estate and Personal Property.	
	1860.	1866.
Alabama	$495,237,078	
Arkansas	219,256,473	38,723,449
Florida	73,101,500	
Georgia	645,895,237	
Louisiana	602,118,568	225,000,000
Mississippi	607,324,911	
North Carolina	358,739,399	150,000,000
South Carolina	518,138,754	90,888,436
Texas	365,200,614	120,793,763
Virginia	793,249,681	327,580,561
Total	$4,708,262,215	952,986,209

It will thus be seen that the wealth of these ten States was $4,708,262,215 in 1860. The wealth of Arkansas, Louisiana, North

Carolina, South Carolina, Texas, and Virginia at the same census was $2,886,703,489. In 1866 that wealth was reduced to $952,986,209 or to *one-third* of the value in 1860.

LATEST ESTIMATE OF SOUTHERN STATE DEBT. (Official.)

Alabama	$ 6,130,910 00	November 12, 1867
Louisiana	12,852,601 14	June 20, 1868.
North Carolina	19,480,500 00	April 8, 1868.
South Carolina	8,576,320 44	April 1, 1868.
Virginia	44,855,915 38	June 19, 1868.

DATES OF THE ORDINANCES OF SECESSION.

1. South Carolina....................December 20th, 1860.
2. Mississippi........................January 9th, 1861.
3. Alabama..........................January 11th, 1861.
4. Florida...........................January 11th, 1861.
5. Georgia..........................January 19th, 1861.
6. Louisiana........................January 20th, 1861.
7. Texas............................February 1st, 1861.
8. Virginia..........................April 17th, 1861.
9. Arkansas........................May 9th, 1861.
10. North Carolina..................May 20th, 1861.
11. Tennessee.......................June 8th, 1861.
12. Missouri........................August 12th, 1861.

www.ingramcontent.com/pod-product-compliance
Lightning Source LLC
Chambersburg PA
CBHW031934230426
43672CB00010B/1920